MAHIR ŞAUL

Understanding Africa's Rural Households and Farming Systems

About the Book and Editor

In this book, the difficult problems of agriculture in sub-Saharan Africa are examined by the farming systems approach, which aims to improve food production under adverse conditions through agronomic and social science research conducted on the farm. Particular attention is paid to household decisionmaking processes that affect the way households and farms respond to changes in agriculture incentives and technologies, the nature of the farm household as a production and consumption unit, and the division of economic spheres between men and women. The advantages of merging farming systems research with "household economics" theory and studies of kinship organization are also explored. This combined approach highlights new areas with great potential for addressing the problems of African agriculture. The contributors are members of international research institutes, African agricultural agencies, and donor agencies as well as university professors from a variety of disciplines.

Joyce Lewinger Moock is associate director of agricultural sciences at the Rockefeller Foundation and coauthor of *Higher Education and Rural Development in Africa: Toward a Balanced Approach for Donor Assistance.*

Understanding Africa's Rural Households and Farming Systems

edited by
Joyce Lewinger Moock

Foreword by Bede N. Okigbo

Westview Press / Boulder and London

Westview Special Studies on Africa

Copyright © 1986 by Westview Press, Inc.

Published in 1986 in the United States of America by Westview Press, Inc.; Frederick A. Praeger, Publisher; 5500 Central Avenue, Boulder, Colorado 80301

Library of Congress Cataloging-in-Publication Data
Main entry under title:
Understanding Africa's rural households and farming
    systems.
    (Westview special studies on Africa)
    Bibliography: p.
    1. Family farms—Africa, Sub-Saharan—Addresses,
essays, lectures. 2. Households—Africa, Sub-Saharan—
Addresses, essays, lectures. 3. Rural families—
Africa, Sub-Saharan—Addresses, essays, lectures.
I. Moock, Joyce Lewinger. II. Series.
HD1476.A357U53 1986   338.1'0967   85-32318
ISBN 0-8133-7175-9

This book was produced without formal editing by the publisher.

Printed and bound in the United States of America

6   5   4   3   2   1

Contents

Foreword

More than 45 years ago, E. P. Prentice wrote in *Hunger and History* that "Mankind evidently has walked with Hunger and Want. These have been his daily companions throughout European history and, could we discover the facts, we would learn that they have been his companions during his whole history."

Today, this statement appears to be more nearly true of the developing regions of the world—and especially Africa, with its current food crisis—than of Europe and the United States, where, thanks to science and technology, nations are able to produce most of their food requirements and can purchase the rest of their needs using foreign exchange earnings from exports of other commodities and industrial products. Plenty and surpluses, rather than hunger and want, are the current companions of Europeans and U.S. citizens. This is not so for Africans and the people of most developing countries.

Farming systems research (FSR) is evolving as an effective, popular research tool in efforts aimed at achieving increased agricultural productivity through the rapid, widespread adoption of technological innovations. Its popularity appears to derive from the perception that FSR rightly addresses the problems of limited-resource farmers, who constitute the majority of the farming population in developing countries. In fact, FSR generally addresses the problems of all categories of farmers, at least initially, through special diagnostic surveys to determine strategies and priorities in research. Researchers then often identify as a "target" those farmers who would experience difficulties in adopting technologies developed through conventional disciplinary research—research that rarely gives due consideration to the socioeconomic factors that FSR can identify. FSR also makes it possible to identify component subsystems and technologies in the production systems of target farmers where intervention has the greatest chance of success in rapidity of adoption. Because FSR facilitates understanding of the farmer's overall environment, production system, and constraints on increased production, it leads to the development of technologies that are relevant to the farmers' needs and circumstances. This characteristic has endeared FSR to donors who support projects designed to increase agricultural production and improve rural welfare in developing countries.

Several chapters in this book demonstrate the need for researchers to focus on intra-household processes in order to gain a better understanding of the farming household's economy and relevant household activities; such an understanding would aid in the development of methods to enhance the relevance and probability of adoption of improved technology. FSR emphasizes the role of social scientists, especially anthropologists. The considerable effort currently being devoted to this exercise suggests in part that the complexity of African farming systems was previously not fully appreciated.

Implications for FSR in African Agricultural Production Systems

A farming system, or agricultural production system, is a bioeconomic activity in which the farmer or farm family manages certain resources to produce food, feed, fiber, shelter, and other necessary products. The farmers' objectives include not only production for subsistence and sale but also activities to "kill time" and break the monotony and tedium of living in rural areas. Although the main objective is usually to produce for subsistence and, increasingly, for cash, there are also subsidiary objectives that may be achieved in varying degrees on a given farm. A farming system may involve growing one or more crops, rearing one or more species of animals, or mixing to varying degrees the production of commodities with the rearing of animals. In Africa, a farm may be owned and managed by a single individual or farming family; if a family is involved, more than one family member is usually involved in farm work. Farming objectives may vary for different commodities in different parts of the farm or community; likewise, the objectives of the individuals involved in farming may vary. As a result, decisionmaking processes may involve several individuals, each with his or her own objectives in growing different crops in different situations and with different statuses and roles in the community. Because members of the farm family may be involved in farm work only part-time, their farming activities may be supplemented with a range of other activities, including wine tapping, cotton weaving, drumming, and marketing farm products or consumer goods.

African farming systems usually consist of more than one field system, or micro-environment, located at varying distances from each other and from the homestead. In each of these field systems, there may be variations in the types of commodities produced, the number of individuals at work, the intensity of farming, and the timing of activities. The various field systems under one farm family are often not farmed only by members of the family. The farm activities may involve not only division of labor among the family members but also interactions with other members of the community or adjacent communities. There are even situations where members of different families may own some crops in a field that is being farmed by another family under the prevailing land tenure system.

The situation is even more complex owing to the close ties that exist between family members, whether they are involved in farming or not, and the extended family system. Even among pastoralists, the situation in Africa is not simple. Their interactions with crop producers (or agriculturists) and their movements from place to place from one season to another result in a more complex situation than exists in other developing regions.

These complexities are further compounded by the continuous changes taking place in the wider society, including the growing commercialization of production, new agricultural production systems that interact and compete with traditional systems, interactions between rural and urban areas, and world economic conditions that may adversely affect African economies. Such complexities point to the need for a strong systems approach in research and development.

Importance of an Interdisciplinary Approach

Until the last several decades, agricultural research on Africa was largely conducted along traditional disciplinary lines. Except for some progress in increasing the productivity of certain plantation and arable cash crops in particular situations, e.g., tropical highlands, this approach did not succeed in developing efficient alternatives to the prevailing farming systems. The failure of the traditional "top-down approach" resulted in research to find more effective strategies for increasing agricultural productivity. As this book shows, FSR involves interdisciplinary studies of the farmers' overall environment, taking physical, biological, and socioeconomic factors into consideration; the dynamics of their production systems in relation to the environment; input/output relations; and constraints on increased production. These studies provide a basis for determining research strategies and priorities, both on the farms and at the research station, so that technologies are developed that will be relevant to the farmers' needs and dynamic circumstances. The nature and complexity of African farming systems make FSR—in which specialists in physiochemical, mechanical, biological, and socioeconomic disciplines interact among themselves and with farmers in studying the system, designing technology, and testing and evaluating new methods—more appropriate than disciplinary research.

Today's changing circumstances and the special complexities of African agricultural production clearly warrant a farming systems approach. It must be noted, however, that some increases in agricultural productivity were made in Africa without a significant amount of interdisciplinary research among social and biological scientists. For example, the introduction of new plants such as maize and cassava played a major role in increasing food production before the advent of agricultural research in Africa. In the colonial era, an increase in the output of plantation crops, such as rubber, cocoa, and oil palms and of such arable crops as cotton and groundnuts was achieved through individual commodity-based research. Increases in productivity were also achieved in favorable environments, such as the tropical highlands, where technologies and production systems were more amenable to horizontal transfer and adaptation because of relative similarity than they were in the lowland, humid tropical forest and savanna areas.

The International Agricultural Research Centers and FSR

The international agricultural research centers (IARCs) and a small number of national institutions have pioneered in the development of FSR. The institutionalization of FSR was, in my opinion, a necessary and welcome development in Africa. There is a general trend worldwide toward adoption of a systems approach as a philosophical framework for dealing with complex problems, not as a "panacea" but as a realistic and pragmatic way of seeking solutions.

Each IARC has a well-defined mandate in relation to the commodities and related production systems under its jurisdiction and its ecological zone of concern. Sometimes its mandate is not commodity based but focused on a specific problem, e.g., animal diseases or food policy. In some cases, farming systems are specifically included in an IARC's mandate. But priority subsystems, commodities, and component technologies in a given area do not always tally with the IARC's mandated problems, commodities, or systems of concern. For example, both the International Rice Research Institute (IRRI) and the International Institute of Tropical Agriculture (IITA) have only food crops in their mandates, but production systems for animals and crops outside their mandate are prominent in the locally prevailing farming systems. IARCs must give priority to developing methodologies and principles that apply to major benchmark areas and related production systems. Conversely, national institutions need to develop capabilities based on these principles and methodologies so that they may tune technologies more finely to local situations and problems. Too often, however, these national institutions, charged with ensuring that technologies developed at the IARC are finely tuned to specific local conditions and that problems outside the mandate of the IARC are addressed, lack the manpower and other resources necessary to accomplish this task.

Since the major review in 1978 by the Consultative Group on International Agricultural Research/Technical Advisory Committee (CGIAR/TAC), practitioners of FSR have been more confident about the relevance of the principles and methodologies of FSR. Despite the progress made in defining FSR and justifying its methodologies, the IARCs, which play a vital role in providing training and support for national programs, have not taken all possible steps to eliminate uncertainties about FSR or to strengthen it on a continuing basis. Among the actions they might take are (1) to minimize the limitations on FSR posed by the IARCs' mandates, possibly by establishing linkages with universities or with national institutions; (2) to institutionalize FSR on a more permanent, rather than temporary, basis; (3) to provide training in FSR as part of general agricultural training, more intensive training for specialists in disciplines relevant to FSR, and "in-service" training; and (4) to assure the professional advancement of persons engaged in FSR.

Conclusion

As the papers in this volume suggest, FSR and intrahousehold studies can lead to the development and use of appropriate agricultural technologies, more effective agricultural support systems, and improved government policies. Supporters have poured hundreds of thousands of dollars into these micro-studies. But an expanded investment, more time, and more systematic efforts to incorporate FSR into national programs may be needed for supporters' hopes and expectations to be realized.

Bede N. Okigbo
International Institute
of Tropical Agriculture

Acknowledgments

Many people helped to make this book possible. Katharine McKee commented on the papers at various stages in their development and suggested areas for revision. Henry Romney assisted in producing the final manuscript and arranging for publication. Laura Nagal and Linda Grandjean oversaw the numerous practical details of communications with the authors and the publisher and the preparation of the manuscript. Helen Handley checked and consolidated the bibliography. Most important, Jane Wilder Jacqz, our gifted consultant editor, did an extraordinary job of sharpening the writing and proving that social science jargon can, with care, be translated into English. The Rockefeller Foundation and the Ford Foundation supported the Intra-Household Processes and Farming Systems Analysis Conference with generous grants, and the Rockefeller Foundation also provided funding for the preparation of the book. The International Institute of Tropical Agriculture (IITA) offered to serve as the distributor of the book in Africa.

I am extremely grateful to the Conference participants for attending the meeting, held March 5–9, 1984, at the Rockefeller Foundation's Bellagio Study and Conference Center in Lake Como, Italy, and for sharing their experiences and concerns. They are George Abalu, Jocelyne Albert, Alva App, Sara Berry, Maimouna Diallo, Jean-Marc Gastellu, John D. Gerhart, Jane I. Guyer, Goran Hyden, Christine W. Jones, Uma Lele, Olga Linares, Allan Low, Katharine McKee, Charles Mann, John Mellor, D. W. Norman, David Nygaard, Thomas Odhiambo, C. Okali, Pauline E. Peters, Mandivamba Rukuni, Laurence Stifel, J. E. Sumberg, Helga Vierich, Abraham Weisblat, and Ruth Zagorin.

Joyce Lewinger Moock

Introduction

Joyce Lewinger Moock

The papers in this volume examine the relationship between farming systems research and studies of household decision-making as each bears upon the improvement of food production in Africa. Both types of research are gaining currency as national governments and the international development assistance community recognize the need to rehabilitate African agriculture and to understand more precisely the severe constraints faced by an economically rational smallholder sector.

Despite the several billions of dollars worth of development assistance given to Africa over the past two decades, the data base regarding African agriculture at the household level remains distressingly thin and fragmented, and the information that does exist is underutilized. To a large extent, this problem can be attributed to a bias in development strategies favoring industrialization, or large-scale commercial agriculture as the spearhead of economic growth. With attention focused away from smallholder farming, there has been relatively little motivation on the part of the agricultural research establishment, or of the donors who bankroll it, to examine fully the complex nexus of social and biological transactions that underlie agricultural practices in rural Africa. In addition, the scarcity of skilled indigenous manpower with solid training and/ or experience in local rural development issues has prompted highly centralized agricultural planning that has relied in large part on Western assumptions about the nature of Africa's farming households and production strategies.

The deepening economic crisis in many African states has highlighted the importance of a reliable agricultural surplus as a basic condition for industrial growth and for expanding rural income-generating, off-farm enterprises. Hard questions are now being asked about whether current agricultural policies, extension services, and technology transfers are capable of creating such a surplus among the household-based cropping and herding communities that form the mainstay of African agriculture.

1

Moreover, as lessons from the post-independence years accumulate, it is increasingly clear that the absence of any effective links between the development designs of national governments and the investment decisions taken by millions of smallholder food-producing households is a major impediment to economic growth and social welfare.

Farming systems research offers considerable potential for bridging this gap by providing a realistic assessment of the conditions under which different types of production units operate. Despite the diversity of activities and approaches described as "farming systems research" (FSR), there is a common objective: to make smallholder farming households the clients for agricultural research and to help develop viable technologies (or support services and policies) that are based on an intimate understanding of family resources and needs and that efficiently incorporate the constraints and flexibility of the current production system.

The FSR concept evolved during the years following the Green Revolution in Asia and Latin America when it became apparent that the basically centralized, "top-down" orientation of the international agricultural research community was not suitable for reaching resource-poor farmers, who are responsive to profit incentives but wary of technologies that may involve increased risk. While many conditions on the research station typically reflect those of resource-endowed farmers, they generally have little in common with the problems experienced by poor farmers—e.g., labor bottlenecks, lack of timely access to inputs, unreliable markets and unfavorable physical environments—including topography and soil conditions. In addition, farms operated by the resource-poor are often more complex than those of wealthier farmers in that they commonly feature intercropping rather than monocropping, smaller and often fragmented landholding units, heavier crop-livestock interaction and greater dependence on off-farm employment for supplemental earnings.

Farming systems research, in contrast to the typical technology transfer model, starts with the farming household and its agricultural production strategies. Through multidisciplinary assessment of the physical environment in which the application of technology occurs, of farmers' goals and preferences, and of the external social environment within which the producers and consumers who occupy farming households make their decisions, FSR practitioners seek to bring on-station scientists and development planners closer to understanding the perspectives of the large disadvantaged segment of their clientele. Under FSR, the critical test of technological innovation is not productivity or even efficiency per se but whether new practices are adaptable, profitable, and sustainable.

As a short-term approach to agricultural improvement, farming systems research has particular appeal in Africa because of the current lack of robust food production packages or of supportive policies that can move the region's resource-poor farming systems to the "high-tech" agriculture associated with the Green Revolution. Clearly, FSR is not a substitute for basic scientific research nor strategies aimed at the radical transformation of African agriculture. But with tens of millions of impoverished families dependent on fragile agricultural systems for their subsistence and a large portion of their cash earnings, incremental improvements in production and production stability are the sine qua non for coping with unchecked birth rates and for giving Africa valuable additional time to develop a longer-range solution to its agricultural problems.

The enormous variation in local resource conditions and associated patterns of domestic production arrangements found in Africa, however, presents some difficult challenges. Agricultural decision-making, the central focus of FSR, is a complex phenomenon in Africa where household members are highly specialized by age and sex in the tasks that they perform and in their spheres of economic responsibility. Husbands and wives, for example, often farm independently, mobilize different factors of production and manage separate budgets. The social status of senior family members may entail kin-related obligations, such as hiring more laborers than needed, that affect the investment of accumulated wealth in ways that conflict with agricultural improvement. Also, individual income-earners within the household often retain full or partial control over their own earnings.

Moreover, the membership of farming households may be difficult to define owing to the prevalence of extended, and frequently polygynous, family systems and the seasonal mobility of labor responding to off-farm employment opportunities. The overlap (or "nesting") of farm management units in Africa and the high incidence of individualized decision-making and control over resources within units makes the conventional notion, of a simple coordinated household group in which welfare gains are distributed equitably among all members, very misleading. Further complications arise when one attempts to sort out linkages among different types of households, since labor relations and other forms of exchange also tend to be more individualized than is assumed in Western-based household models and since gender is often a key mediating factor.

Recently, a body of studies concerned with the dynamics of household decision-making in Africa has emerged that reveals a great deal of information about the social phenomena in which FSR practitioners should be interested. These studies focus on the interplay between production and consumption activities within the household and emphasize time as a scarce factor. The research covers a number of interrelated issues: the nature of off-farm employment sought by various family members throughout the year and its conflict with the cropping calendar; whether income is pooled; whether separate male and female economies exist within the household; how time is spent, especially by women, in field crop and livestock production, home garden cultivation, fuel and water collection, childcare, food preparation, marketing and participation in community political events; the substitutability of labor among family members; and the ways in which production resources are mobilized across family groupings. Because major changes in farming practices often require significant adjustments in the amount and timing of labor inputs within and possibly between households, it seems important that these complex factors affecting production decisions are taken into account when predicting a new technology's impact on rural communities.

Household decision-making studies, which have largely been conducted by anthropologists and nutritionists, and by economists interested in what is sometimes called the "new household economics," can enrich farming systems research by helping to define appropriate units for analysis, to place time values on non-farm activities that compete with food production for labor inputs, and to specify the distributive effects of changes in farm practices on individual members of the household. Information, however, has a cost in terms of both time and money, and it is not altogether clear how much of this type of detail is needed, nor when it is needed for farming systems research to do its job.

In March 1984, the Ford Foundation and the Rockefeller Foundation organized a conference to assess the state of knowledge regarding household decision-making dynamics in Africa and to elucidate the ways in which these processes relate to farming systems research and agricultural policy. A group of scholars and practitioners concerned with FSR, as well as persons involved more directly in the traditions of anthropology, economics, political science and agronomic science, met at the Bellagio Study and Conference Center (Bellagio, Italy) for the better part of a week to discuss the merits and problems of making household behavior analysis a primary component of the agricultural research and development process for smallholder farming.[1] The papers in this volume were selected from presentations at the meeting and reflect, in their revised state, views exchanged across the conference table.

Although all the papers are empirical in nature, they can be divided roughly into three categories. The first set focuses on disciplinary or methodological contributions to FSR and household studies (Low, Guyer, McKee). The second presents recent field studies of household behavior in Africa (Jones, Savané, Peters, Vierich, Okali and Sumberg). The third concerns specific aspects of micro-level agricultural research in the region, e.g., the historical specificity of Africa's peasant agriculture (Hyden), the structure and application of FSR in Africa (Norman and Baker, Gerhart), implications for training (Rukuni), and implications for policy (Berry). The material is drawn from many parts of the sub-continent and covers a wide variety of crop, livestock and small ruminant production systems.

All of the papers recognize the importance of bringing insights from household decision-making studies to bear on some of the questions posed in farming systems research about the characteristics of African farming families. In particular, they point out the need to link differences in behavior among households to variations in their structure and composition as well as to the resulting time values placed by various family members on off-farm and household maintenance activities. The case studies in this book show that, given the high degree of specialization within the African household, the appropriateness of new technology will depend in part on who performs what tasks, who controls what resources and who has which kinds of family responsibilities to meet with their income. The studies also indicate that to overlook women's roles in both the farm production process and the wider decision-making processes of the household can have unfortunate consequences for efficiency and can result in welfare losses for the entire family.

The papers, however, identify a number of substantive and pragmatic problems that arise in attempting to create a critical synthesis of household decision making analysis and FSR which might usefully inform agricultural policy and development. An underlying objective of the Bellagio meeting was to test whether such a synthesis is feasible at this time, by exposing scholars and practitioners from relevant research traditions to each other's methods and approaches. While anthropologists, for example, stress the need for paying attention to the ways in which non-market relations control access to production resources in the agricultural systems of partially monetized economies, how can such qualitative insights be quantified for use in formal economic analysis? If, as many of the papers argue, joint objectives at the level of the household do not necessarily prevail in Africa, resulting in an absence of allocative efficiency, what guidelines can FSR practitioners follow to identify the appropriate units of analysis? To what extent should technology development be held accountable for achieving welfare distribution goals within the household? What types of data are needed to predict the likelihood, speed and nature of socio-economic adjustments to short-run inequities within the family? How can we use participant-observation methods, usually requiring relatively long immersion in the rural area under study, and historical analysis of production strategies to enrich the rapid survey techniques characteristic of farming systems studies?

The meeting did not provide precise answers to all such questions, but there was considerable value in posing them. Many questions were discussed concerning the breadth and detail of research needed for FSR to achieve worthwhile results. Most participants felt that there are diminishing returns to in-depth socio-economic studies within the FSR framework but that, with a firm understanding of an area's human organization, shrewd analyses of the local economy could be developed from rapid reconnaissance survey methodologies.

From the spirited discussions in Bellagio, five central themes emerged and are reflected in the papers presented in this volume. The first, raised initially by Low, stresses the importance for farming systems research and macro-economic policy of the two-way relationship between agricultural productivity and household welfare. Drawing on Hyden's thesis that universal access to land and lack of a labor surplus in most parts of Africa have resulted in specialization within, rather than between, households, Low argues that members of farm families are often heavily engaged in non-farm activities, including household maintenance and child-care, and that these compete directly with on-farm uses of labor, compromising farm production. The papers by Guyer, Jones, Okali and Sumberg show that, given the sharp division of labor and responsibility by age and sex within the household, and given the individual control of income, members of the domestic unit do not necessarily use the same criteria for evaluating new technology.

A number of papers in the volume accuse FSR of paying insufficient attention to the multiple objectives of individual farmers within the household; FSR is also said to base farm-level analysis on incorrect assumptions about intra-household dynamics. Norman and Baker point out, in response, that giving attention to these areas when the theoretical basis for analysis is insufficient and efficient methodological tools are lacking may cost too much in relation to the benefits derived from maintaining a sharp, problem-solving focus and obtaining quick results. The conference also made it clear that the field of intra-household analysis is still new and that many problems exist in defining the critical units of analysis amid an array of intersecting domestic spheres, in identifying the appropriate decision-maker with respect to proposed innovations, and in measuring and giving value to household resources—especially the allocation of time.

The second theme to emerge emphasizes the complex linkages between intra- and inter-household variables in determining resource access and control. Since the farming system is a response to external environmental factors, as well as the product of farmers' goals and resource allocation decisions, conference participants argued that one must look outside the household to explain its adjustment to changes in economic opportunities and incentives. Too often, household-level studies provide only static portraits of behavior, captured at one moment in time. Unless one links households and their members with social spheres of interaction in the wider society, it is hard to understand what causes them to shift their production strategies over time. The papers by Peters, Hyden, and Vierich indicate that viable production and income-generating strategies by individual farming households depend upon their being embedded in supra-household networks. According to Peters, "These supra-household linkages may take the form of mutual aid or have the character of patron-client relations. Whatever the form, it is clear that access to key resources or to basic factors of production lies outside the household as often as it lies within it—even in the short run."

But if FSR teams are to trace the flow of rights, obligations and resources that shape tradeoffs between different cropping and livestock systems and between off-farm and non-farm activities and if they are to judge how household and community composition helps to determine that flow, they must have clear analytic frameworks and compact methodologies for carrying out their investigations. Here again, as several papers point out, there are few shortcuts readily available—few substitutes for sophisticated, time-consuming field work on these subjects.

Gender issues in farming systems research and agricultural policy were the third theme to permeate both the discussions at Bellagio and the papers. A concern about gender issues in agriculture is often interpreted to mean an interest in designing technology suitable for the conditions under which women work and for their food production responsibilities. But interest in gender relations also derives from the explanatory power of gender as a primary organizing principle of society, including the society's agricultural production. The household analysts represented in this volume point out the significance of gender not just as a means of categorizing labor or household headship, but as a basic key to understanding structures and actions, including production relationships within and across households, the setting of goals and priorities, the mobilization of resources, willingness to take risk, and the rights to benefits derived from increased farm production.

Many questions were raised in Bellagio about whether it is possible to discern general patterns in women's roles across agricultural systems and about the types of information needed to understand existing interactions between women's household activities and market-related activities and to predict their future course. The current knowledge base, represented by the small sample of literature in this volume, points to the need for FSR and agricultural policy generally to give greater attention to the agricultural roles and responsibilities of women. Examples are accumulating of poor farmer responses to agricultural development projects in Africa because gender issues were not adequately understood by project sponsors. Jones provides a dramatic illustration of this situation. Evidence is not yet in hand, however, that would answer some of the most important questions about how gender issues bear on the larger context of agricultural development. We know little about the conditions leading to previous shifts of gender roles or about how they might change under new conditions; about whether women can realize gains in welfare only as a direct result of their own activities, as opposed to the activities of the household unit; or about the extent to which, and the circumstances under which, gender, as distinct from other factors of socio-economic differentiation, influences agricultural production behavior. It is worth noting in regard to this last point that, according to Savané and Vierich, gender divisions themselves are subject to variations by social class and by the labor composition of the household over time.

Although the complex issues surrounding women's roles within the household and agricultural development are slowly being unraveled, we clearly need to learn a great deal more about the ways in which social relationships are reinforced, or redefined, in Africa as part of household strategies for gaining or defending access to productive resources. While several Bellagio participants expressed concern about the difficulty of fitting gender concerns into the closely focused agenda for farming systems research, others such as Guyer contended that, "It is not a question of grafting on a new factor, but of having recourse to a whole other framework of analysis, one which holds fewer factors constant and, as a result, can address long-term change."

The fourth theme highlights the insufficient role that FSR and household studies have played to date in strengthening agricultural policy. This topic provoked the most heated debate of the conference.

Both Gerhart and Hyden note in their papers that attention to the human aspects of agricultural development has been one of FSR's most important conceptual contributions. The systems perspective helps to bring agricultural research closer to the users of agricultural technology by demonstrating that farming is a complex enterprise, integrating physical, biological and socio-economic components. In some parts of Africa, the farming system is sufficiently flexible at the micro-level so that technology, finely tuned to local circumstances, can have, in and of itself, a major impact on production efficiency. But it is more often the case that changes in support services and policy are also needed to achieve progress toward a more productive and stable farming system.

It is hard to deny that policy has a major role to play in solving problems that relate to the distribution of benefits.

Yet, several conference participants argued that, in practice, FSR remains a micro-level approach that helps farmers operate better under resource-poor conditions rather than changing those portions of their circumstances that are amenable to policy intervention. They also noted that farming systems economists are usually more concerned about building links with technical scientists than with economists in such areas as marketing or macro-policy. The FSR representatives at the meeting took issue with the strongest of these statements but explained that to the extent these criticisms were justified, the problem results largely from the fact that FSR teams are often based at crop research institutes which focus on production constraints and have little direct interest in policy.

A parallel argument can be presented with regard to household studies. Berry's paper notes the many ways in which household rights and responsibilities shape farmers' responses to policy interventions and the ways in which such interventions, in turn, can affect patterns of resource acquisition, allocation and control. However, the value of household studies for policy improvement is frequently limited, either by the conceptual isolation of the domestic unit from social phenomena in the wider society or by the highly esoteric, non-practical form in which such studies are often presented.

The papers in this volume offer considerable evidence that a great deal of micro-level information is needed in order to manipulate the social environment in a scientific manner. As biological scientists are striving to create new technologies suited to local agro-climatic conditions, national governments should be able to anticipate the social problems that may arise from these innovations and to predict what complex adjustments families and societies may need to make. Farming systems research and household studies have enormous untapped potential for offering assistance in this regard.

The fifth theme seeks to unite the virtues of a cost and time efficient farming systems research approach with the need to understand the complex relationships that affect production decisions and, in the long-run, determine technology's impact on rural households and communities. The conference recognized that FSR has encountered great difficulty in incorporating socio-economic studies into its framework, mainly because the pressures of funding cycles do not permit adequate analysis of large quantities of data. In addition, as Rukuni notes, the present dearth of social scientists in national agricultural research programs who possess the requisite training and experience to conduct interdisciplinary, problem-solving research, emphasizing subtleties of detail, has impeded the building of rigorous socio-economic analysis into FSR methodology. In order to institutionalize FSR at the national level, it seems necessary at this time to offer a minimum content of socio-economic concepts needed for short-term research about technology adoption.

McKee's paper responds to this dilemma by outlining three levels of household decision-making analysis which can complement current farming systems work: simple studies which fit directly within the FSR framework; in-depth analyses of specific issues raised in the course of farming systems investigations; and basic, long-term studies which illuminate the processes of agricultural change and build a pool of knowledge as a foundation for technology development and policy formulation. In regard to the third level of analysis, Rukuni's paper reminds us that "a good bit of household and social analysis has already been done and is ongoing in Africa, but African researchers have few effective links for keeping up-to-date with developments elsewhere on the continent . . . farming systems researchers in Africa would benefit from a network providing access to some of the longer-term in-depth studies that are often missing from or given low priority by on-farm research."

These are a few of the highlights of the Bellagio conference and the papers selected from it. The volume, which explores the advantages of merging separate micro-level research traditions and reflects a dialogue among disciplines, negotiates some rocky conceptual and methodological terrain. Nevertheless, it provides a fertile source of new ideas and hypotheses that allow more relevant and valid enquiry into the micro-bases of current agricultural transformation processes in Africa. It also shows that Africa's deep-rooted agricultural problems require interdisciplinary attention and a new effort to place locale-specific studies within the context of the larger human and institutional forces that are shaping agrarian change on the African continent.

Notes

1. The conference was organized by the author, in collaboration with Katharine McKee, a program officer of the Ford Foundation. The original idea for the meeting came from Abraham Weisblat, then a staff member of the Agricultural Development Council, New York. Participants included university scholars, biological and social scientists from international agricultural research institutes, members of African national research organizations and professional staff from donor agencies.

1

The Invisible Economy of Smallholder Agriculture in Africa

Goran Hyden

The most alarming aspect of African agriculture today is not its declining performance in the last decade but the very limited prospects of any improvement in the future. This paper discusses the constraints on African agricultural productivity, the historical specificity of African economic and political development, the independent nature of Africa's economy and its ambiguous role in development, and the urgent need to adopt new agricultural strategies, drawing in part on the farming systems approach, if African governments are to avoid losing control of their own economic bases.

Introduction

Although figures differ, there is general agreement that the trend has been downward since the early 1970s. According to a recent African survey (ECA 1983, 8-9) for the whole of that decade, when Africa's population was expanding at an average annual rate of around 2.8 percent, total food production in Africa was rising by no more than 1.5 percent. Food self-sufficiency ratios dropped from 98 percent in the 1960s to approximately 86 percent in 1980. This means that, on average, each African had about 12 percent less home-grown food in 1980 than 20 years earlier. With food production stagnating and demand, particularly for cereals, keeping pace with population growth, the volume of food imports between 1970 and 1980 increased by an average annual rate of 8.4 percent. In 1980, imports of food grains alone reached 20.4 million tons, costing African countries over $5 billion (not including heavy ocean freight costs). Food aid to Africa in 1980 was 1.5 million tons.

Although national data on African agricultural output may paint an incomplete picture, it would be wrong to brush aside such statistics and assume that there is no agrarian crisis. To be sure, as Sara Berry reminds us (1983, 4) national aggregates and indices on which we tend to base our judgments derive from foreign trade statistics, data on domestic purchases of agricultural commodities by official marketing agencies, and agricultural censuses or surveys, i.e., officially sanctioned activities. Because smallholder farmers tend to opt out to the official system[1] and resort to parallel markets where prices are more favorable, production may be significantly higher than official records suggest. Nevertheless, the tendency of small producers to withdraw from the official system is at the core of the present crisis: by exercising their "exit" option, African peasant farmers are limiting official policy choice and implementation. Government structures lose their ability to reverse the deteriorating trends. As a result, the severity of the crisis grows and the prospects for a turn to the better lessen.

This is one reason why it is difficult to share the optimism expressed in the 1981 World Bank Report outlining measures to accelerate development in sub-Saharan Africa. The authors are correct in arguing for economic policies that are more attractive to peasant farmers but they are far too confident that, with such policies and increased foreign aid, Africa's economies will begin to show sustained growth. Neither the official economy nor relevant public sector institutions can perform the wonders anticipated by the Bank. After 25 years of independence, governing and policy-making institutions in Africa have taken on the political and social color of the continent's own material realities. Government ministries in Africa no longer resemble the Western model of rational-legal bureaucracy (Moris 1976, 1981).

In this situation, improvement in public management is not likely to be achieved by adopting training and development devices from experiences in other world areas, as proposed in the 1983 World Development Report. Some experiences may be transferred to Africa on a selective basis, but the lessons to be learned from abroad are more likely to be historical than immediately translatable into operational and methodological guidelines. The real lessons to be learned come from Africa's own experience to date.

It is a great mistake to assume that Africa is already part of the mainstream of international development: that it is accessible to policy interventions which have proved successful elsewhere. We are not sufficiently sensitive to the structural constraints—and opportunities— that are peculiar to African societies. Development economists and, more recently, their political economist colleagues have all described and analyzed Africa as if it were already an integral part of world capitalism. Whether portrayed as "rational peasant" or "proletarian," the African smallholder has been assumed to function in a predominantly capitalist setting. As a result, the international debate about development in Africa has centered on such issues as "the adverse effects of capitalism" and "the prospects for socialism."

Because African states joined the international community at a time when these issues were prominent in world development, their acceptance of this predominant credo was inferred. To obtain foreign aid, African leaders necessarily danced to tunes played by the dominant forces on the global scene. As a result, they have been led down a blind alley. They have distanced themselves from the economic facts of their own countries. Caught in the dark, together with their donor friends, they face a hard and painful return to reality. That is why declining performance today may be only the initial warning signal of an even worse crisis. It is also why we must discard conventional concepts and models and, instead, begin to analyze African society in its own terms.

Understanding Hidden Processes

Understanding micro-processes in Africa, including farming systems and intra-household processes, may give us a better understanding of how society at large operates and of the public institutions that have been created to govern African society. Focusing on such micro-processes may seem strange, but the knowledge of Africa gained in the last three decades has given us little understanding of how macro-processes are, and can be, influenced by forces operating outside the national government.

The generalizing and abstracting modes of social science inquiry have been predominant in the literature on African development, and it is time to temper this approach with the sensitivity to historical specificity that characterizes humanistic study. This poses an especially difficult challenge to the student of African agriculture. The data base for Africa is thin, and there is great variation in the organization of social and productive life (Guyer 1981). Farming systems are highly locale-specific. For these and other reasons, the researcher would be well advised not to take theoretical assumptions for granted but, rather, to develop new hypotheses or questions that allow more relevant, valid inquiry.

In some respects, researchers today are in the same position as the early anthropologists, although our goals are different. Unlike them, we are not concerned only with the culturally exotic nature of African society. Our focus on the grassroots is not an end in itself. It is the instrument through which we may be able to unveil the hitherto hidden processes prevailing behind official policy-making structures in Africa. Farming systems research and intra-household analysis may, at first glance, appear to be a tiny peephole but they are like a microscope: through this instrument we can perceive social phenomena that have so far been largely unrecognized by observers of the African scene. By looking through the microscope, we can gain a better understanding of Africa's complex social processes and economic transactions.

The Historical Specificity of Africa

Africa's political economy has a peculiar and anomalous character. But the road to recognition of Africa's historical specificity has been long and winding.[2]

When independent African states came into being some 25 years ago, the world was bubbling with faith in progress. Captivated by scientific and technological success, the postwar generations in both West and East lost their sense of proportion. Against the background of an almost religious faith in secularization through the expanded uses of science and technology, they lost sight of the finite, temporal and historical nature of man's position in society. To liberal, positivist scholarship in the 1950s and 1960s, history had become irrelevant and thus superfluous. The express intent of much writing about Africa, in the context of this optimistic "modernization" approach, was to demonstrate the universal applicability of theoretical assumptions and, thus, enhance the respectability of indigenous African institutions. Many scholars discounted the exotic nature of African society and argued that the way Africans organized their lives wasn't so different, after all, from what was happening in the rest of the world. Although this view was important at both the academic and political levels, it was oriented primarily toward an uneducated Western public.

In the late 1960s and early 1970s, a radical refutation of the modernization paradigm emerged. This view was also characterized by an ahistorical perspective. Equipped with Lenin's writings on imperialism and Gunder Frank's crude application of that theory to Latin America, students of Africa began trying to prove that African economies were subjugated by world capitalism. Although this brought attention to social and economic processes that had been ignored in previous studies, there was a tendency to apply, far too simplistically and uncritically, conventional categories and concepts borrowed from Marxist theory. Any social confrontation was quickly perceived as a "class conflict," and any major anti-capitalist move by an African government became, if not a "revolution," at least proof of a socialist transformation. Like the earlier "modernization" theory, this was a way of studying Africa through Western glasses.

In the last few years there has been a gradual shift toward a more objective and sensible form of Marxist scholarship, which has opened the door to greater recognition of the historical specificity of the African political economy. It is significant that this emerging school has been inspired by scholars outside the Anglophone academic community. Particularly important has been the contribution by French anthropologists and historians concerned with the transformation of indigenous forms of organization and production in Africa over the last century.[3] Working independently, Asian scholars have advanced similar arguments (Banji 1973).

Grouped together in what is now known as the "articulation of modes of production" school, these new scholars recognize the existence of precapitalist modes of production in rural Africa. They have until now concentrated their analysis on how these precapitalist modes in interaction with capital are either dissolved or preserved and on the implications of these tendencies.[4]

With this latest orientation in scholarship, the dust of the great debates of the 1960s and 1970s has finally settled. It is now increasingly possible to identify the factors that give the African political economy its peculiar and anomalous character. Although we are still at an initial stage, I would like to comment on three factors that determine not only agricultural development in sub-Saharan Africa but also, indirectly, the character of broader social, economic and political processes on the continent: the absence of intermediate technology, the relative autonomy of the peasant producers and the absence of agricultural surplus labor.

The Absence of Intermediate Technology

There is no indigenous tradition in Africa of land alienation and concentration similar to that found on other continents. This phenomenon arose only in colonial times and was important mainly in territories with a considerable number of European settlers, notably Kenya and Rhodesia. Africa never developed truly feudal societies or produced anything like the highly regimented forms of small-scale agriculture that permitted the rise of the great Asian civilizations. To be sure, there was an ongoing process of social differentiation in both precolonial and colonial days, leading to apparent differences of wealth in most societies; but even in places with feudal tendencies, like Buganda, Ashanti, northern Nigeria and Ethiopia, the trend to feudalism was clearly feeble. Precolonial agriculture in various parts of Africa remained technologically simple and was characterized by limited scope for surplus extraction. Although colonial authorities turned the bulk of the African peasants into commodity producers and brought about considerable changes in farming systems, agriculture remained, at the time of independence, an activity largely controlled by peasants with access to their own land.

A major reason for the virtual absence of land alienation and concentration in sub-Saharan Africa is that societies did not acquire the technological means to realize it. As Jack Goody argues, in the absence of the wheel, plow and all other concomitant aspects of an "intermediate technology" for agricultural development, sub-Saharan Africa was unable to match the improvements in skills and productivity and, consequently, the changes in specialization and stratification that marked agrarian societies, e.g., in medieval Europe or the Far East (Goody 1971). Africa developed its own empires and kingdoms, but the ones that sustained themselves over any length of time did so by appropriating a surplus from the slave trade or other forms of long-distance trade.[5] When such trade declined, so did the power of the rulers. The absence of an "intermediate technology" may also explain why, for example, the British failed to develop a feudal system of land tenure in Buganda and, instead, reverted to a policy of promoting small-scale peasant production.[6]

Although African farmers are engaged in commodity production, usually for the world market, their systems and forms of production are still characterized by low productivity levels per unit of land. Activities are not structurally differentiated according to a strategy of specialized production, nor is labor specialized. Money wages are still a marginal phenomenon in the rural economies in many parts of Africa. Peasant farming is embedded in a multiplicity of occupations and tasks, and, although African villagers are increasingly differentiated by property, kinship and occupational emphasis, they are, as Hart (1982, 78-79) emphasizes never so specialized that it would be possible to identify production units in which all major branches of the economy are not somehow inextricably linked. Specialization exists only among members of the household.

The low productivity of peasant agriculture on the continent is manifested in the cumulative discrepancy between African production rates and rates achieved elsewhere in the world. While the world average for the output of cereals is about 2,000 kg per hectare, Africa's average reaches only half that figure—and, because of gains in productivity in other Third World countries, the gap is growing. For roots and tubers, the difference is less dramatic but still a cause of concern: while Africa's average of approximately 7 tons per hectare has remained stagnant for many years, the world average has shot up and now reaches 11 tons per hectare. The low productivity of African agriculture can also be deduced from its low levels of fertilizer consumption. The latter stands at only 3 kg per hectare of agricultural area while fertilizer consumption in Latin America and Asia is respectively over 8 kg and 26 kg per hectare of agricultural area (ECA 1983). These figures should be judged against the fact that, although Africa's potential arable land is estimated at about 1.7 hectares for each African person, only about 0.55 hectares per person is being utilized at present. Implied in these figures is that, compared with Asia, African agriculture remains extensive and may require fewer inputs, but it is precisely this form of agriculture that has the smallest scope for significant productivity gains, particularly when carried out on marginal lands as in the Sahel.

Impressive improvements in peasant agriculture have occurred in many parts of Africa since 1900, but these have usually resulted from demographic and ecological circumstances rather than farsighted government policies. In the highlands of Kenya, for example, the catalyst of change has been growing population pressures, which have forced peasant farmers to adopt new land-use practices. Relatively good soils have facilitated the transformation to more intensive forms of cultivation. Colonial policies, notably those based on the Swynnerton Plan, which sought to create a class of yeoman farmers by giving them title deeds to their land and encouraging cash cropping, no doubt helped to accelerate this process, but it would be wrong to attribute the transformation of peasant agriculture in Kenya to only those interventions (Cowen 1981, Leys 1975). Spontaneous social forces then at play, including the Mau Mau rebellion, were equally important.

The Relative Autonomy of the Peasant Producer

The second factor shaping African agricultural development and social, economic and political processes in Africa is the relative autonomy of the individual producer.

As a result of the transformation to more intensive forms of cultivation in central Kenya, cited above, the Kenyan peasant is quite heavily dependent on the regular provision of inputs for his farming and, in this respect, is extensively incorporated into the market economy. Because he has become dependent on the ability of the official system to serve him reliably and efficiently, he is forced increasingly to accept the dictates of the official system. He is also increasingly at the mercy of those who manage the economic system because he can no longer withdraw from it without risk of a substantial loss in his economic and social status.

This may be the road that all of Africa's peasant farmers will one day travel, but at this point in time it would be wrong to assume that the bulk of Africa's farmers are captives of official economic systems. Most peasant producers enjoy an unusual degree of autonomy from other groups in society, mainly because of the rudimentary technology that still characterizes most peasant production.

Members of African farming households are engaged not only in production but in socially necessary labor. In addition to tilling the land, they do a great many other things both during the farming season and after it. Although the following description from West Africa may not apply universally, it sums up much of what peasant households do to sustain themselves.

> They build and repair their houses; they prepare food and fetch water, fuel and other domestic supplies; they spin, weave, and sew clothing; they keep animals, slaughter them, and tan their hides; they make tools, pots, baskets, furniture and ornaments; they generate remedies for their ills; they run their own systems of conflict resolution and work hard to keep a variety of spiritual agents appeased (Hart 1982, 78).

Not every household member does everything. Husbands and wives combine to carry on most tasks falling within the sphere of the household economy; children are drawn in to care for crops, animals and smaller children, and combinations of relatives or neighbors help each other with farming, construction and other heavy jobs. Although villagers normally have an astonishing ability to ensure everyone's livelihood, the absence of a key household member can have adverse effects on other family members. If the male head of the household seeks urban employment and maintains little contact with his rural family, the burden on his wife may be unbearable; agricultural production may decline, and the children may become victims of malnutrition.[7] Even the absence of children at school often means inadequate care for crops, animals and smaller children. (In this situation, where all household members are engaged in socially necessary labor, the margins for maneuver are very limited; it is no wonder that a pro-fertility orientation prevails [Caldwell 1976].)

The fragmentation and autonomy at the level of each unit of production are reinforced by the fact that there is no independently systematized knowledge underpinning the prevailing modes of production.[8] The necessary knowledge is in the producer's head, and it is normally transmitted from one generation to another through apprenticeship rather than formal training. Production is often cleverly adjusted to local conditions and usually ecologically sound, but man's relation to nature in this situation is one of symbiosis rather than manipulation.[9]

In the absence of product specialization, there is very little exchange of goods among the various units of production. Also, there is no structural interdependence that brings production units into reciprocal relations with each other, leading to a refinement of the means of production.

Because there has been little surplus product, smallholder agriculture has proved an inadequate base for the elaborate development programs adopted since independence. Even more noteworthy, however, is the method by which surplus product is appropriated in a system dominated by independent peasant producers.

Under feudalism and capitalism, for example, appropriations of surplus product are made in the immediate context of production, on either the landed estate or in the factory. In these systems, the state is functionally and structurally linked to the productive demands of the economy and can be used by the rulers to steer and control society. The submerged classes have no choice but to respond to the dictates of the system at large.

In a mode of production where independent producers prevail, relations are every different. When the productive and reproductive needs of peasants are met without the support of other social classes, relations between those who rule and those who till the land are not firmly rooted in the production systems as such. Instead, appropriations of surplus product are made by the state through taxes, representing simple deductions from an already produced stock of value.[10] The relationship between peasant and state becomes tributary rather than productive and implies a much more limited degree of social control. From the point of view of the individual peasant producer, the state is structurally superfluous, and it is not difficult to understand that the African farmer perceives many public policy actions aimed at improving his agriculture as "foreign" interventions. Because the peasant is so extensively in control of his own production and reproduction on the land, he can escape government policy demands to an extent that is certainly denied to either a tenant under feudal rule or a worker under capitalism. There is growing evidence that peasants in Africa are using this "exit" option, particularly in instances where government policies are viewed as a threat or as being void of any apparent benefits to the producer (Berry 1983).

What emerges is that African governments are structurally much less well-placed to affect agricultural development than governments in either Asia or Latin America. Their access to the peasant producer is limited and must often be accepted on the latter's terms, i.e., the peasant determines whether anything is going to be implemented. For this reason, it is an unfortunate anomaly that virtually all responsibility for agricultural development is concentrated in government and its extension services. This perpetuates a "top-down" approach that stands very little chance of yielding anticipated results. Informed policy must recognize that the solution to Africa's agrarian crisis cannot be found in government-directed measures only.

The Absence of Agricultural Surplus Labor

The third factor that gives African development its historical specificity is that urbanization and industrialization are taking place at a time when agricultural surplus labor is still lacking in the rural areas. This phenomenon has led to strong informal linkages between urban and rural areas that are not found in societies where productivity gains in agriculture have rendered superfluous a growing proportion of the agricultural labor force.

In the early days of colonial rule, authorities used compulsion to recruit labor for productive work outside the peasant household. Forced labor and harsh methods were at the bottom of many early uprisings against colonial authority and a continuous source of tension in relations between colonial governments and African peasant producers.[11] Since compulsory labor offended the sensibilities of some metropolitan legislators, this method was eventually abandoned in favor of taxation. Taxation, an indirectly coercive method, was subsequently used extensively throughout Africa to cause rural area males to leave their residences and seek paid employment. To ensure stability in the work force, migrant laborers on plantations or in the towns were often recruited from far-distant places so that they could not easily maintain contact with the social networks in their home areas.[12]

Today, the social stigma attached to being a migrant is very different from the days of colonial rule. Urbanization has been rapid, particularly since independence. Between 1960 and 1980 Africa experienced the world's highest rural-urban migration rate. From a level of less than 20 percent in 1960, Africa was nearly 30 percent urbanized in 1980, implying an annual growth rate of about 5 percent or almost double the growth rate of the total population (ECA 1983). In the early days of rural emigration, village elders may have feared a permanent loss of male labor but such fears have proved exaggerated. Migrants have not given up links to their home communities in the rural areas. As so many studies have demonstrated,[13] urban migrants almost invariably claim that they plan to retire in their home village and, in pursuit of this objective, they remit a considerable amount of money, not only to sustain family members left behind but also to invest in agricultural improvement and to purchase new land.

With rapidly rising population, this pattern may soon disappear in certain parts of Africa but, because town is to most Africans still only a place to live and not "home," the social orientation of the bulk of Africa's urban population has remained rural. City-dwelling Africans have not developed the specific urban orientation that is typical of townspeople in other parts of the world. Thus, Elkan's observation that it is wrong to equate the growth of towns in Africa with the growth of an urban proletariat seems as valid today as it did in 1960 (Elkan 1960). Current statistics tell us little about the extent to which the towns are capable of developing new forms of social orientation and social action; but it is certain that, compared with the urban centers of colonial days, they have, in the process of accepting an accelerating influx of rural immigrants, become increasingly ruralized. The distinction between rural and urban life has grown less apparent, and forms of social interaction and modes of conducting business increasingly reflect indigenous—originally rural—practices.

To be sure, there are differences among different parts of Africa. West Africa had already developed its own towns as enclaves for long-distance trade before the advent of colonial rule, but, because of a decline in trade and European neglect of these centers, they failed to develop a distinctly urban character or orientation. In this respect, there was less alienation of urban migrants in West Africa than there was in East Africa during colonial days. The urban migrant in southern Africa seems to be more alienated from his rural origin than his counterpart in East or West Africa. Colin Murray has shown with respect to migrant laborers from Lesotho that the costs of divided families have been high in virtually all cases (Murray 1981). This may be explained both by the regimented, proletarian conditions under which migrants must live in South African cities and by the legacy of underdevelopment that characterizes much of the countryside in southern Africa, where there are few incentives to invest money in productive activities. Similarly, a study of urban migration in Zambia shows that, compared to other parts of Africa, the number of respondents claiming that they want to retire in the rural areas is exceptionally low (Hedlund and Lundahl 1983). Concomitantly, southern African migrants remit money to their families in rural areas less regularly and tend to abandon them more frequently than migrants in other parts of Africa.

The extensive influx into the urban areas of people, both rich and poor, who through ownership of and access to land maintain a rural orientation—combined with the absence of a firmly established ruling class and, thus, an elite culture—gives an inevitably populist character to African society. There are strong informal ties between town and village that are not found in societies where a growing proportion of the agricultural labor force is being rendered superfluous by increased agricultural productivity. Surveys which focus on only the official flows of funds from urban to rural areas in Africa, and which assume that income differentials based on official statistics reflect African social realities, generally miss the mark. In most African countries there is a net flow of resources through informal channels from urban to rural areas. Some resources are used for social maintenance purposes but others represent investments in agricultural development. These transfers take place both within the context of a single family, where the male head works in town and other members are rurally based, and within community-based social networks—some officially registered as welfare

or improvement associations, others being ad hoc groups mobilized for
a specific event or project. Although these networks and linkages are
increasingly reported in the literature, their macro-economic and political
significance have scarcely been recognized. Because they are largely
"invisible," i.e., do not show up in official statistics, are fluid and are
difficult to get a handle on, they tend to be ignored by economic analysts
and policymakers alike.

An Economy Apart: Not Capitalism Nor Socialism

Despite the greater openness and pragmatism of current scholarship on
Africa, there is still an underlying assumption that, to serve its own
interests, capitalism has subjugated other forms of economic and social
organization in Africa. Even advocates of the "articulation of modes of
production" school—which recognizes the existence of precapitalist modes
of production in rural Africa—argue that, where capitalism has failed
to transform precapitalist formations, these are preserved in the interest
of capitalistic growth, i.e., that capitalism feeds on the weaknesses of
outdated indigenous structures. This excessively centrist (metropolitan)
view of Africa, which reduces indigenous formation to a passive role
in development, is part of the "positivist" orientation that has characterized both Marxist and non-Marxist scholarship on Africa to date.

Although capitalism has played havoc with social formations throughout Africa in the last century, its grip over most African societies is
still marginal. Capitalism has opened some new doors to progress, and
closed others, but it has not so transformed Africa's social and economic
map that it can take for granted its own dominance. The social transformation initiated by capitalism during the colonial period is still far
from complete. Precapitalist forms are resilient. They have, in fact,
become more significant recently as African governments have initiated
strategies aimed at curbing the influence of capitalism. The principal
effects of anti-capitalistic policies in countries like Tanzania and Mozambique have been not a transformation to socialism but a reinvigoration
of the precapitalist forms held at bay by the colonial presence. The
limited interest of foreign companies in African investments has also
tended to reinforce the resurgence of precapitalism. To assume a unilinear
progress toward the further incorporation and subjugation of Africa
under capitalism would be wrong.

The "articulation of modes of production" school has not fully explored
the concept of the mode of production as an abstraction of a particular
set of economic organization and social behavior. If we accept that a
precapitalist mode is still active in rural Africa, then we should investigate
its effects on the governance of society.

Because production systems are cellular and the forces of production generally rudimentary in rural Africa, macro-economic structures have less influence on organization and behavior than they would in a feudal, capitalist or socialist setting, where penetration by the system makes external influences on the peasantry far more decisive. In rural Africa, the internal dynamics of each household are relatively more important and determines economic and social organization.[14] In southern Africa, for example, Low has found that, although rural households are quick to take up the cultivation of higher-yield varieties of basic grains, they do not seek to increase their earnings from agricultural production. Rather, they reduce the time spent on agriculture and shift their efforts to off-farm activities. By taking advantage of their links to town as well as village, they are effectively undermining government efforts to raise agricultural production nationwide (Low 1984, 288-311).

The "Economy of Affection"

African peasants operate within a type of economy that must be conceptualized independently from either capitalism or socialism. I call it the "economy of affection."

It must be said from the outset that the term "economy of affection" does not refer to fond emotions per se. Rather, it denotes networks of support, communications and interaction among structurally defined groups that are connected by blood, kin, community or other affinities, e.g., religion. The economy of affection links in a systematic fashion a variety of discreet economic and social units that, in other respects, are autonomous. This type of economy, which springs from the needs and dynamics of micro- rather than macro-structures, becomes important in any society where the producer has not yet been cut off from access to the control of his own land. In most parts of the world, the economy of affection has been reduced to an historical artifact; the "moral economy" that Scott (1976) described in Southeast Asia for example, has been effectively overpowered by other economic forms. This is generally not the case in Africa.

In most African countries, productive and reproductive processes at the household level are still very much embedded in the economy of affection. Despite the autonomy of the production unit, members of each household generally cooperate with each other, presumably to safeguard physical and social reproduction under conditions where the margin of survival is very small. Economic forms and activities developed in precolonial times have not disappeared. In fact, their protective role was enhanced in many parts of Africa as the colonial powers imposed new demands on rural society. But because such cooperation is not an inherent, permanent part of the production system, it tends to be ad hoc and informal rather than regular and formalized. Cooperating groups constitute "invisible" organizations that are brought to public attention only through careful research.

As Jane Guyer demonstrates, it is difficult to explain the great variety of cooperative forms (Guyer 1981). One hypothesis is that the material conditions of production play a major role in determining the character of such organizations when these conditions are demanding and impose definite constraints on reproduction. In such cases, the lineage organization tends to be predominant. Where material conditions are more propitious, there is greater variety in the forms of cooperation, within and among households.[15] Here, social differentiation is likely to be more apparent and the economy of affection more versatile.

The economy of affection does not disappear in a society with social differentiation as long as the means of production are shared among a multitude of smallholders. This is why, despite social changes in the rural areas during colonial and post-colonial days, the economy of affection has survived and in some respects, grown in strength. Many of its organizational forms have successfully adapted to changing situations. The self-help work group, the burial society and the rotating credit society all have their origin in the economy of affection. Such groups play a crucial role, often unacknowledged, in rural development today. For example, a recent case study identified no fewer than eight single-purpose, small-scale organizations, each catering to a specific productive or reproductive need, in one Tanzanian village in a relatively well-developed area (Rugumisa 1973).

As a 1983 survey of community-based organizations in Third World countries demonstrates (Ralston, Anderson, and Colson 1983, 64-111) the indigenous criteria for organizing—whether "lineage," "age-grade" or some other affinity—are important to progress. Organizations based on lineage (and extended family connections) have helped local entrepreneurs to succeed in both West and Central Africa.[16] Although this seems to be less true in East Africa, the age-grade system has often served as a valuable substitute in that area (Marris and Somerset 1972; King 1977). Whatever the pattern of organization, the economy of affection serves as a vehicle for the perpetuation of communal groupings, and these enjoy much greater legitimacy in African society than the formal state structures. The prevalence of the economy of affection has, for example, prevented effective appropriation by the state of any part of the surplus generated by successful trade or manufacturing, and the diffuse nature of the social groups generated by this type of economy has provided many loopholes for escape from the tax collector.

The economy of affection does not manifest itself in rural areas only. Because there is no ruling class that has cut its ties with its rural base, the tentacles of the economy of affection are pervasive also in urban areas. Evidence suggests that in both East and West Africa, urban-rural linkages are sustained and promoted effectively both within individual households and at intermediary levels through various associations. Instead of being plowed back into the public purse, resources and services are often channeled through informal support networks from urban areas to rural areas for social maintenance and investment purposes. (This is less evident in southern Africa, especially in countries where a large proportion of the male labor force are migrant workers in South Africa. The predominance of capitalism and the sterile, rigid nature of South Africa leave little room for the emergence of an economy of affection. Although remittances by migrant workers to their home countries are significant, they take place through official channels and are subject to more effective government control.)

The Politics of Local Networks

As Peter Ekeh (1975) has shown, the moral standards prevailing in African society stem from the nature of the local political economy. Rights and obligations are still defined primarily in relation to precapitalist structures associated with a system of smallholder peasant production. The state realm is generally regarded as an arena from which one seeks to make gains, if possible, to enhance patronage relations.

It is the prevalence of this orientation that gives African politics its peculiar character. The "politics of affection"—or "clan politics," as Cruise O'Brien (1975) calls it—is the product of a society where social differentiation has not yet crystallized into a distinct division between those who own the means of production and those who serve them as workers. Africa today is witnessing only the earliest vibrations of this social transformation, and it still tends to be encapsulated in the communalist relations. Although class relations may one day spring from the womb of the economy of affection, it is the latter which currently determines African social relations.

Social differentiation on the African continent is a complex process characterized by the contradiction between the private ambitions of the budding bourgeoisie and the communal pressures restraining the emergence of a true capitalist ethos. These pressures remain strong because, as long as Africa's leaders do not effectively control the means of production, they can sustain their own power and influence only by following the rules of the economy of affection. They cannot take their power for granted but, instead, must constantly invest in ways of preserving it. African leaders do not command a system equipped with subtle policy instruments which will enable them to realize their private and public interests. Although such measures as price incentives may have effects, the most important step is manifestation of direct support for the relevant communal realm.

It is a gross oversimplification, and in many respects misleading, to view the accumulation of wealth as merely a capitalist or neo-colonial manifestation. Accumulation strategies in Africa, as Sara Berry (1983) has also noted are directed more toward building up power over resources than toward increasing their productivity.

Whether the official policy orientation is capitalist or socialist, property rights are politicized rather than privatized and are used by the budding bourgeoisie to safeguard their own position. As a result, the politics of affection is characterized at all levels by investments in patronage relations. The head of a household invests in the purchase of land for his wives and his offspring, even if this means proliferation of ownership to include many small plots operated at low productivity levels. If new land is not available, existing plots are sub-divided to achieve the same end. In Kenya, for example, where privatization of land ownership was institutionalized in the 1950s, the sub-division of existing plots and the accumulation by individual households of many plots, physically distant from each other, have probably reduced the scope for any significant future productivity gains in agriculture (Haugerud, ms.).

Similar strategies are pursued by the business entrepreneur who, in order to safegurad his own position and respond to the social pressures of his home community, tends to invest in many small enterprises, which absorb labor at low levels of productivity, rather than in the improvement of productivity within one or two operations (Berry 1983; Norcliffe 1983). The manager of a public enterprise may find his hands more tied, but he too feels the social pressures and responds by steering investments to his home area and by hiring people to whom he has an obligation under the economy of affection. Even the civil servant finds it difficult to escape these pulls, particularly since he must serve a politician whose legitimacy is almost wholly dependent on being able to mobilize his inter-personal networks. Considerable sums of public money are, in fact, invested in "political maintenance." As a result, it is not surprising that public finance is in a mess. Problems of financial management in Africa do not stem primarily from lack of talent and experience. They originate in the politics of affection, with its emphasis on channeling public funds to local constituencies, irrespective of efficiency or considerations of effectiveness as expressed in official goals. Without countervailing forces, there is little prospect of improvement in Africa's management of public finance.

We must not use our microscope to enlarge the economy of affection out of proportion to other forces influencing economic and social trends in Africa. If I seem to have given it excessive significance, this can be attributed to my belief that we must give greater prominence to those forces that are indigenous to Africa. The move in that direction has been slow since people like Polly Hill (1972) many years ago turned against the positivist inclinations of development analysts and called attention to the importance of understanding micro-processes. But recent macro-economic crises have created a more favorable climate for attention to the hidden factors of development. The current scholarly and professional concern with intra-household processes and farming systems is one strong manifestation of this change.

Potential Contribution to Rural Development

The potential of local interpersonal networks for rural development must be explored further. An increasing number of studies have shown the contribution of these networks to both social security and agricultural development. Against the backdrop of declining performance by the state in rural development, particularly in terms of improving agricultural productivity, we must ask whether appropriating funds from the wealthy through heavy taxation or other forms of reduction in net income, in order to invest in rural development, is really a viable strategy.

Persons legitimately concerned with growing income differentials have undercut their own work by focusing only on direct public interventions in the formal sector. This orientation has ignored the potential role of unofficial flows of funds from the urban to the rural areas through the economy of affection. We know that public investments in rural development do not stem the flow of people to the urban areas—in fact they may reinforce it—and we also know that the vast majority of urban residents in Africa send considerable amounts of money to their rural homes. Strategies based on curbing urban incomes in the interest of vast public investments in rural development seem to be particularly ill-timed in the contemporary African setting. Tanzania is an obvious example. Official *ujamaa* strategy has made the sustenance of urban livelihoods very difficult and has reduced the potential contribution of local interpersonal networks to development. Forced by material realities, people have resorted to the relations of affection to protect themselves and safeguard their own survival. To defend themselves against misconceived and ill-timed public policies, they have increasingly diverted flows of money to unofficial channels, effectively depriving the Tanzanian government of its ability to control the destiny of the country.

Where society is denuded by design or default of local networks and organizations based on the relations of affection, oppression and exploitation within rural households tend to be reinforced. Certainly, studies from Tanzania indicate that the exploitation of women in rural households has increased as members of rural households are obliged to operate in the context of government-designed new villages.[17]

The economy of affection can play its most useful role when the forces of production associated with precapitalist modes of production are refined and material conditions result in a more dense organizational setup, i.e., when precapitalist modes of production are gradually trans-formed under the influence of external forces, including capitalism, and there is a new division of labor and a further differentiation of roles. The introduction of new technology, for instance, may change the position and status of individual members of the rural household. Studies from various parts of Africa, drawing on Boserup's work (1970), suggest that women lose economic power and social status in this process. This is certainly the point made by Shimwaayi Muntemba in her study of women in agriculture in Zambia (Muntemba 1982; Nash 1983). But such a loss of power and status is not inevitable, and the whole process is influenced by a range of factors. For example, women are more likely to be losers if external forces have a strong influence at a time when the forces of production level is limited. Similarly, if macro-economic policies discourage the growth of indigenous groups and organizations, the likelihood of womens' ending as losers is also great.

Other studes have shown, however, that with growing social differ-entiation, the opportunities for women tend to be enhanced. This is particularly apparent if the analysis of the division of labor goes beyond commercial and subsistence agriculture. As Kenneth Little shows with reference to West Africa (Little 1973) colonialism opened up new op-portunities for commercial agriculture and wage labor, both of which were monopolized by men. But the growth of urban centers, with their predominantly male populations, generated a demand for goods and services that women were able to supply on a commercial basis, notably prepared food and sex. Women also began to fill the distribution gaps in trade beyond the local level. Because this trade often became quite profitable, women were able during the colonial period to increase their economic independence and social status in ways that had been impossible when the precapitalist mode of production alone was operative. This point is also supported by studies from East Africa. Zinat Bader, for instance, shows how Haya women in northwestern Tanzania were able to enhance their independence by breaking out of traditional roles and, through practicing prostitution in urban centers of East Africa, accumulate enough capital to return home and establish themselves as landowners (Bader 1975). In her analysis of strategies adopted by women in Uganda to increase their independence, Christine Obbo cites similar examples

(Obbo 1980). Even if men monopolize export-crop activities, women usually have opportunities in the secondary and tertiary sectors opened up by the advance of commodity production. The fact that women have been particularly successful in the manipulation of their sexual attractiveness does not mean that their advancement must be confined to that field. With greater understanding of macro-level forces and with macro-economic policies providing incentives for women to enter into new activities, e.g., the provision of credit and technical assistance, the female labor force can be more productively engaged.

The growing involvement of rural households in the market economy is not a bad trend provided individual members of these households can make their advances using the relations of affection. But it would be wrong to assume that such advancement is totally uncontroversial. As Boserup has shown, where simple agricultural technology prevails, the bulk of the work is performed by women (Boserup 1970). Women tend to do less agricultural work than men only when intermediate technologies like plowing cultivation are introduced. It is important therefore to view women's advancement in the secondary and tertiary sectors in relation to what happens in the agricultural sector. Without changes in technology that may further alter the division of labor on the land, agricultural productivity—and particularly food self-sufficiency ratios—may continue to decline. The solution to this problem must go far beyond such ideas as providing female extension staff in order to achieve greater interaction with women farmers.

The family system prevailing in African society is at the heart of the matter. When a woman marries in Africa, she is not so much incorporated in her husbands' lineage as linked with him in a cross-cutting conjugal unit. Husband and wife are not, as is generally the case in Eurasia, bound in some form of conjugal community, nor does the marriage make them a corporate entity. The economic and social spheres of action of husband and wife tend to be discrete and, as a result, their financial activities are often also quite distinct, even when there is no plural marriage (Goody and Tombiah 1973, 1-58). Whether this should be attributed to the precapitalist modes of production, as Boserup (1970) does or to the absence of established social hierarchies, as Goody (1973) does the economy of affection tends to perpetuate this form of social organization. For instance, the strains of a long physical separation of a wife from her husband resulting from urban migration are reduced not only by the monetary remittances by the husband but, above all, the support provided by other members in the rural community during the absence of the husband.

Although there are tendencies toward nucleating families in African society, the predominant demographic behavior is still shaped by the presence of an economy of affection. For example, the urban worker tends to look at family size against the backdrop of existing support structures in the rural areas. Although he may, as a worker, be absorbed by capitalism, his demographic behavior shows little sign of being influenced by that system. As a result, the physical separation of husband and wife caused by urban migration does not lead to any reduction in family size. Even poor women left on the land to care for large families prefer many children, mainly because they regard their offspring as necessary labor.[18] Neither poverty nor wealth seems to be a factor influencing fertility in a downward direction.

The household is perhaps the principal reason why one must be cautious about predicting any significant productivity gains in African agriculture within the next generation. It is likely to remain a slippery actor, difficult to influence in either the agricultural or demographic field. Even so, efforts to promote greater integration and, in the long run, increased government ability to shape the behavior of the rural population, will have to take into consideration the economy of affection.

Role of Farming Systems Research

It is particularly important that the constraints and opportunities of rural Africa are investigated more closely in the light of prevailing material and social conditions. Farming systems research (FSR) has the advantage of drawing attention to the locale-specific determinants of agricultural development and of providing a better basis for effecting changes in policy outlook. This does not mean, as the advocates of the approach are first to admit (Norman 1982), that FSR is a panacea. There is a tendency for farming systems research to focus primarily on the agricultural extension system as if this institution were the most important agent of change in African agriculture. But bureaucratic agencies may not be capable of internalizing the results of farming systems research or of translating them into alternative strategies. FSR's principal value may be to highlight the limitations inherent in more conventional extension approaches. Although farming systems practitioners tend to have more far-reaching ambitions, such an achievement is important if it paves the way for other agricultural policies, including price incentives, that induce the peasant farmer to embark on new activities, regardless of whether these locally-initiated ventures relate to existing farming systems.

An important complement to farming systems research is the development and strengthening of organizations that enable rural producers to realize their own activities more effectively and to claim public resources—from extension services and other relevant agencies—with greater self-confidence. This means that there must be a greater willingness on the part of governments and donors to discover the organizational potential hidden in the economy of affection. In countries like Kenya and Zimbabwe, community-based organizations are being increasingly incorporated into mainstream development work with the support of intermediary voluntary agencies.[19] Instead of starting cooperatives that serve the interest of the state and compel the cooperators to adhere to a specific organizational model borrowed from other parts of the world, these intermediary bodies are taking the trouble to prepare the members for greater common responsibilities and to help nurture the organization into a cooperative mold.

Conclusion

Because of the cellular production system and the fragmentary nature of the economy, both highly dependent on locale-specific social and material conditions, development work in Africa is far more demanding and difficult than elsewhere in the world. In industrialized countries the production environment permits effective manipulation of variables that influence change in one direction or another and facilitate the transferability of a particular experience from one place to another. The various components making up the "system" have fallen into place, and the consequences of intervention in a component can be anticipated and subsequent steps planned. These conditions also exist to some extent in the semi-industrialized countries of the Third World and in societies where agriculture is more mechanized and irrigated than in Africa. Comparatively, the African environment is particularly difficult to plan and manipulate for development purposes. The discouraging experience of two decades of development planning and the frequent failures in implementing individual project designs—often prepared by the best professional consultants—provide ample evidence of this. There is reason to heed Robert Chambers, who said several years ago that investment in good project design is by no means the guarantee of success in Africa that many professional planners and analysts think (Chambers 1969). This point has been taken further more recently by David Korten, who argues that the emphasis on a "blueprint" approach, derived from a successful pilot effort, rarely leads to effective implementation (Korten 1980). The "blueprint" approach is far too narrow to incorporate the factors that determine project execution and overlooks, for example, the many complex issues associated with building organizational capacity to achieve the desired objective.

Insofar as cooperative types of organization are concerned (Hyden 1983), African governments may find more encouragement in the "greenhouse" approach, which stresses the importance of providing a more hospitable climate for the growth of indigenous organizations. This approach implies the need to retreat from a strategy of nationwide interventions, based on singular policies, and to focus instead on investments in various types of support activities important to the growth of local economic activities.

A change to the "greenhouse" approach would be only the first step on a long road toward progress, which would no doubt be characterized by its own strains and disappointments. Nevertheless, given the social and material realities prevailing in rural Africa, policies must be developed that facilitate the emergence of new linkages among rural production units and between production units located in the countryside and units in the towns in order to enhance the prospects of a manageable development system. An approach of this kind would enable the political economy of smallholder agriculture to grow more nearly on its own terms by providing incentives for peasant producers to move forward at their own pace.

Although this implies slow, incremental change, there is little room for any "quantum jump" as long as much of African agriculture remains essentially precapitalist. There may be some countries that are less dependent than others on the constraining factors of precapitalist production, but generally speaking there seems to be little prospect that the "blueprint" approach can be successfully applied prior to the effective implementation of a "greenhouse" approach. Africa's "hundred flowers" must be allowed to bloom before they are pressed for prosperity. Only then can we fully understand the potential for cross-fertilization of experiences from other continents.

Notes

1. Relevant studies include: Uma Lele and W. Chandler, "Food Security: Some East African Considerations" in A. Valdes (ed.), *Food Security for Developing Countries* (Boulder, Co.: Westview Press, 1981); Barbara Harriss, "There is Method in My Madness—Or is It Vice Versa?", *Food Research Institute Studies*, Vol 17, No 2 (1979); R. Jeffries, "Rawlings and the Political Economy of Underdevelopment in Ghana", *African Affairs*, Vol. 81, No. 324; G. Hyden, *Beyond Ujamaa in Tanzania: Underdevelopment and an Uncaptured Peasantry* (London, Heinemann Educational Books, 1980).

2. A review of these paradigmatic shifts and their influence on African studies is made by John Lonsdale in his "States and Social Processes in Africa: A Historiographical Survey" in Vol. XXIV; No. 2/3 (1981) of the *African Studies Review*. An attempt to link these shifts to changes in the economic climate affecting African countries has been made by Chris Wrigley in "Sketch Maps

of African Economic History," a University of Nairobi History department seminar paper presented on December 14, 1978.

3. See, for instance, Claude Meillassoux, *Anthropologie economique des Gouro de Côte d'Ivoire* (Paris, Mouton 1964); Catherine Coquery-Vidrovitch, "Recherches sur un mode de production African" *La Pensee*, No. 144, pp. 61–78; Subsequently translated pp. 90–111 in Peter Gutkind and Immanual Wallerstein (eds.), *The Political Economy of Contemporary Africa*, (Beverly Hills, CA, Sage Publications, 1976); also Jane Copans and David Seddon, "Marxism and Anthropology: A Preliminary Survey" in D. Seddon (ed.), *Relations of Production: Marxist Approaches to Economic Anthropology* (London, Frank Cass, 1978).

4. Originally developed by the French political economist, Pierre-Philippe Rey, the arguments characterizing this debate are well summarized and analyzed by Aidan Foster-Carter, "Can We Articulate 'Articulation'?," in J. Clammer (ed.), *The New Economic Anthropology* (New York, St. Martin's Press, 1978). *Peasant Tobacco Production in Tanzania: The Political Economy of a Commodity Producing Peasantry* (Uppsala, Scandinavian Institute of African Studies, 1979).

5. See, for instance, Robin Law, *The Oyo Empire c. 1600-c. 1836: A West African Imperialism in the Era of the Atlantic Slave Trade* (Oxford, Clarendon Press, 1977); Richard Roberts, "Long-Distance Trade and Production: Sinsani in the Nineteenth Century", *Journal of African History*, Vol. 21, No. 2 (1980); and Catherine Coquery-Vidrovitch, "Research on an African Mode of Production" in Seddon *op. cit.*, pp. 261–288.

6. For an account of the attempt to deal with the peasant in Buganda and the consequences of these policies for class formation, see Mahmood Mamdani, *Politics and Class Formation in Uganda* (New York, Monthly Review Press, 1976).

7. For a case study of this tendency in Zambia, see Shimwaayi Muntemba, "Women as Food Producers and Suppliers in the Twentieth Century: The Case of Zambia," *Development Dialogue*, 1982:1/2.

8. Florian Znaniecki has a discussion of this point in his book, *The Social Role of the Man of Knowledge* (New York, Octagon Books, 1976).

9. In my own writings, I have usually referred to existing precapitalist modes of production in Africa under the common label of the "peasant" mode, the reason being that those who appropriate the surplus are themselves dependent on the peasant producers and lack the means of effectively enforcing their own will on these producers. The hegemonic culture, therefore, also tends to reflect peasant values rather than form a distinct "high culture" that is associated with more deeply stratified class societies. Because of the controversy surrounding the conceptualization and labeling of any precapitalist mode of production in Africa, I have refrained from using my own label while at the same time, stressing the precapitalist nature of the predominant modes in rural Africa.

10. This point is further elaborated by Barry Hindess and Paul C. Hirst, *Pre-Capitalist Modes of Production* (London, Routledge and Kegan Paul, 1975).

11. See, e.g., Ronald Robinson, "European Imperialism and Indigenous Reactions in British Africa, 1880-1914" in H. L. Wesseling (ed.), *Expansion and Reaction: Essays on European Expansion and Reactions in Asia and Africa* (Leiden,

Leiden University Press, 1977), pp. 141–163; Terence Ranger, *Revolt in Southern Rhodesia 1896-97* (London, Heinemann Educational Books, 1967); and John Iliffe, *A Modern History of Tanganyika* (Cambridge, Cambridge University Press, 1979).

12. For a general overview of the question of forced labor, see E. J. Berg, "The Development of Labor Force in sub-Saharan Africa," *Economic Development and Cultural Change*, Vol. XIII, No. 3 (1955); for a case study of Tanzania, Justinian Rweyemamu, *Underdevelopment and Industrialization in Tanzania* (Nairobi, Oxford University Press, 1973), esp. Chapter 1; on the question of long-distance labor, see M. A. Bienefeld, "Trade Unions, the Labor Process and the Tanzanian State," *Journal of Modern African Studies*, Vol. 17, No. 4 (1979).

13. Cf. e.g., John C. Caldwell, *African Rural-Urban Migration: The Movement to Ghana's Towns* (New York, Columbia University Press, 1969); John C. Mitchell (ed.), *Social Networks in Urban Situations* (Manchester, Manchester University Press, 1969); Joyce Moock, "The Content and Maintenance of Social Ties Between Urban Migrants and Their Home-Based Support Groups: The Maragoli Case," *African Urban Notes*, Number 3 (Winter 1978-79); Thomas Weisner, "The Structure of Sociability: Urban Migration and Urban Ties in Kenya," *Urban Anthroplogy*, Number 5 (1976); and Richard Sandbrook, *The Politics of Basic Needs: Urban Aspects of Assaulting Poverty in Africa* (London, Heinemann Educational Books, 1982).

14. Although this is not the place for a lengthy review of Chayanov's theory of the peasant economy, his point about the relative autonomy of the peasant household as an economic and social entity may be more relevant to the political economy of Africa than even the conditions prevailing in Russia at the turn of the century. Because his analysis was caught up in internal Soviet debates after 1917, it has hardly been treated with the objectivity that it deserves. The growing attention paid to Chayanov by economic anthropologists and political economists working on Africa is encouraging.

15. This may explain why Meillassoux in his analysis of societies in the Sahel tends to identify the material conditions as determining variations in social relations in African society—see his, *Maidens, Meals, and Money* (Cambridge, Cambridge University Press, 1981)—while Wolf, in focusing also on peasant societies where the material conditions are more favorable, is ready to attach more importance to inter-group relations and other facets of the economy of affection in explaining variations among systems of peasant production. For an elaboration of this point see his "The Mills of Inequality: A Marxian Approach," in G. Berreman (ed.), *Social Inequality: Comparative and Development Approaches* (New York, Academic Press, 1981), pp. 41–57.

16. See, for instance, Polly Hill, *Migrant Cocoa Farmers in Southern Ghana* (Cambridge, Cambridge University Press, 1963); John M. Janzen, "The Cooperative in Lower Congo Economic Development" in David Brokensha and Marion Pearsall (eds.), *The Anthropology of Development in Sub-Saharan Africa* (Lexington, Ky., Society for Applied Anthropology, 1969), Monograph 10, pp. 70–76; William Ogionwo, *Innovative Behavior and Personal Attitudes: A Case Study of Social Change in Nigeria* (Boston, G. K. Hall & Company, 1978).

17. Several cases are quoted by Ophelia Mascarenhas and Marjorie Mbilinyi, *Women in Tanzania: An Analytical Bibliography* (Uppsala, Scandinavian Institute of African Studies, 1983).

18. This comes out in interviews with rural women in Kenya; see Priscilla Reining et al., *Village Women: Their Changing Lives and Fertility: Studies in Kenya, Mexico and the Philippines* (Washington, D.C., American Association for the Advancement of Science, 1977), pp. 11–110.

19. Interesting work along these lines is conducted by Partnership for Productivity in Kenya, Silveira House and the Savings Development Movement in Zimbabwe.

2

Components of Farming Systems Research, FSR Credibility, and Experiences in Botswana

D. W. Norman and D. C. Baker

The farming systems approach and its primary subset activity, farming systems research,[1] are products of the 1970's.[2] They developed because of the partial or complete failure of other approaches to create technologies relevant for use by limited-resource farming families in relatively unfavorable environments.[3]

This paper will define the farming systems approach; identify the attributes of farming systems research (FSR), and discuss relationships among FRS methodological issues, FSR credibility and intra-household processes. The dilemma facing FSR field teams seeking to establish and maintain their credibility is illustrated by examples of research experiences in Botswana.

Defining the Farming Systems Approach

Although terms used in describing the farming systems approach are often person-, institution- or country-specific, a certain commonality in terms of philosophy, methodology and implementation has emerged.[4]

Distinguishing Features

A distinguishing feature of farming systems philosophy is its emphasis on increasing the overall productivity of the farming system. It is assumed, at least implicitly, that improved productivity in the agricultural sector is a sine qua non for addressing the entire range of private and societal goals—such as improving the welfare of rural families. (It is tangential but interesting to note that the popularity of the farming systems approach follows closely on the heels of donor agency disappointment in integrated rural development and basic needs strategies, largely because those approaches failed to identify an "engine of development.")

A second feature of farming systems philosophy is an assumption that increased productivity in the agricultural sector must be achieved by developing and disseminating improved practices (technologies) or by developing more relevant policies and support systems (external institutions). The root cause of farmers' resistance to proposals for changing their farming practices is said to be the incompatibility of technologies and policies with agro-ecological and socio-economic-political environments rather than farmer irrationality or managerial mistakes. In its emphasis on improved technology and farmer rationality, the farming systems approach is thoroughly "Schultzian."[5]

A third identifying feature is the belief that, even where the well-being of rural populations has improved due to introduction of improved technologies, neither the size nor the distribution of benefits has matched expectations.[6] This result is generally attributed to neglect in traditional research approaches of the "human element" in farming systems.[7]

The farming systems approach postulates that this checkered pattern of success will not be altered until linkages among the various participants in the research process—sponsoring government or agency, research institution, extension service and farming families—are strengthened and mutual accountability is increased. The farming systems approach seeks to ensure two-way linkages between various participants in the research process through a pragmatic "bottom-up" orientation. This approach to research in low-income countries is analogous to techniques used by commercial firms for measuring their success in sales: they first try to determine what their customers want and then formulate a product to fulfill the demand.

While the primary objectives of "bottom-up" research strategies have clearly been tailoring improved technologies to potential farmer customers and, ultimately, greater production and improved welfare, there has also been recognition that farmers have something valuable to contribute to technology development. An essential feature of the farming systems approach, and a major reason for donor agency interest in this approach, is the realization that listening to farmers and observing what they do can help to improve the potential for increased efficiency in the allocation of research resources.

The "bottom-up" orientation of the farming systems approach is manifested in two types of developmental strategies: (1) farming systems research (FSR), involving the development and dissemination of relevant, improved practices (technologies) through conducting on-farm research and working directly with the farmer, and (2) farming systems perspective (FSP), involving influencing the development of policies and support systems that create an appropriate incentive structure for adopting technologies that will improve the productivity of farming systems.

Given the right institutional setting and linkages, both FSR and FSP are possible. However, FSP has usually not been operative, mainly because programs based on the farming systems approach have generally been located in agricultural research institutes—primarily crop-oriented—that are often poorly linked to planning or policy-making agencies. Programs using a farming systems approach have almost always concentrated on FSR, and policies and support systems have been treated as parameters rather than variables amenable to manipulation. An approach that treats policies and support systems as variables would clearly permit consideration in research of a wider range of possible improved technologies, although methodological and implementation issues become more complex as the ratio of variables to parameters increases.[8]

Farming Systems Research: A Definition

As indicated earlier, the term FSR has often been used loosely. There are programs called "FSR" that are not FSR, and there are programs not called "FSR" that are indeed FSR.

Applied FSR produces recommendations that are suited to particular local situations. It involves on-farm research and working directly with farmers. Longer-term technical problems identified through farm-level research are fed up to the experiment station. Farmers' perspectives on policy and support-system problems are also fed upwards.

There are four conceptually distinct stages in the farming systems research process (See Figure 2.1):

a. The *descriptive* or *diagnostic* stage when the actual farming system is examined in the context of the "total" environment in order to identify the constraints that farmers face and to ascertain the potential flexibility in the farming system in terms of timing, slack resources, etc. An effort is also made to understand farmers' goals and motivation that may affect their efforts to improve the farming system.

b. The *design stage* in which a range of strategies is identified that are thought to be relevant in dealing with the constraints delineated in the descriptive or diagnostic state. Heavy reliance at this stage is placed on obtaining information from the "body of knowledge." This "body of knowledge" is derived from experiment station-based research, researcher-managed (RM) and researcher-imple-

FIGURE 2.1
The Farming Systems Approach

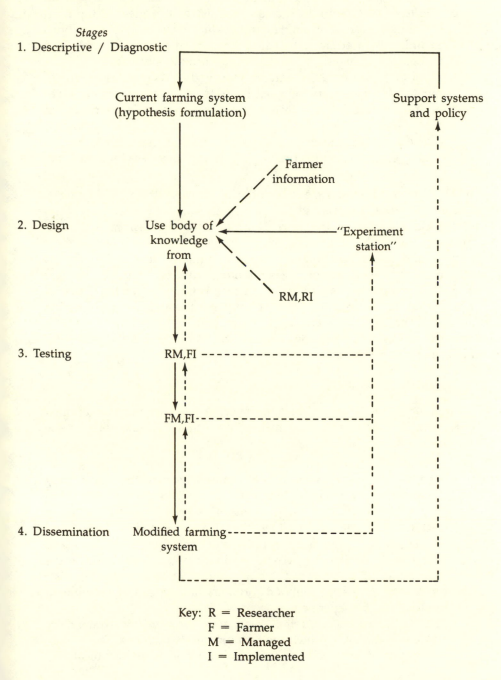

Stages
1. Descriptive / Diagnostic

Current farming system
(hypothesis formulation)

Support systems
and policy

Farmer
information

2. Design   Use body of
knowledge
from

"Experiment
station"

RM,RI

3. Testing   RM,FI

FM,FI

4. Dissemination   Modified farming
system

Key: R = Researcher
F = Farmer
M = Managed
I = Implemented

mented (RI) type trials off the experiment station and knowledge obtained from the farmers themselves.

c. The *testing stage* in which a few promising strategies arising from the design stage are examined and evaluated under farm conditions in order to ascertain their suitability for producing desirable and acceptable changes in the existing farming system. This stage consists of two parts: researcher-managed (RM) but farmer-implemented (FI) type tests followed by tests where farmers themselves are responsible for both test management and test implementation (FM, FI).

d. The *dissemination stage* in which the strategies that were identified and screened during the design and testing stages are implemented.

In practice, there are no clear boundaries between the various stages. Design activities, for example, may begin before the descriptive and diagnostic stages end and may continue into the testing stages as promising alternatives emerge during trials at the farm level where farmers and researchers interact directly. Similarly, testing by farmers may mark the beginning of dissemination activities. Thus, the process of FSR is recognized as being dynamic and iterative (repeating), with linkages in both directions among farmers, researchers and funding agencies. The iterative characteristics can improve the efficiency of the research process by providing a means for fine-tuning improved technologies to a specific locale.[9]

Applied FSR

In addition to being a multi-stage, iterative research process, applied FSR has a number of important methodological attributes. Among these are the following:

a. The farm (system) is viewed in a comprehensive manner. A farming system adopted by a given farming household results from allocation by its members, with their managerial know-how, of the three factors of production to which they have access (land, labor and capital) to four processes (crop, livestock, off-farm enterprises and household maintenance activities)[10] in a manner which, within the knowledge they possess, will maximize the attainment of their goals. The means of livelihood and households are intimately linked and cannot be separated.

b. The farming system itself is recognized as being determined by the environment in which the farming family operates. The "total" environment in which the family operates includes technical and human elements. Technical elements determine what the potential farming system can be.[11] The human element determines what the actual farming system, a subset of the potential defined by the technical element, will be.

c. The choice of priorities for research derives from an initial study of the whole farm and its environment. However, provided the concept of the whole farm and its environment is preserved, not all factors determining the farming system need to be considered variables. Some may be treated as parameters. Similarly, research on a farm sub-system is legitimate FSR, provided connections with other sub-systems are recognized.

d. Evaluation of research results explicitly takes into account linkages between sub-systems. Adoption of an integrative function increases the potential for exploiting complementary and supplementary relationships between resources and enterprises and the derivation of solutions compatible with the needs and capacities of farming families.[12] Ensuring that the integrative and beneficial relationships are adequately considered and exploited (and that human as well as technical determinants of farming systems are considered) requires an interdisciplinary team—technical and social scientists—working together at all four stages of the research process.

e. Predicting the suitability and eventual impact of technologies can, and should, be an integral part of agricultural research. The suitability or relevance of improved agricultural technology[13] at the farmers' level has commonly been assessed in an ex post sense (afterwards) using various methods of acceptance testing, diffusion rates and the like. Although ultimately such ex post assessments provide the best tests of the suitability of an improved agricultural technology, efficient use of research resources indicates that it makes sense to try to assess the potential suitability of technologies before they are disseminated. The first three stages of the farming systems research process explicitly focus on this task. Conceptualizing a farming system provides a systematic basis for forming evaluation criteria.

f. By including farmers FSR taps the pool of knowledge in society, enabling research and, hence, developmental strategies to build on the good points of present farming systems while, at the same time, minimizing time spent "rediscovering the wheel," e.g., the value of intercropping in many parts of Africa.

g. FSR recognizes locational specificity of technical and human elements. This requires disaggregating farming families into recommendation domains (homogeneous subgroups) and developing strategies appropriate to each. In particular subgroups farming families should have similar social customs, access to support systems, marketing opportunities, present technology and resource endowments, and, therefore, similar paths to improved productivity and welfare.

h. Finally, FSR complements and does not compete with other research approaches.[14] With reference to this complementarity, FSR contributes in two ways: 1) Fine-tuning, through adaptive testing at the farm level, technologies developed on experiment stations. Successful testing, it is hoped, leads to successful dissemination and improvement of farming families' welfare, and 2) Testing at the farm level results in closer specification of requirements for improved technology development that can be fed back to experiment station-based research programs outside the FSR program itself. This should contribute to development of improved technologies that will increase the welfare of farming families in the future.

Farming Systems Credibility

A major problem for farming systems research is that, because of its youthful nature, a conventional methodology is still emerging at the same time that donor agencies are pouring millions of dollars into FSR programs and developing country governments are rushing ahead with plans to establish FSR units.

Herein lies the dilemma. On the one hand, funding agencies perceive the farming systems approach and FSR, in particular, as potentially time- and cost-efficient means of developing technologies and policies that are relevant to limited-resource farming families. To obtain credibility with donors and ensure continued long-term funding, FSR teams need quick results. On the other hand, FSR's credibility with technical scientists in international and national agricultural research institutes, with national policymakers and extension services, and, most important, with farmers depends more on the suitability of a recommended practice (technology) than on whether it was developed in one or two seasons—although even FSR's farmer clients will lose interest if tangible, relevant results take too long.

Designing Cost- and Time-Efficient Methodologies

In view of the credibility issue and limited availability of research resources, three important principles have been emphasized in designing cost- and time-efficient methodologies:

a. Reducing the time required to move through the four research stages. The methodologies applied, in addition to ensuring a fast turnaround, need to be practical, replicable and inexpensive (Byerlee et al. 1981). Complex procedures that require scarce, highly qualified individuals to collect and analyze data and to design and test solutions should be avoided as much as possible (Zandstra 1979).

b. Maximizing the return from such research by making results more widely applicable. This means defining recommendation domains as broadly as possible. The extent to which improved systems can be transferred or extrapolated to other areas directly affects efficiency.

c. Using "second best" or "best of readily available solutions." Traditionally, research in agriculture has emphasized the concept of developing optimal practices. When one considers the heterogeneity existing in the total environment, however, costs in terms of finance and time to obtain optimal recommendations for each possible variation would be astronomical. Therefore, the emphasis of FSR has been on developing improved technologies that are better than most, but not necessarily the best, for each environment (Winkelmann and Moscardi 1979).[15]

As recently as two to three years ago, there was general consensus favoring the above principles. However, a debate is now emerging between "purists," who argue that the short cuts being attempted in the pursuit of "time- and cost-efficient methodology" are unacceptable compromises which could do more harm than good,[16] and "practitioners," who worry more about a loss of credibility if the process is perceived as being too long or, even, too "scientific." A purist might point out there are limits to reducing the time required to obtain results, particularly if the "body of knowledge" is weak. Also, there are many who feel that more attention should be given to the substantial variability existing in the real world. The quality and quantity of rural households' resource bases and the goals of farming households often diverge widely.

Two circumstances have combined to undermine the earlier consensus. First, as farming systems research moved out of the international agricultural research centers (IARC's) and into national research programs, it became necessary to consider increasing the number of variables to parameters in analyses of constraints on farming system productivity. Increasing the number of variables leads naturally to consideration of the complex of factors influencing rural welfare and to diffusion of the earlier focus on technology development. In brief, FSR is asked to do much more in a national setting than it is in the research center.

Second, because of the popularity of farming systems research, FSR programs were rapidly established in many countries where there was not a backlog of available technologies that could be extended to farmers with only minor modification through FSR. The availability of such technologies derives largely from experiment station based-research. A lack of these improved technologies means delays, while research priorities are fed back to experiment station-based researchers, in improving the welfare of farmers. In such cases, FSR has taken on a specific role, often quite minor relative to the full range of problems facing agricultural ministries, and concern with and expectations for quick results have been succeeded by hopes for any results that can really make a difference.

A third factor might also be noted, namely the large gap between the principles of the farming systems approach and the way FSR programs are being implemented. The failure to address Farming Systems Perspective (FSP) is only the most obvious example. Conventional FSR methodology, to the extent that it exists, often seems to take lightly the concern with environmental determinants and complexity inherent in the farming systems approach. In order to ensure fast turnaround time, conventional methodology has stressed informal exploratory surveys, possibly followed by a single-visit formal survey, quickly followed by on-farm trials. Also, research is often focused on one or a few "leverage points."

In practice, the leverage point selected in FSR has reflected the mandate of the sponsoring agency as much as it has farmers' priorities. Even where this has been avoided, research foci have tended to reflect the disciplinary training of FSR team members—usually agronomists and economists. This has meant that such "bottom-up" principles as determining "farmer priorities" and "study of whole farming systems" have been replaced with focused diagnoses of technical and economic "constraints on adoptions."

The obvious gap between the principles of the farming systems approach and applied FSR, as it is practiced, has led many "purists" to ask: why don't FSR "practitioners" try to be more sophisticated in their approach? In other words, why not act more in accord with systems philosophy?

Household Processes and FSR

As far as FSR credibility and methodology in relation to households and intra-household processes are concerned, there are three areas of specific interest: definition of a family unit, relationships between family units and relationships within family units. In each of these areas, there are trade-offs between credibility resulting from cost- and time-efficient research results and the credibillity that derives from understanding complex relationships which affect production decisions and from making better ex ante (advance) assessments of a technology's impact on rural communities.

Definition of a Family Unit

The problem of defining a decision-making unit—a family or household unit in the context of most farming systems research—has been the focus of much discussion in Africa, where the extended family system has traditionally been prevalent. For FSR teams it is obviously desirable, all other things being equal, to identify a single, distinct economic or sample unit representing a production decision-making unit (*exploitation agricole*; Kleene 1976) that is in most cases synonymous with a consumption unit (i.e., the farming family). To obtain some correspondence between the two is important in societies where much labor on the family farm is from family sources and much production is consumed within the household. But in Africa complications arise in defining the family because of the progressive breaking up of traditional family systems (Nicolas 1960), the increased significance of individual decision-makers within families (Kleene 1976) and fluidity in the composition of families resulting from changes in the level and composition of economic activity at different times of the year (Hill 1972).

These trends have a number of important implications for applied FSR. (Norman, Newman, and Ouedraogo 1981). Among the implications for FSR are the following:

a. It has been suggested that introduction of cash crops encourages the breakup of family units, largely as a result of increased contact with the outside world, monetization of the economy and a consequent weakening of traditional hierarchical structures. FSR teams must be concerned with the potential disruption of rural communities and the distribution impacts of technologies that tend to increase the relative productivity of resources used on cash crops as opposed to staple food crops.

b. In many parts of Africa fields farmed by families are divided into common and individual fields. Common fields—controlled by the family head—have traditionally provided food for all members of the family. As an increasing proportion of fields comes under control of other family members, there is a decrease in the obligations of family members to work on common fields—and food from the common field to meet subsistence needs can no longer be assured. Given the fact of individual control of fields, the notion of a simple, integrated decision-making unit becomes untenable. For FSR teams this means having to assess who is the appropriate decision-maker for which enterprise while, at the same time, understanding the factors that constrain individual decision-making because of the still present, but declining, authority of the family head. The multiplicity of decision-makers within family units presents a special problem for extension programs (the dissemination stage of FSR) because such programs tend to be directed at family heads.

c. In many areas the breakup of families is resulting in small farms (although with similar land-per-resident ratios); increased fragmentation of fields; younger and relatively inexperienced family heads, and, often, increased dependent-per-worker ratios, with resulting poor net worth and cash liquidity levels. Such trends raise questions about the appropriateness of certain types of technology and processes. For example, can oxen traction be introduced as a replacement for hand hoe tillage in areas which might be technically suited but where farm size averages only two to three hectares?

FSR teams need an approach enabling quick identification of sampling units. Do simplistic definitions lose too much relevance for most farming families (i.e., "cost" too much) in relation to the "benefits" of getting a quick turnaround in terms of results? Some people think the answer to this is "yes."[17] Incorrect specification of a sampling unit (which will usually tend to be biased toward a smaller unit than in the extended family system in Africa) will mean that relationships usually considered within the household will mistakenly be considered as between-household relationships. It can also mean that dependent relations in supra-household networks are ignored by FSR teams and, as a result, some may be made worse off by recommendations to "independent" relations to change their practices.

Between-Family Relationships

As suggested above, FSR methodology characteristically divides the "heterogeneous" farming population into "homogeneous" sub-groups or recommendation domains. Once this is done, however, researchers tend to focus on a small sample of individual farming family units thought to be representative of the recommendation domains rather than explicitly consider relationships between farming families, both within and between recommendation domains.

Traditionally, villages in the semi-arid areas of West Africa, whether in a nucleated or dispersed settlement pattern, had a strong sense of community, often with a strong hierarchical system of control (Remy 1977; Ramond, Fall, and Diop 1976) This control was not considered to be very exploitative, however, especially since individuals only possess usufructuary rights to land (Hill 1972; Maymard 1974).[18] Haswell (1975) has pointed out that communities had a "shared poverty" concept, with poverty being primarily determined by the technical element—climate and soil. However, recent population increases, concomitant with increasing contact with the outside world, have resulted in a breakdown of community spirit, an increase in individualization and less assumption of responsibility for other people.

In Botswana, a sharing of resources between families has traditionally been important for resource-poor households. Rainfall is sparse and uncertain. A critical determinant of stand establishment, and hence yield, is timely planting after a rain. Timely access to traction is a crucial ingredient of this timeliness. Households lacking traction can gain access through hiring, borrowing, cooperative resource-sharing agreements or family help. In any of these arrangements, a household is likely to have less control over the timing of plowing (primarily with respect to a "planting" rain) than will households owning their own traction and equipment. But there are significant differences in the rights and obligations associated with each alternative means of gaining access which affect the possibility of doing timely planting. At the least dependent end is the person who can borrow traction animals. If that person can keep them for the whole plowing season, he can operate as effectively as a household that owns traction. In the middle, if a family can work out a cooperative agreement whereby labor is exchanged for access to traction, a reciprocal obligation is created, giving the traction-short household rights with respect to timely access on alternating rains. At the most dependent end, households with weak social linkages have to hire traction and generally have little say over when the plowing is done.[19] Effectively, owners of traction therefore potentially have control over the hirers. Helping the owners without consideration of possible harmful effects on "borrowers" could polarize society.[20]

If the goal is growth in productivity with equity, it is extremely important to develop strategies that will be sensitive not only to heterogeneity in the technical element but also in the human element. A critical ingredient is understanding interdependencies between family units. Again, the challenge for FSR is to find cost- and time-efficient methods of doing this.

Relationship Within Families

Because of time and cost considerations, FSR teams have sometimes paid little attention to within-household or family issues. There is once again ample documentation from Africa that intra-household relations are changing over time, sometimes aided by the adoption of new technologies and by implementation of new infrastructure. The relative deprivation of women in Gambia has been well documented by Haswell (1975).

In assessing the potential suitability of a technology, it is essential to assess possible changes in work loads, responsibilities and reward systems, particularly between the sexes. In Botswana, for example, one key recommendation being advanced by the extension service is to plow early—either on the first spring rains or during the preceeding winter.[21] However, the recommendation fails to consider the different impacts this has on various members of the household. Responsibilities for arable production activities are differentiated between men and women in Botswana, as is so often the case in Africa. While men mostly do the plowing, women are responsible for weeding—and, indeed, most other crop production activities. Where early plowing is done, the subsequent burden of weeding appears to be significantly increased. Although the men's work load may be decreased since they will have fewer plots to plow—if, as is expected, they can get better stands on the plots they do plow—women may be forced to shift to double weeding instead of single weeding as at present.

Potential changes in the relative productivity of resources used in crop, livestock and off-farm enterprises must also be assessed in relation to their impacts on relationships within families. Again, we cite Botswana as an illustration. In Botswana, not only do crop activities tend to be sexually differentiated but responsibilities for livestock and various off-farm enterprises are also generally divided among members of the family. For example, if men are present in a family, they usually take responsibility for livestock while women are traditionally responsible for beer brewing. This differentiation becomes important for a FSR team since there is often extensive cross subsidization of activities within households. The use of money from cattle or beer sales to hire traction for plowing is most commonly observed. Unfortunately, the present risky nature of arable production means that a crop failure is as likely, or even more likely, than a return equal to the value of the cash investment in plowing—let alone any consideration of the opportunity costs of other labor and non-labor inputs. Thus, various household members are in the position of subsidizing activities often controlled by other members with little expectation of benefit. FSR teams must consider these relations when deciding whether to promote recommendations that call for an intensification of arable production, even if they believe that the investment would probably produce a large net benefit over time.

The problem once again is the need for a resource-efficient methodology to handle these issues in the context of research programs that have highly focused mandates to develop and test agricultural production technologies.

Experience With FSR in Botswana

Botswana provides a vivid example of the dilemma facing FSR field teams in establishing and maintaining credibility. The productivity of most of the land is extremely low, and there are no "quick fix" technologies on the shelf. Even at experiment stations, technical researchers are struggling with the uncertainty and complexity of technical solutions for low-resource farmers. Because there have been too few researchers to push ahead with basic and commodity-specific research, efforts aimed at fine-tuning traditional practices have been out of the question.

Efforts to improve the productivity of cropping systems will require dealing with several interrelated problems. Possibly the greatest single determinant of overall productivity is how effectively farmers make use of limited amounts of water. The availability of labor and capital (particularly draft animals and tractors plus relevant equipment) are particularly important in facilitating more efficient use of available water by improving the "timeliness" of operations and traditionally, extending the area cultivated per household.

It is not surprising that efforts to address the combination of factors constraining arable productivity in Botswana necessitate an understanding of household processes affecting resource allocations and farmer objectives. The social context of production decisions clearly influences decisions to invest in production.

The Agricultural Technology Improvement Project

Although there is general agreement among practitioners on the principal characteristics of FSR methodology, program implementation differs significantly from one project to another, mainly because priorities and activities must be adapted to the environment in which the research is carried out. Steps taken in the Central Agricultural Region of Botswana, by the Agricultural Technology Improvement Project (ATIP),[22] are outlined below.

The primary task in the first year of the ATIP program was to design and implement a viable, integrated technical and socio-economic research program. A wide range of technical investigations and six surveys were designed and carried out.

Under an agreement with the Government of Botswana, research was concentrated in two villages, Shoshong East and Makwate. Fieldwork began with exploratory surveys by two interdisciplinary teams, each consisting of at least one agronomist and one agricultural economist. Although the teams' interviews were informal and unstructured, they compiled checklists of information on practices and problems. Debriefing meetings were held each evening to review findings and identify key issues for future exploration.

The exploratory surveys identified six recommendation domains according to whether farmers owned, managed or borrowed their draft power (tractor, oxen or donkey) or whether they hired it or shared it with other farmers—mainly because farmers' arrangements for draft power were perceived as a critical factor affecting their ability to plant in a timely way and, as a result of early planting, obtain higher yields.

After identifying the recommendation domains, researchers developed a 16-question sample frame census designed to elicit information on the characteristics of farming families in the two villages. Also taking into account sex, cattle and fencing, researchers selected households representing the major recommendation domains to participate in whole farm studies and on-field trials.

The whole farm studies consisted primarily of a multiple-visit resource-use survey and on-field investigations. The resource-use survey covered five key areas of farm management: cash flows by month; income analysis at the whole farm and enterprise level; opportunity costs of resources including non-cropping activities, household maintenance activities and off-farm work; participation in formal and informal markets, and the role of animals in the farming system. The survey has now been administered to a small sample of farmers (27), and there is extensive interface between survey questions and direct technical measurements, including measurements of farmer and climatic production inputs and of crop production response and outcome.

Three single-interview special-subject surveys were also administered on draft arrangements, extension agent activities and crop management practices. The draft arrangements survey covered the social organization of plowing, including obligations incurred by farmers as a result of different draft arrangements and farmers' views of those arrangements.

In the latter part of the cropping season, a questionnaire was distributed to all extension agents in the Central Agricultural Region to determine whether the problems identified in the two research villages were typical of problems throughout the region. This survey also yielded information on extension agents' activities and on constraints affecting their effectiveness.

Of all the surveys conducted, a crop management survey administered at the end of the cropping season was probably most useful. This provided information on household structural characteristics, the plowing situation, crop enterprises, crop husbandry practices, resource constraints, farming hazards, and food supplies and preferences.

While these research activities were being carried out, field technology schemes currently being investigated elsewhere in Botswana were tested on 25 farmers' fields. To address the key issue of poor stand establishment, different planting methods (involving different patterns of seed placement) were tested.

During the second season, ATIP Mahalapye[23] emphasized diagnosis and the design and testing of technologies. It continued whole farm studies and expanded the on-field trials. Five special-subject surveys have dealt with farmers' cropping plans; post-plowing weed development; soils and root penetration; village institutions, infrastructure and services, and cowpea cultivation practices and utilization.

The procedures being followed by ATIP in Botswana are constantly changing as researchers seek an effective approach to increasing arable productivity and farmers' welfare. Although we shall continue to modify our approach as new circumstances arise, it is already apparent that the research strategy adopted in Botswana differs in some repsects from applied FSR elsewhere, especially in the design and use of sample frame censuses, whole farm studies encompassing a multiple-visit resources survey and technical field monitoring, and several special-subject surveys.

Principles Underlying ATIP Approach

Three principles underly the approach adopted in Botswana:

1. We believe that FSR in practice has sometimes tended to deviate too much from the principles of FSR methodology. To develop and maintain credibility, particularly in the harsh environment found in Botswana, we need to take into account the complexity and heterogeneity of both the technical and human environment affecting crop production. In practice, this means increased attention to whole farm studies over time. Small-sample, multiple visit surveys have a role to play not only in providing data on resource use at different times of the year, in different years, by households with different resource endowments but also in generating discussion issues and a knowledge of farmer problems to promote improved farmer-researcher interaction. The emphasis on technical monitoring data—collected by the same enumerators as the

resource survey—allows us, we believe, to get a clearer picture of interactions over time among resource endowments, resource use patterns, technical managerial practices and technical outcomes than is possible through a combination of single-visit surveys and on-farm experiments.

2. The principles of pragmatism and iteration need to be applied to selection of research methods as well as to topics of research. Applied FSR has been very pragmatic in focusing on one, or a few, leverage points in a farming system. However, we feel the emphasis on cost- and time-efficient results has sometimes focused too much on the establishment of on-farm trials. It is often difficult to get clear results from on-farm trials, and logistical problems can be severe. There is no single answer as to whether formal or informal approaches, structured or not, survey or direct measurement is best. Even with on-farm trials, there is no single role for researchers and farmers in different trials. The range of approaches used in our special-subject surveys reflects the iteration and flexibility in methodology we feel is necessary.

3. Although an approach is needed which is sufficient to deal with the complexities of rural socio-economic networks—and which will take better account of factors limiting the acceptability of technologies—the approach should not stray from a focus on the primary mandate of developing and testing technologies to improve the productivity of farming systems. In Botswana, ATIP has an even narrower specific mandate (to focus on arable production technologies and the arable/ livestock interface) but we still feel it is important to accept the limits of our mandate. In large part this reflects a necessary compromise when working toward interdisciplinary cooperation. Technical problems are so severe in Botswana that there is a temptation for technical scientists on FSR teams to try to develop research agendas which can unravel the complexity of the technical environment. The challenge of under- standing basic technical relationships is as interesting to technical sci- entists as the challenge of addressing the complexity of social production environments is to social scientists. If social scientists working in the context of FSR teams move beyond their specific "pre-screening tech- nologies mandate," then they must acknowledge the equally compelling disciplinary interests of their technical science colleagues. Given the extremely low productivity of arable land in Botswana and in a spirit of compromise—necessary to the functioning of an interdisciplinary team—we have agreed to concentrate on technology development and pre-screening, even though there are a wide range of policy and support system issues which are potentially relevant to agricultural development in Botswana.

Conclusion

Despite a systems philosophy, applied FSR in practice has relied on the appeal of time- and cost-efficient research. Therefore, dominant FSR methodology has stressed informal contacts with farmers, single-visit verification surveys and on-farm trials. Technical and economic criteria have dominated. Moreover, research foci have been determined by research mandates of particular ministries, donor agencies or research institutes. This has resulted in a "constraints adoption" research rather than a true bottom-up "farmer priority" approach.

We believe a degree of broadening is necessary in applied FSR. On the other hand, we are concerned about detailed research into farmer welfare and the social and political environment of production. Results of detailed research on the social relations of production, including intra-household processes, tend to emphasize the complexity of rural settings and limitations of technical solutions. While this may be a necessary message for governments and donors to hear from social scientists, it is not one likely to encourage continued interest in costly, applied field research teams and funding of FSR projects.

Individuals participating in FSR, therefore, are faced with a pragmatic trade-off. A "purist" view of the complexity of rural production decisions may not only conflict with the interests of donor agencies and national research ministries, it may also alienate technical scientists on research teams. Even technical scientists who make great strides toward considering farmers' objectives, resource endowments and location-specific constraints will have a hard time accepting a substantial allocation of research resources for the study of social processes unless there is a clear pay-off in terms of pre-screening technologies. While ignorance of the social organization of production is likely to result in lost credibility, because of either low adoption rates or undesirable distributional consequences, we cannot ignore the disciplinary interests of our technical colleagues if we are to gain the advantages of interdisciplinary cooperation.

We feel that one must do sufficient, sophisticated micro-research on resource endowments and resource allocation decisions to make both informed judgments about the suitability of technologies and ex ante assessments of the impact of technology. Since household organization and supra-household linkages are vital aspects of social relationships affecting access to and use of resources, these must be understood. But we would draw the line at the point where research is no longer directed toward the primary mandate of FSR: to pre-screen and adapt technologies designed to increase the productivity of farming resources.

The point we would stress, based on our experiences thus far in Botswana, is that a line must be drawn. Farming systems research is not a panacea for solving the problems of development. Farming systems approach activities, including both FSR and Farming Systems Perspective (FSP), can complement, help integrate and improve the pay-off of other activities by providing a "bottom-up" approach. But hanging too many "ifs" and "buts," "dos" and "don'ts" on FSR will hasten its demise. The question we must ask ourselves is what will happen to efforts to create a "bottom-up," pragmatic research approach that highlights both farmers' perspectives and system interactions when donor agencies tire of unrealistic promises made on behalf of FSR and turn to a new fad.

Already on the horizon are calls for increased attention to micro-macro linkages and the need to shift to an emphasis on FSP (Eicher 1983). While we recognize limitations of a "technical fix" mentality behind FSR and see the need for a more balanced approach, we can envision an overreaction to the limited gains of micro-oriented technology development programs and an outpouring of funds for macro-oriented policy analysis programs.

Our current assessment is that FSR can be effective in developing and pre-screening technologies and at the same time can provide data needed to evaluate micro-macro linkages. But this will entail shifting from an emphasis on the speed with which trials are on-field, or even the speed with which one or a few technologies are pre-screened, to an emphasis on uncovering what causes resistance among farmers to proposed interventions, even if this leads to results relevant only in a longer-term horizon. It is not apparent that donor agencies will accept even this shift in the emphasis of FSR. At the same time, though, it is clear that FSR teams cannot afford to get lost in academic studies of social complexity and dynamics. Such a shift in emphasis could lead to abandonment of the "bottom-up" strategies associated with the farming systems approach and a repetition of the mistakes made in the "macro-planning" period of development thinking.

Notes

1. The term "farming systems approach" refers to a broad strategy or philosophy of research. "Farming systems research" encompasses specific farm-level activities: farming systems description and diagnosis and technology design, development, testing and dissemination. These and other terms are defined in the paper.

2. Although the farming systems approach is new in the developing world, earlier versions have been practiced in the United States since the 1920's (Johnson 1982).

3. These approaches, discussed in detail elsewhere (Norman, Simmons, and Hays 1982), involved the transfer of technology from developed countries largely located in temperate zones and the use of technology "building blocks," elements that had made technology development successful in developed countries.

4. Key references on the farming systems approach include Byerlee and Collinson (1980), Byerlee *et al.* (1981), Gilbert, Norman and Winch (1980), Harrington (1981), Hildebrand (1976), ISRA (1977), Moreno and Sanders (1978), Norman, Simmons and Hays (1982), Perrin *et al.* (1980), Shaner, Phillipp and Schmel (1981), Technical Advisory Committee (1978), Zandstra (1979) and Zandstra *et al.* (1981).

5. Schultz (1964) contended that farmers producing with age-old techniques are generally efficient in the use of their resources even though poor. Although many questions have been raised about the notion of a "traditional agriculture" where no new factors have been introduced in a long time and about empirical "tests" of farmer efficiency, the basic belief that farmers are "efficient but poor" has survived. In recent years, farmers' "indigenous knowledge" and rational adaptations to their environments have been stressed. The resulting implication— that if farmers' resources are improved and if suggestions contribute to farmers' objectives, they will either fit the suggestions into the farming system or reject the suggestions as being inappropriate—is in the Schultzian spirit.

6. The Green Revolution is a good example. Although its production success should not be ignored, distribution problems engendered by new technologies have been widely portrayed, in South Asia, for example, as worsening many farmers' positions vis-à-vis other farmers' achievements. (Saint and Coward 1977.)

7. The human element determines what a farming system will be, as a subset of the potential defined by the technical element. This human element can be divided into two components, or groups of factors: "exogenous" factors (the social milieu in which the farming household operates) and "endogenous" factors (land, labor and capital, along with management). The exogenous factors are largely beyond the control of individual farming households but influence what its members can do. They include (1) community structures, norms and beliefs, (2) external institutions or support systems and (3) miscellaneous influences such as location and population density. Endogenous factors are under the control of individual households and are used to derive a farming system consistent with their goals, subject to the boundary conditions imposed by the technical element and the exogenous factors. Additional explanations of the determinants of farming systems are available in Gilbert, Norman and Winch (1980) and Norman, Simmons and Hays (1982).

8. In addition to being differentiated on the basis of variables to parameters, FSR programs can also be classified as "upstream" (developmental) and "downstream" (applied). "Upstream" FSR programs have a developmental orientation, are mainly experiment station-based and really do not provide results that can be immediately adopted by farming families. "Downstream" types of FSR programs have an applied orientation and aim at developing and introducing strategies that will improve the productivity of farming systems for target groups

of farming families immediately and in the near term. Not only methodological issues but also the scope of a FSR program will be partly determined by the mandate of the institution in which it is located; the effectiveness of linkages with other institutions and agencies, and available resources, i.e., time, skill, finances, etc.

9. This attribute has been illustrated in work on an improved cotton package in northern Nigeria (Beeden, Hayward, and Norman 1976, and Norman, Simmons, and Hays 1982).

10. Household maintenance activities include cooking, washing, fetching water, gathering firewood, tending livestock, repairing dwelling structures, etc. Such "non-production enterprises" both contribute to household welfare and utilize the labor resources of a household. These activities are still sometimes ignored by applied FSR teams.

11. The technical element includes both physical factors (water, soil, solar radiation, temperatures) and biological factors (crop and animal physiology, disease, insect attack, etc.).

12. The farming systems practiced by farmers traditionally have always recognized such relationships, e.g., between crops and livestock, the need for staggered planting dates, etc.

13. In general terms, a suitable agricultural technology is a way of doing things (combining resources to carry out processes) that is compatible with environmental constraints, including human and technical constraints, and that contributes to the goals and aspirations of the group or individuals using the technology. A suitable improved agricultural technology is one that is adopted by farming households and improves the efficiency with which they do things. Although intuitively comfortable, such a micro- or household-oriented definition may not suggest adequate criteria for judging a technology's suitability at the societal level. Further specification may be needed.

14. Although FSR and experiment station-based research are conceptually complementary, FSR is often perceived as competitive in terms of research resource allocation.

15. Some of the ways in which these principles are being applied in each phase of the research sequence are discussed elsewhere (Norman, Simmons, and Hays 1982). An attempt to apply the principles in Botswana is described in Baker *et al.* (1983).

16. Indeed, the very act of joining an interdisciplinary team inevitably means making adjustments in the operational and methodological strategies that are sometimes anathema to "peer groups" firmly embedded within individual disciplines.

17. Behnke and Kerven (1983), for example, argue: "To create an artificial tight definition of the household in such societies is not, therefore, merely to 'tidy up' the data; it is to systematically misconstrue the long-term economic environment in which individuals operate, and to ignore the way in which individuals manipulate their social environment. Such manipulation underestimates the social dimensions of economic behavior and restricts economic analysis to narrow calculation of the relative efficiency of different productive techniques."

18. Others, however, have questioned the lack of exploitation in traditional societies (Ernst 1976; Kafando 1972). Nevertheless, for reasons given in the paper, we believe that the potential for exploitation is likely to be exacerbated as time goes on.

19. As is true with any structural representation of social relationships, each of the above situations manifests itself in different ways depending on other factors influencing the household networks and on the particular individuals involved.

20. Examples illustrating the adverse impacts of technology introduction on inter-familial relationships abound in West Africa, e.g., the introduction of oxen in Mali (Ernst 1976) and the introduction of irrigated tomatoes in northern Nigeria (Agbonifo and Cohen 1976).

21. The primary reason for plowing early is that opened land will allow increased water infiltration.

22. Prior to the start of the ATIP program, there were three FSR-type projects in Botswana.

23. A second ATIP FSR team started research in the Francistown Agricultural Region during 1982-83.

3

Farming Systems Research, Productivity, and Equity

John D. Gerhart

Introduction

This paper states the broad case for farming systems research as a useful activity aimed at increasing agricultural productivity and equity. The choice of the term "agricultural productivity" rather than "agricultural technology" is intentional since the generation of suitable new technology per se is only one part of the process. It is the contention of this paper that the distinction between technology per se and actual on-farm productivity remains an important distinction, one which must continually be re-emphasized in the agricultural research process if the benefits of agricultural research are to reach the majority of poor farmers in the developing countries. The paper advocates research on farming systems as a relatively inexpensive way to make agricultural research more relevant to farmers' conditions.

Particular attention is paid to the role of social scientists in that research. The argument is made that, if researchers want to understand better how new technology will be achieved, they must broaden their research framework to include such factors as family labor utilization, family decision-making, the role of livestock in the household economy, the importance of off-farm income and employment, and the disposition of farm products. In order to achieve this understanding, researchers must explore intra-household processes more fully, a field hitherto reserved largely to anthropology. Early efforts to introduce anthropologists into agricultural research in the international centers are reviewed briefly and some conclusions drawn about the contributions which they can make and have made.

Why Concentrate on Agricultural Productivity?

The case for continuing to work on developing new agricultural technology is straightforward. First, food production in the developing countries is not keeping pace with population growth. The Third World's 1973 food trade surplus of $1 billion became a $14 billion deficit by 1980. This deficit was generally worst in sub-Saharan Africa. Second, although total world production has risen, the poorest food deficit countries lack the purchasing power to continue buying food imports from the surplus countries. Third, within the developing countries, the poorest segments of the population lack the purchasing power to obtain adequate calories and protein. For many of the poor, increasing agricultural production represents their best (or only) opportunity for meeting their food requirements and for earning case incomes to meet other needs. Even the landless poor depend on the purchasing power of agricultural producers to find employment, either as agricultural workers or in the rapidly expanding rural non-farm service sector. The multiplier effect of higher farm incomes is the best source of new employment in most poor countries. Indeed, industrial development in the developing countries depends largely on the purchasing power and the foreign exchange generated by the agricultural sector. If we are concerned about eradicating poverty in either the urban or the rural sector of the developing countries, we must be concerned with increasing agricultural productivity.

Increasing agricultural productivity also merits attention because it is an effective way of achieving higher incomes. There is abundant evidence of the ability and willingness of small farmers to respond to new agricultural technology provided that it is socially and economically beneficial to them, does not contain an unacceptable level of risk and does not require complementary inputs which are not obtainable. Where the diffusion of new technology has been limited, it is usually because the proposed technology is not beneficial, entails important risks to the reliability of food supplies or requires additional inputs (often of water or fertilizer) which the poorer farmer cannot afford. There are also cases in which wealthier farmers were quicker to adopt new innovations but where smaller farmers followed soon behind. In the case of hybrid maize in Kenya, for example, adoption rates between large and small farmers were indistinguishable after the first two years. There are even some cases (including vegetable production in Egypt) where small farmers have a comparative advantage in adopting new technology, usually because of greater labor self-sufficiency within the family. The old colonial concept of "the unresponsive traditional farmer" now has one of the best-nailed coffins in the world.

There are, of course, many constraints to increasing agricultural productivity. Most farmers in the developing countries are "resource poor"; they lack the land, water, implements, labor and/or management necessary to farm successfully. More often than not, they live in marginal environments with poor soil, high temperatures, high levels of disease and pests, low or unreliable rainfall, severe slopes, serious soil erosion or other natural problems. Since agricultural research has traditionally focused on the best farming areas, the technology for resource-poor areas is not well developed. National research agencies tend to serve the more prosperous farmers or to concentrate their scarce resources on the areas that will give the greatest production, which are naturally the more productive areas. In almost every country, additional research of all kinds is needed for resource-poor areas and for resource-poor farmers in all areas. This is especially so because technologies tend to be location-specific; what works in one area may well not work in an ecologically different environment or even in the absence of basic economic infra-structure such as input distribution, veterinary services or marketing channels.

The first need, therefore, is simply for more research on more aspects of agricultural development in more localities. The International Food Policy Research Institute (IFPRI) estimates that in 1980 national research programs in 76 developing countries spent a total of $890 million (in 1975 dollars) on the work of almost 36,000 scientists. Yet 62 percent of expenditure and 46 percent of the scientists were located in only five countries (Brazil, Argentina, India, Nigeria and Mexico). And this expenditure equalled only 0.56 percent of the value of agricultural output in the producing countries. With a few exceptions, most national ag-ricultural research agencies are characterized by poorly trained staff, low levels of incentives, spotty supervision, inadequate material support, excessive diffusion of effort and high rates of staff turnover. Few have sufficient links with the producers. Given the financial difficulties of most developing countries, it is not surprising that a long-term activity such as scientific research is often the first to face budget cuts.

The Role of International Agricultural Research Centers

The international agricultural research centers offer a partial answer to this problem. They provide genuine economies of scale in the collection, maintenance and development of genetic materials, as well as in the conceptualization of research programs and the training of national research scientists. They also offer much higher levels of staff stability, support services, research direction, strong supervision, a professional work environment and reasonable financial continuity. They contain a critical mass of scientists and a multidisciplinary work environment, most of which national programs lack. Yet the international centers cannot substitute for national programs. Moreover, the centers themselves are restricted by their mandates from taking on too much direct technical assistance; they have financial constraints of their own; their very strength invites invidious distinctions with national programs, and they are often too station-oriented in their own work. The centers need more socio-economic understanding, more off-station research, a much better understanding of family labor and non-farm family livelihoods, a greater recognition of the role of livestock in farming systems and greater capacity for promoting work on improved water management and on small scale mechanization.

Initially, the international centers concentrated on those crops and those areas where they could achieve the most substantial results. This meant primarily irrigated wheat and rice. Now, however, the centers are focusing more explicitly on resource-poor areas. The International Rice Research Institute (IRRI) and the International Center of Tropical Agriculture (CIAT) devote relatively more of their time to upland, rainfed crops than they did previously, while the International Center for Agricultural Research in Dry Areas (ICARDA) concentrates solely on low rainfall areas of the Near East and the International Livestock Centre for Africa (ILCA) primarily on semi-arid livestock production in Africa. By explicitly choosing to work on low-rainfall crops such as cassava, sorghum, cowpeas, lentils, chickpeas and the like, the centers have gone part way toward redressing the imbalance of research toward more prosperous farmers. Although immensely important in resolving research inequities at the regional or ecological level, this focus does not resolve the biases toward larger and more prosperous farmers capable of using new technologies, especially when the technologies require complementary inputs, knowledge or marketing outlets which are differentially available.

One of the most encouraging developments of the past decade in agricultural research, both within the international centers and elsewhere, is the movement to make research more directly relevant to farmers' conditions through the prior description and diagnosis of existing farming systems and the analysis of constraints to increased production which farmers face. The origins of this work are many and diverse; careful and exhaustive surveys of traditional farming systems by such pioneers as David Norman in Northern Nigeria, Michael Collinson in Tanzania and Peter Hildebrand in Guatemala eventually led to simplified diagnostic procedures. Under the leadership of Don Winkelmann, social scientists at the International Maize and Wheat Improvement Center (CIMMYT) have developed perhaps the best known sequence of steps for diagnosing constraints and hypothesizing research interventions that could lead to higher productivity. Alternative versions of farming systems research have now been developed at most of the international centers and by several donor agencies. At least four farming systems newsletters exist, and several universities, including Kansas State, Florida, Kentucky, and Michigan State, are specializing in the field.

What Is Farming Systems Research?

Farming Systems Research (FSR) has become almost a fad among development agencies. There is considerable variation in its definition and use, and a growing literature on the subject. For the purposes of this paper, I have chosen the definition used by the ICARDA farming systems program (ICARDA 1982, 3):

> FSR is a process that identifies problems limiting agricultural productivity and then searches for solutions to these problems. This process recognizes the resources and constraints of the farming families (who are both producers and consumers) and seeks solutions that are relevant, useful, and acceptable to these families. Research is undertaken by multidisciplinary teams of scientists that interact continually with the farmers for whom the research is intended. This approach should ensure that the research produces appropriate technologies and, therefore, will be more easily and quickly adopted.

FSR normally passes through four stages: (1) diagnostic surveys of existing farming systems to identify constraints and provide characteristics of representative farmers; (2) design of experimental innovations, whether biological, mechanical, or economic, to overcome these constraints; (3) the testing of innovations on farmers' fields, and (4) the introduction of the innovation(s), together with necessary infrastructural support (e.g. training, demonstration, supply of inputs, marketing, etc.).

Farming systems methodologies can have useful results in two fields. One is the design of research and the other is the design of policy. On the research side it enables the scientist to make a "short list" of targets of opportunity, what CIMMYT calls "biological leverage points." These are points in the farming process which are amenable to alteration by agricultural research and which are likely to fit easily into any given system because they have already been identified as addressing constraints in that system. The "short list" can then be used to help set priorities for the research system as a whole. In practice, this should lead to a better, quicker, more complete diffusion of innovations than would otherwise be the case.

An example from CIMMYT's East Africa program may illustrate the process. Farmers in central Tanzania achieved low yields of maize because of drought at the end of the season. The extension service advised them to plant early, but the farmers did not follow this advice. Research station trials proved conclusively that early-planted maize did better, and the extension service insisted on its recommendation. A diagnostic survey revealed that the farmers were not planting early because they planted a bean crop first to insure their food supplies during the long growing season. A shorter-maturing maize variety would significantly alleviate the labor conflict and increase the probability of getting a crop within the period when adequate rainfall was available. The maize breeders had a new objective, which could be achieved relatively easily and which would be readily acceptable to farmers.

This type of problem is characteristic of agricultural research when it is done on a research station without farmer involvement. If research funds are available, constraints, whether they be labor, pests, fertility, draft power or lack of moisture, can be removed by utilizing (respectively) hired labor, insecticides, fertilizers, machinery or irrigation. If the constraints are removed, breeding and selection are likely to be concentrated on genetic potential. It is logical that a longer-maturing plant will produce more vegetative matter and higher yields, within whatever absolute constraints are imposed by daylight and temperature. Yet these longer-maturing varieties may not fit well into a farming system which is also producing other crops and animals. On-farm surveys, done correctly, can avoid this problem and give the scientists a "short list" of research objectives which will greatly improve the relevance of their research program.

Implications for Policy Making

Farming systems research can also point to changes in policy or in economic infrastructure which are necessary for the adoption of agricultural innovations. In Jordan, for example, field trials indicated that weeds were competing with wheat for scarce winter rainfall. An infrastructure survey showed, however, that very few farmers had access to the sprays and herbicides needed for efficient weed control. Moreover, the survey showed that many male heads of households were migrants working in the Gulf States and that 90 percent of the farmers were using customized tractor operators to plow their land. An extension program aimed at male farmers would reach only the small percentage wealthy enough to operate their own farm machinery. Instead, a program aimed at introducing spraying equipment to custom operators could reach many more farms, while reducing labor requirements for weeding. Launching an extension campaign without knowledge of the characteristics of the farming families would have been ineffective. Hence, farming systems research can be a cost-effective way of redirecting agricultural policy as well as agricultural research.

Most important, FSR relates research and policy together in a fashion which is immediately practical and useful. It tends to be ex ante rather than ex post in its analysis. This is a departure from much traditional social science research, including both anthropology and economics, which tends to analyze the nature of rural poverty with the technology taken as a fait accompli. Such research is usually descriptive in nature and often uninformed about the technical aspects of agriculture. Just as the biological scientist is not trained to look at the composition of family labor and its distribution around the agricultural calendar, so the social scientist is even less capable of identifying plant diseases or of hypothesizing what genetic improvements might allow an increase in production. FSR provides a pragmatic, non-threatening method of carrying out multi-disciplinary research in a context most likely to produce a usable research product. Moreover, unlike traditional social science research, it has a very powerful built-in method of self evaluation, namely whether or not output is increased among the families in the region under study.

An additional reason for working on farming systems research is because of its potential for directing technological development toward specific populations, whatever their characteristics. If donors, researchers or governments want to reach resource-poor farmers, female-headed households, malnourished children and perhaps even landless laborers, they must have a much better understanding of the socio-economic conditions of rural life. They should also have something to offer such disadvantaged groups in terms of relevant technology and should know how new technology may affect the livelihoods of people in the areas where it is to be introduced.

Again, an example may illustrate the possibilities. In Syria, ICARDA is looking at the possibilities of mechanized harvesting of certain crops. A study of rural women, carried out by an ICARDA staff member as part of her master's thesis, found that much of the labor in question was undertaken by very poor Kurdish women from the northeast who migrate seasonally to earn cash incomes on the more prosperous farms in the west. An introduction of mechanization might displace these workers without providing a comparable alternative. The benefits of mechanization had to be weighed against the losses in employment of this disadvantaged group and/or alternative livelihoods sought for them. Through the process of carrying out farming systems studies, one can enlist the support and knowledge of agricultural scientists in addressing social and economic problems which would not normally have come to their attention. To the extent that farming systems research incorporates attention to intra-household variables, it offers a means to monitor technology's impacts on individuals, as well as households of different categories, and to understand the incentive systems (and hence the responses) that result from application of new agricultural technologies. This can enhance achievement of both productivity and equity goals underlying the widespread concern with developing innovations appropriate to smallholder farming.

It is important to note that a farming systems perspective is not limited to the situation of small farmers. A farming systems approach is also appropriate in dealing with the circumstances of large farmers. The use of a farming systems approach in itself, therefore, does not solve the problem of skewness of resources toward larger, more capable, more powerful or more advantageously placed farmers. What it does do is to enable the motivated researcher to direct his or her efforts toward farmers in specific environmental or socio-economic situations by defining the characteristics of a given stratum of farmers; delineating their resource constraints, and hypothesizing, designing, and testing technologies applicable to their circumstances. Moreover, this can be done without having to rely on the "trickle down effect" of a generalized, or an input-intensive, technology. Increasingly in the international centers, for example, low input intensity is being specified as a criterion for new technologies.

It is this ability to "target" innovations toward disadvantaged groups that accounts in large measure for the increased interest of donors in farming systems research. The disadvantaged groups can include resource-poor farmers, farmers in drier areas, farmers who lack complementary inputs, farmers who are not on irrigated land or who are at the tail-end of irrigation systems, farmers on badly eroded slopes, farm families headed by women, families where the men are away from the farm and other subclasses of farmers who may be either ethnically or geographically disadvantaged. By using diagnostic surveys and on-farm trials, one can identify those constraints that face any particular disadvantaged group and hypothesize both the technological and policy changes which would be necessary to assist that group.

To identify constraints and hypothesize changes effectively, we must have greater knowledge of the characteristics of these groups—what it is about their resource availabilities, their family labor situation, their decision-making patterns, their capitalization, their skill levels, their pattern of livestock ownership and/or their food preferences—that affects their interest in and ability to adopt agricultural innovations. Both the desire to improve the diffusion of agricultural technology and the desire to reach disadvantaged groups come together in the desire to make greater use of intra-household studies within agricultural research. It is at this point that the agricultural scientist must move outside the traditional biological sciences to seek expertise from social scientists in order to understand the characteristics and behavior of the agricultural research clients and to be able to design innovations for any given population.

Making Farming Systems Research Effective

Carrying out farming systems research in a national context is not an easy process. Since agricultural research is a highly location-specific process, one must build capacity in as many locations as research is needed. Just as hybridization is a process for inventing locally-adapted plant varieties rather than a single, universally-applicable variety, so FSR is a process for analyzing locally different farming situations, not a prescription for all farming situations. If it is to be conducted successfully, a number of factors must be taken into account, including the following:

First, since FSR entails communication across disciplinary lines, it must necessarily involve biological and social scientists throughout the research process. Contracting out the social science research to a local (or foreign) university will not overcome the existing disciplinary apartheid and will not bring about the mixing of the biological scientists' optimism (about what can be done) with the social scientists' realism (about the dangers of doing it). Although biological scientists can be taught social survey methodology, they are less readily able to identify or measure the opportunity costs of one farm activity versus another or versus non-farming activities. For the time being, farming systems research must be explicitly multidisciplinary.

Second, "social scientists" means more than economists. Anthropologists add a qualitative and holistic perspective which is badly needed. This is especially true as family labor is shown to be important in determining the adoption of new technology. The old paradigm of the "able bodied male household head" is a thing of the past in those parts of the world (including southern Africa, the Middle East and much of South Asia) where the migration of male workers has made women the functional heads of many rural households. In many situations, because of religious or other restrictions, intra-household studies must be carried out by women. If men are not available in the household, farming technology must be designed explicitly for women, and extension strategies must be aimed at and often carried out by women. Because of their formal training in kinship relations with explicit emphasis on gender and its relationship to work roles, anthropologists are well qualified to conduct such studies.

Third, while FSR can generate improved technology by linking the researchers to the farmer in a more systematic way (through diagnostic surveys, on-farm trials, and demonstrations), it is difficult to advocate new technologies without a better understanding of government policies on agricultural production, input distribution, marketing and the like.

As an example, CIMMYT studies in Algeria and ICARDA studies in Jordan have both shown that input availability was a major constraint to technological change. Without changes in pricing and input distribution policies, improved technologies are not likely to be adopted successfully. Both national and international centers should establish more direct means of influencing national policymakers.

Fourth, because national programs are the weak link in the chain of agricultural research, they should be given priority in developing capacities in this field. This requires not just financing FSR studies in local situations but much more systematic efforts to develop local capacity through training and supervised field experience. In most cases, job descriptions and terms of reference are also needed for social scientists within research agencies. Trying to introduce FSR into a skeptical scientific research agency by putting in relatively junior, poorly trained or inexperienced economists, in their first professional posting, will not achieve a successful result. Since FSR researchers, by definition, must work largely off the research station, they tend to require those very inputs (vehicles and travelling allowances) which are in short supply; in order to avert hostility and discrimination by research administrators, FSR researchers should be largely self-contained regarding transport and extra administrative expenses. Because FSR uses farmers' fields, it is relatively cost effective; to compromise that effectiveness from the outset, by cutting corners in providing mobility, makes little sense. Although strengthening national programs should have priority, the international centers should not be ignored. On the contrary, these centers offer attractive benefits in providing guidance, supervision and training in FSR methods.

Fifth, the introduction of FSR methods into national or international research programs is more difficult than it appears since FSR implicitly criticizes the way that research priorities are presently set. Done correctly, however, FSR can make both research and extension easier by making the technology more congruent with existing practices and/or less risky for the farmer to adopt. This does not mean that extension can be ignored altogether. FSR studies should be designed in such a way that they explicitly consider how the new technology should be diffused. Experiments in extension are important for this purpose. Extension without a tested, improved and beneficial innovation, however, is an expensive and frustrating exercise.

Anthropologists and FSR

I have until now argued that research can be made more relevant to small farmers by the explicit study of small-farm conditions, i.e., farming systems research. If FSR is only a "gimmick" to encourage a more holistic, interactive view of the farm situation, it appears to be an effective one. But if FSR is going to be used for identifying and designing technologies relevant to specific classes of farmers—especially those disadvantaged by location, size or lack of access to resources and skills—we must ask what components are needed? What subjects require additional study, and what skills are useful?

Initially, farming systems studies focused on expanding the horizons of the researcher from a single crop to mixed cropping systems. Another early emphasis was on the sequencing of crops, including the labor bottlenecks created by the overlap of agricultural activities at peak seasons of the year. Gradually, livestock activities were incorporated into FSR studies. This was particularly the case in the Middle East and North African countries, where cereal-forage systems predominate and where farmers' strategies are often built around providing summer forage for the animals. Crops are not uncommonly grazed under, and straw prices regularly exceed those of grain. More recently, FSR studies have expanded to include studies on consumer preferences, nutrition, food storage practices, household decision making, credit, mechanization, non-farm activities, labor migration and other factors affecting both the need for and the adoption of new technologies. Many of these subjects of study go beyond the traditional competence of not only the biological scientist but also the agricultural economist, the other main practitioner of farming systems-type research.

Recognizing the need for studies of family labor, family consumption patterns and family decision–making, agencies conducting farming systems studies have increasingly sought out both the methods and the skills of the "human sciences," anthropology and sociology. Because of the growing involvement of anthropologists in farming systems research, it may be interesting to review briefly here the kinds of issues anthropologists have to date addressed in their work at international research centers, the contributions they have made, what skills they have provided that were otherwise lacking and how their contributions have been received by scientists lacking the same perspectives.[1] Not surprisingly, there has been a wide range of experience reflecting different approaches and, in some sense, different conclusions.

The introduction of anthropology into the international agricultural centers parallels that of economics, which began perhaps a decade earlier. Like the economists before them, the anthropologists have had to "prove" the utility of their discipline, even though it ranges more widely than most. Although the presence of economists may have helped to smooth the path for the anthropologists, the road to "acceptance" of the anthropologists generally has been even more difficult than it was for the economists.

This may be because biological scientists are unfamiliar, if not uncomfortable, with the necessarily non-quantitative nature of most anthropological research; because anthropologists have generally lacked experience that the economists had when they joined the centers, and/or because the time available to the anthropologists to "prove" the value of their contributions has been too short to show long-term results. (Most anthropologists hold one- or two-year postdoctoral appointments.) Aware of time constraints, some anthropologists have tended to focus on discrete, even independent, projects that could make a useful contribution in the time available.

In spite of difficulties, there have been numerous successes in the use of anthropologists. At least three centers have hired anthropologists to fill core positions; others are meeting their needs by engaging anthropologists on short-term contracts. Attributes of anthropology and anthropologists cited favorably by the centers include the holistic nature of anthropological methods, a broader sense of what questions to ask, greater attention to the quality of information received, more careful and more effective ways of formulating questions, better targeting of sample surveys and on-farm trials toward intended beneficiaries, better selection of collaborators, better assessment of reactions to recommendations, more attentiveness to non-farm factors, more awareness of organizational factors affecting individual adoption practices, greater flexibility in exploring farmer motivations, less pro-innovation bias and more commitment to the training of collaborators. Among the few negative traits mentioned were occasional lapses into jargon and a danger of "slipping toward the norms of the disciplines and the applause of professional peers."

Several commentators have mentioned that satisfactory working relations in multidisciplinary research are a two-way street and that, when social science staff are cast in a purely service-oriented role, low staff morale and problems in retaining an effective capacity have tended to result. One commentator observed that a social scientist may be willing to remain on the side line while the learning is interesting or when the scientist is working on his/her own project but that the "handmaiden relationship is not one that will keep talent on for very long." Working relationships have been most productive when there was flexible leadership, tasks were concrete and clearly defined, jargon was eschewed and there was strong support from the top.

Conclusion

Specific issues in which intra-household studies can contribute to the design of improved agricultural research include the disposition of family labor; the management of livestock for both commercial and subsistence purposes; the processing of agricultural products, whether for sale or home consumption; decision-making within the household on the disposition of non-farm income; decisions to migrate or engage in off-farm employment, and other factors. From the experience of the international centers, however, one can hypothesize that, however good the quality of the research, such studies are unlikely to have a major impact on agricultural research per se unless the biological scientists are involved in their design and their interpretation. Experience would indicate that biological scientists are more enthusiastic about participating in such research than in absorbing its lessons without having participated. We must concern ourselves not only with what is studied but also with the process by which these studies are carried out.

There is increasing evidence that development activities of many types require multidisciplinary approaches in order to achieve new levels of understanding, and participation by disadvantaged elements in society. Such fields are agroforestry, water management, public health, low-cost housing, and appropriate technology in agriculture and other fields require a mix of social, economic and technical disciplines. Of all these fields, farming systems research may have already gone the farthest in testing the utility and the limits of multidisciplinary research. For those concerned about improving the application of improved technologies to poor populations, the experience of farming systems research may well have a wider importance than its utility to agriculture alone.

Notes

1. This summary is based on information gathered from several sources, including responses to inquiries directed by the author to research leaders and/ or social scientists at all of the international agricultural centers. Replies were received from four economists, two biological scientists and three anthropologists who were working, or had worked, at six different centers. The experience of two other centers was known to the author. I have also drawn on two excellent papers prepared for The Rockefeller Foundation by Robert E. Rhoades and Robert Tripp detailing the experiences of the two centers, CIMMYT and the International Potato Center (CIP), which have made the most extensive use of anthropologists and two anthropological publications with a special interest in this field, *Practicing Anthropology* and *Culture and Agriculture*.

4

On-Farm Research and Household Economics

Allan Low

Introduction

Although there is in theory a close relationship between the two new philosophies of farming systems research and household economics, this relationship has not been sufficiently recognized or adequately developed in practice. This paper focuses on the need to orient on-farm research methodologies toward household economics concepts.

By "on-farm research," I mean the aspect of farming systems research in which CIMMYT[1] is currently engaged, namely "on-farm research with a farming systems perspective." This involves farm-level research to (1) understand farmers' circumstances, (2) generate hypotheses about how best to improve farm productivity in the near term given the farmers' circumstances and current technical knowledge, (3) design and test on farmers' fields new technologies based on these hypotheses or (4) direct station research toward more relevant programs if the technical base is lacking.

By "household economics" I mean the concept of household production behavior that has its basis in the new theory of consumer choice developed by Becker (1965), Lancaster (1966) and Muth (1966). This new theory sees households as production/consumption units in which market goods and household resources (mainly time) are combined in a household technology to produce intermediate non-market goods ("Z goods") which are then consumed in combinations that generate maximum utility (or satisfaction or welfare) for the household.

On-farm research is aimed at seeking ways of increasing farm production, for either the market or home consumption. On small African farms, crop or livestock production is organized within the context of the farm household, which is both a production unit and a consumption unit. The production of non-market goods forms part of this production/

71

consumption milieu. A high proportion of available household resources are used in household production activities, including not only household maintenance or child care but also such socially necessary activities as exchange labor to ensure access to the essential non-market resources of land and labor.

If farm production is increased through technologies that use more household resources, fewer resources will be available for household production. This implies that either more farm goods will be consumed or the proceeds of increased farm production will be used to purchase market goods. The appropriateness of new technologies clearly depends not only on the extent to which they increase the productivity of household resources used in farming but also on a comparison of current production with potential future production (the investment/security aspect) and on a comparison of the subjective value of the non-market household production goods that have been foregone with the utility and/or price of the substitute goods consumed (the consumption aspect).

Logically, household economics theory and the study of intra-household processes should form an important part of on-farm research methodology, but this is not the case. On-farm research methodology tends to concentrate on the interactions among different farming activities and, although some attempt is made to account for the opportunity costs of time and funds used in non-farm market production, little attention is given to the opportunity costs of resources used in non-farm non-market production, investment and consumption. Moreover, the relationship between agricultural productivity and household welfare is generally perceived as a one-way process and assumed to be positive, i.e., increased agricultural productivity is perceived as leading to increased household welfare. But welfare is a function of the total mix of monetary and non-monetary, tangible and intangible goods. Moreover, perceptions of welfare affect the goals of farm-household members and, in turn, their allocation of resources and management; thus, welfare is not only a function but also a determinant of agricultural productivity (Caldwell 1983). Where household welfare and the household's commitment to farming are affected by non-farm factors, e.g., the wage employment market, access to consumer goods and household composition, these factors become relevant for on-farm research aimed at generating appropriate technology.

On-farm research results are indicating the need to think more in household terms. The new household economics perspective and an appreciation of intra-household processes can contribute to the effectiveness of on-farm research methodology and help move us beyond the notion of a one-way linkage between farm income and household welfare.

The Development of On-Farm Research Methodologies

The need for on-farm research developed as a result of the observation that much of the technology developed from station research programs was not adopted by small farmers in developing countries. One reason for this lack of adoption was that the technologies being produced were not consistent with the circumstances of many small farmers. They were inappropriate for a number of reasons:

a. The natural circumstances (soils, topography, climate) facing small farmers in specific situations vary from location to location and are generally different from those on research stations;

b. The institutional support services needed to supply inputs were either nonexistent or unreliable;

c. The costs and risks of using the new technologies were too high for small farmers relative to the benefits; and/or

d. Small farmers had multiple objectives stemming from their need to consume much of what they produced, to minimize risk and to maximize returns to heterogeneous resources such as family labor, whose opportunity cost varies at different times in the season and according to individuals.

By contrast, the on-station researcher's environment is characterized by particular—often favorable—natural circumstances, availability of inputs, little concern with cost or risk and generally a single objective: to increase output per unit of land.

On-farm research methodology is aimed at sensitizing agricultural researchers to the circumstances of their farmer clients. Apart from getting researchers to conduct experiments on farmers' fields, it was recognized that farmers' circumstances are determined by both physical and social factors. This led to the need for interdisciplinary interaction between social and technical sciences. It was also recognized that family farming systems tended to be complex. Within the farm context this complexity was especially evident in tropical areas with long growing seasons, where intercropping and multiple cropping were practiced.[2] The recognition that family farming systems are complex led to the need to adopt a systems perspective in which interactions between activities could be accounted for. Again, this contrasts with the commodity- and disciplinary-orientation of station-based research.

The characteristics of on-farm research, then, are that it is based on first-hand interaction between farmers and researchers, it is interdisciplinary and it encompasses a systems perspective.

The Aims and Methodology of On-Farm Research

The aim of on-farm research is to increase farm production through the generation of appropriate technology in the near term. The strategy for achieving this aim is based on the adaptation of existing technology so that it better fits the needs and circumstances of small farmers in developing countries.

The starting point is to gain an understanding of the farming system and to identify key research opportunities that are likely to give a substantial pay-off in the near term. On-farm researchers are increasingly relying on unstructured exploratory surveys (or sondeos) for rapid understanding of the farming system(s) in an area. The technique used is characterized by a high degree of researcher participation in farmer interviews and field observations (Collinson 1981; Hilderbrand 1981). A multidisciplinary team of researchers interviews farmers in an informal and interactive manner. The aim of the interviews is to focus quickly on areas where there is research potential for adapting current technology so that the technology will be more consistent with farmers' circumstances and in ways that are likely to improve farm productivity.

Findings from the exploratory survey are used to generate hypotheses about how current technology can be adapted in ways that are consistent with these circumstances. These hypotheses may be tested in more formal, verification surveys in which emphasis is placed on the collection of quantitative data to test the hypotheses.

On the basis of results from the formal surveys (or in their absence) research opportunities are identified, given priority according to farmers' needs and probable pay-off, and screened for systems compatibility. The two or three most promising opportunities are designed as trials to be set out (tested) on farmers' fields.

The guiding principle of on-farm research is that data collection is designed as a sequential process. The objective of this research is limited and clear: to generate appropriate technology in the near term based on the use and adaptation of existing information and a knowledge of farmers' circumstances.

The Consideration of Intra-Household Processes

On-farm research focuses sharply on the farm, with minimal consideration given to non-farm household activities and decision-making processes. Research concepts and techniques of analysis have tended to concentrate on how farmers' adoption of new technologies is influenced by natural circumstances, institutional support or cash costs and risks. Farmers' multiple objectives have been less thoroughly treated, partly because there is little theoretical basis for analyzing the multiple market and non-market objectives of a household[3] and partly because the other factors can be handled within the context of the farming system. The need to adjust input rates (e.g. fertilizers, plant population) to fit local soil suitability or a new crop to an existing cropping system can be established without reference to non-farm activities and intra-household decision-making processes.

Taking account of farmers' multiple objectives, however, implies extending the area of analysis from the farm to the farm-household and from concentration on production to more emphasis on consumption. This reduces the focus and complicates the analysis. Nevertheless, experience with on-farm research work in eastern and southern Africa points toward the need to consider household/farm linkages more explicitly in technology generation and suggests that there may be a case for extending the concepts of on-farm research beyond the boundaries of the farm to encompass the larger farm-household unit, despite added complexity and some possible loss of focus.

Some On-Farm Research Findings

Recent findings from on-farm research in eastern and southern Africa demonstrate the linkage between on-farm research and household economics.

The Importance of the Time Constraint

According to household economics theory, the time of its members is the basic resource of households. The opportunity cost of this resource varies over time and at any one point in time among household members of different genders, ages and skills. An implication of the theory is that time and cash are substitutable. Time can be "sold" to generate cash or non-market goods and it can also be "purchased" by spending cash on time-saving inputs.

Diagnostic work in on-farm research is indicating that farmers very often compromise on crop and livestock management, not because of lack of knowledge or cash to purchase inputs or because inputs are not available but because of time constraints.

Often, seemingly appropriate production-increasing innovations are not adopted because of their implications in terms of time. Commenting on the results of experimental work on livestock feeding in the Kenya Dryland Farming Research and Development project, Tessema (1983) concluded that the rate of adoption of innovations was disappointingly poor. He observed that:

- Kenyan farmers valued their leisure more than the gains they could get from clearing bush to encourage good forage growth.
- Most farmers are grazing their crop residues in situ and realize that they are wasting about 40 percent of production by doing this. Since they persist in this practice, it appears that they are choosing the least burdensome way of doing a job even though they know that increased input would give a higher return.
- The growing of fodder crops demands greater labor and oxen time, which the farmer cannot cope with if he must also plow, plant and weed for food crop production. Thus, only a handful of farmers could be persuaded to include fodder crops in their cropping system.

The summary of research thrusts from on-farm research work in southern Africa in Table 4.1 shows the importance of time in evaluating potential technical innovations.

Household Differentiation

Household economics theory relates differences in behavior among households to differences in their characteristics and composition and, in particular, to the way these affect the relative time values of members within a household. On-farm research methodology recognizes that differences in the economic and natural circumstances facing households will affect their ability to adopt, and interest in adopting, particular farm technologies. The identification of different recommendation domains (homogenous groups of farmers) in on-farm research has tended to be based on external factors such as agro-climatic conditions and access to markets or inputs. However, as research proceeds, the importance of internal household factors in determining appropriate technology is beginning to emerge.

In Table 4.2 we see that cattle owners achieved higher crop yields than non-owners. These yield differences are related to management factors. Cattle owners plant and weed earlier, and a greater proportion of them winter plow and apply manure. These management differences are in turn related to internal household factors. As Shumba (1983, 11) states:

> While non-owners and owners obtained the same absolute income from off-farm sources, this represents a much higher proportion of total income for non-owners, who have lower productive capacities in farming because of their smaller labor forces, lack of oxen and greater tendency for the household head to be away. The greater tendency for household heads to be absent in non-owning households is related to the younger age of these households. Job prospects for younger household heads are better

TABLE 4.1
Summary of Research Thrusts from On-Farm Research Programs

Location/Problem	Trials	Evaluation Criteria
Zimbabwe (Mangwende)		
Late maize planting	Minimum tillage/ herbicide	Yield/ha, time costs
Late fertilizer application	Fertilizer management	Yield/ha, time cost, risk
Zimbabwe (Chibi South)		
Staggered maize plantings	Variety × time of planting	Minimum yields, risk
Shortage of oxen	Forage intercropping	Yield/ha, time costs
Malawi (Local Maize)		
Witch weed	Planting time	Reduced weeding requirements
Lack of fertilization	Fertilization	Yield/ha
Malawi (hybrid maize)		
Cob rot and late planting	Time of planting/stalk bending	Yield/ha, disease incidence, other operations at stalk bending time
Botswana (Dryland Oxen Cultivators) Variable germination and poor weed control due to broadcasting	Row planting methods	Returns to oxen and labor and returns to cash
Botswana (Ngamiland Dryland Hoe Cultivators) Small areas cropped due to labor shortages	Pre- and post-emergence herbicides and hand pushed jab planter	Speed of operation farmer acceptance yield/ha.
Zambia Late planting, fertilizing and weeding	Short-maturing varieties zero tillage, fertilizer management	Land not a constraint and returns per unit of land is low priority

Table 4.1 continued

Location/Problem	Trials	Evaluation Criteria
Swaziland		
Poor emergence, low plant population	Modified ox planter	Yield/ha, emergence, fertilizer rates, farmer interest/assessment
Late and inadequate weeding	Granular/liquid herbicides	Yield/ha, time costs farmer interest/ assessment
Lesotho		
Poor seedbeds, late planting	Fall and early winter plowing	Yield/ha, oxen work rates, germination percentage
Poor animal nutrition	Stall feeding of grown forage or bought hominy chop	Weight gains, oxen work rates

than for their older counterparts, and wages provide a relatively low-risk means for young households to generate the necessary funds to hire cattle and purchase fertilizer. The incentive for members of non-owning households to seek wage employment is therefore quite high and, given their already smaller work forces, this further reduces time available for farm activities and contributes to the lower levels of crop management, lower yields and lower farm incomes of non-owners compared with owners.

From a household economics perspective the influence of the domestic development cycle on the productive capacity of farm-households is clear. Oxen ownership is a critical factor enabling better crop husbandry, and the distribution of cattle in this society is associated with household development and maturity, which are related to the other factors mentioned by Shumba and combine to result in poorer crop management by the less mature non-owning households.[4]

Given the relationship between cattle ownership and crop productivity and the decline of cattle in the area owing to a health control breakdown and drought, on-farm researchers have looked toward research opportunities, such as improved feeding, that would increase the size and capacity of the draft cattle pool. However, recognition of the development cycle linkage poses two questions: 1) Would these extra cattle be any better distributed between households? 2) Would having cattle enable

TABLE 4.2
Characteristics of Two Recommendation Domains in Mangwende, Zimbabwe

| | Cattle Ownership | |
	Owners	Non-Owners
Resources		
Family size (persons)	8.4	6.4
Farm workers	3.4	2.8
Size of holding (ha)	3.9	2.9
Area cultivated (ha)	3.6	2.1
% Farms with head working away	7	13
% Farms with head less than 55 years	17	42
$ Farms with women head	12	30
Crop Yields (t/ha)		
Maize	3.2	2.1
Groundnuts	.7	.5
Sunflower	.2	.04
Income Sources (Z$/annum)		
Maize sales	347	168
Vegetable sales	140	84
Groundnut sales	40	26
Off-farm income	159	149
Total income	752	449

less mature households with smaller workforces to practice better crop management and would the relative incentives to seek wage employment be sufficiently reduced to encourage them to do so?

An answer to the distribution question is suggested by the situation in neighboring Botswana, where cattle numbers have increased at 4.7 percent per annum over the last decade and the average herd size has increased from 30 to 43 head. Despite this sustained increased in the size of the draft cattle pool, the proportion of households owning cattle has remained unchanged and more than 50 percent of farmers still do not own their own draft animals.

Women Farmers

As on-farm researchers conduct surveys and establish trials in eastern and southern Africa, they increasingly find themselves dealing with women farmers. At farmers' group meetings women invariably outnumber men, and it is said that 50–70 percent of all farmers in Africa are women.

Because women everywhere are responsible for household production activities (household maintenance, child care, etc.), it follows that much of the agricultural work in Africa competes with household production activities for the allocation of women's time.

On-farm researchers and farm management economists are used to assessing potential technical innovations in terms of the labor demands of competing farm activities and to accounting for alternative market activities by imputing an opportunity cost of time. But the demands of household production are seldom considered, either directly or indirectly through imputing opportunity cost.

Rural household studies are beginning to highlight the large amounts of time allocated to non-farm non-market household activities, especially by women. Often the costs of not performing some of these essential or socially necessary tasks (e.g. fetching water or working in another's field) will be quite high and will significantly reduce the real benefits of technologies that compete for the time of the responsible household member.

Factors affecting who does what within farm-households and the number of hands available for farming clearly have significant implications for the appropriateness of new farm technology. Tessema's observations cited above, to the effect that farmers value leisure more than gains from bush clearing or choose the least burdensome way of feeding crop residues even though they know that an increased input of time would result in higher feed production, are made from a farming systems perspective which lacks a household perspective on farm-household decision-making.

Toward a Household Economic Perspective in On-Farm Research

The application of a household economics perspective can contribute to the effectiveness of on-farm research in three particular areas:

- Understanding farmers' objectives and strategies.
- Defining recommendation domains.
- Evaluating new technologies.

Understanding Farmers' Objectives and Strategies

On-farm research looks at technology development from the farmers' point of view. As Norman suggests, understanding farmers' objectives and values is crucial to this:

The goals and motivations of farmers, which will affect the degree and type of effort they will be willing to devote to improving the productivity of their farming systems, are essential inputs to the process of identifying or designing potentially appropriate improved technologies. (Norman et al. 1982, 25).

While on-farm research recognizes that farmers have multiple objectives, these objectives are generally considered in terms of the farming system. Multiple and intercropping strategies are manifestations of farmers' multiple objectives for cash, preferred staple foods, food security and maximization of returns to farm resources. Non-farm and non-market objectives of farmers have been given less, if any, attention. As Behnke and Kerven state, this concentration on the farming system may have two undesirable results:

First it may encourage researchers to think of those who farm as primarily or solely farmers, and thereby underestimate the role of non-agricultural activities in the larger household economy. Secondly, an exclusive concentration on farming may ill equip FSR to address one of the major issues in agricultural development in Africa: the withdrawal of labor from agriculture due to rural-urban migration (Behnke and Kerven 1983, 9).

In eastern and southern Africa farming is seldom the only source of income and in many cases it is not the major one. Wage employment, beer brewing, handicrafts, trading and teaching are common additional sources of income for rural households. While on-farm researchers are concerned with measuring and increasing farm income, farmers are concerned with stabilizing and increasing their entire welfare, much of which may come from non-farm production. Thus, in order to understand "farmers'" goals and objectives, on-farm researchers need to adopt a household economics perspective and attempt to see how diverse production activities are combined to maximize household utility. To quote Behnke and Kerven again:

The acceptability of a farming innovation cannot be adequately judged solely by its technical and economic impact on farming. It must also be assessed in terms of its positive or negative contribution to the household economy as a whole. This will especially be the case when technical innovations require additional labor or capital that could be invested elsewhere, for example, in the search for urban jobs or in the education of children. (Ibid. p. 10).

Application of a household economics perspective will help on-farm researchers to understand farmers' strategies in a household context and thus to search for farm technologies that are appropriate to the overall, farm and non-farm, circumstances facing farmers. Given a household perspective it is possible to see, for example, that one important risk-reducing strategy adopted by many farmers is the search for wage employment by one or more members of the rural household. Over the last two drought years in southern Africa, households with a wage earning member have suffered much less than those without a reliable non-farm source of income. Clearly where the chances of obtaining off-farm employment are quite good, any farm-based risk avoidance strategy, such as planting an extra area of cassava or tied ridging or mulching or insect control, must be compared with the returns and reliability of obtaining income from wage employment.

Norman (1983, 7) notes that in the case of Botswana it may be necessary to accept that farmers will be reluctant to invest very much (money or time) in crop production because investing in crop production is riskier than putting money/time into livestock or off-farm activities. This insight clearly has important implications for technology generation in Botswana.

Defining Recommendation Domains

The concept of the recommendation domain has become central to on-farm research methodology. A "recommendation domain" is a homogeneous group of farmers who share the same problems and possess similar resources for solving these problems. This group of farmers is expected to adopt (or not adopt) the same recommendation given equal access to information about it. In much of southern Africa, different recommendation domains occur not only because of differences in farmer resources, cropping opportunities, market access and inherent land fertility but also because, at any one time, farm households have different opportunities for non-farm wage employment or other income-earning activities. Often it is the nature and extent to which farm households exploit these non-farm opportunities that most strongly influence farming practices and the aims and objectives of farm production.

It is commonly observed that, within homogeneous agro-climatic locations with similar market opportunities, neighboring farmers with similar income or resource levels will farm in very different ways. Households that are in a position to exploit non-farm income opportunities, by dint of better qualifications, experience or enterprise, will tend not to manage their farming operations in as thorough a manner as their less wage-employment-oriented neighbors. In these farm-households, the aims and objectives of farming tend to be less production-oriented and more social- and security-oriented. Neighbors who are less able to exploit non-farm opportunities will look on farming more in terms of production and income and will tend to give more time and attention to farming activities. The cultivation practices of these two types of farmers will differ, as will relevant interventions and recommendations.

A recommendation domain exercise was recently carried out in Swaziland with the expectation that different farming systems would be observed in the very different ecological conditions of the highveld, middleveld and lowveld areas of the country (Watson 1983). However, it was found that variations in cropping systems within the regions were much greater than the variations between the regions. The within-region variation stemmed from differences in internal household circumstances rather than from external circumstances. Table 4.3 gives a breakdown of these farm-household types according to household characteristics and relates these differences to the typical cropping practices employed by each group and to the potential interventions implied by farm-household circumstances and current practices.

In Table 4.3 the farm household types have been broken down on the basis of off-farm income/resource endowments and labor committed to farming. These factors are not independent. Previous surveys (e.g., de Vletter 1981) have found that there is a strong positive relationship between off-farm income and farm-household resource endowments. There is also an inverse relationship between off-farm income and the time and attention directed to farming. However, some households are able both to exploit off-farm income opportunities and to commit time and attention to farming. Generally these are households where the head is not engaged in off-farm employment but other household members are earning cash away from the farm. Such farm households would fall into Category 1 in Table 4.3. Other farm households may find that they are able to exploit off-farm earning opportunities but, in order to do so, they compromise on time devoted to farming. These fall into Category 2 in Table 4.3.

Category 3 represents households with relatively little potential for exploiting off-farm income opportunities but with a reasonable labor and resource endowment for farming. The last category may be represented by old households or women-headed households, where opportunities for off-farm income exploitation are poor and labor and resource endowments are also relatively low.

We can identify some of the distinguishing features of these household types as is done in column 2 of Table 4.3. On the basis of survey data we can also list the different types of observed cropping practice that apply to each category (see column 3 of Table 4.3). These lead us to suggest different sets of potential relevant interventions for each farm-

TABLE 4.3

Relationship Between Household Characteristic, Determined Recommendation Domains and On-Farm Trials

Farm Household Type	Distinguishing Features	Cropping Practices Fixed Non-Experimental Variables	Potential Interventions
1. Cash/resource rich and labor rich	(a) 4 + adult equivalent in family farm work-force (b) Access to significant non-farm income	(a) Winter or 2 × plough, early plant, 2+ weedings (b) High level of input use e.g. fertilizers (top dressing), hybrid seed, tractors	(a) Top dressing levels (b) Tied ridging (c) Winter ploughing (tractor) (d) Early planting (hybrids) (e) Double cropping
2. Cash/resource rich but labor poor	(a) 4 adult equivalent in family farm work-force (b) Access to significant non-farm income (c) May or may not own oxen	(a) Only one ploughing, late planting, 1 weeding, use of planter (b) High levels of input use e.g. fertilizers and top dressing, hybrid maize, no tractors	(a) Top dressing (b) Botswana plough/planter (c) Botswana improved planter (d) Winter ploughing (tractor) (e) Short season varieties (f) Herbicides
3. Cash/resource poor, but labor rich	(a) 4+ adult equivalent in family farm work-force (b) Poor access to non-farm income (c) Have some own oxen	(a) 2 × plough, early plant 2 × weedings (b) Lower levels of input use, e.g. no top dressing, less hybrid maize, no tractors	(a) Winter ploughling (b) 2 × ploughing (c) Better weeding (d) Double cropping (e) Intensive sweet potato production (f) Cutworm banding and scouting (g) Early planting (h) Fodder conservation (i) Tied ridging

Table 4.3 continued

Farm Household Type	Distinguishing Features	Cropping Practices Fixed Non-Experimental Variables	Potential Interventions
4. Cash/resource poor and labor poor	(a) 4 adult equivalent in family farm work-force (b) Poor access to non-farm income (c) Few if any cattle	(a) 1 × plough late planting, 1 × weeding, hand planting in furrow (b) Low levels of use, local or open pollinated varieties, no tractors	(a) Minimum tillage (b) Tyne plough (e.g. Zimbabwe) (c) Short season varieties (open pollinated)

household type. For example, Type 1 households can contemplate cash-expensive inputs and have the resources and commitment to manage these inputs reasonably well. Group 2 households may have the cash and incentive to purchase inputs but will tend not to manage them so intensively. Thus, fertilizer top dressing may be a relevant intervention for both Group 1 and 2 farm households. But the conditions under which the resource of top dressing is tested should differ significantly for the two groups of households. Trials related to Group 1 households would be conducted with good land preparations, early planting and adequate weed control. The response of top dressing under conditions relevant to Group 2 farm households (poor seedbed preparation, late planting and little weeding) is likely to be very different. Not only that, the relevant evaluation of the trial results may also be different. If Group 1 farm households are surplus producers, the relevant value for any increased production is the market price of maize. For Group 2, deficit producers, the relevant value to place on yield increases will rather be the equivalent food purchase price.

Another example is the introduction of an early maturing short season maize variety for Group 1 farmers. This may open the door for double cropping and, if so, the benefit of an early maturing variety should take the value of the second crop into account. For households in Groups 2 and 4, however, where circumstances dictate late planting, the potential benefit of a short season variety will be that it can better exploit the limited growing period. It should therefore be evaluated in terms of its production compared with current varieties when planted late.

The point of this example is to demonstrate how the specific composition of the household affects the relevance of improved technology. On-farm research methodology takes the farm as the unit of analysis and the farmer as the single decision maker. For example, rather little thought has been given to the question of how the family farm unit is defined and whether it is managed within a nuclear family structure or through an extended family structure. Because household composition can affect the appropriateness of technology, there may be a case for on-farm researchers to pay more attention to the organization of farming households and the definition of farming units.

On-farm researchers in Swaziland included a series of questions in their formal survey designed to establish the organizational structure of each homestead and how this affected farming. First, questions were asked to establish whether the homestead was composed of a single household or multiple households on the basis of the Swazi definition of a household (*tindlu*) as well as on the basis of the number of separate kitchens (*emadladla*) in the homestead. If the homestead comprised more than one household on either count, questions were asked to establish whether the households were farmed separately or together. A household census was completed for each household in the homestead, and subsequent questions in the survey were to relate specifically to the household of the respondent.

In the case of multiple household homesteads (25 percent of the sample), it proved difficult to establish clearly how independently they farmed and to restrict the answers to subsequent questions, on labor inputs for example, to the members of the respondent's household alone. It became clear that some households that were enumerated separately actually formed part of the larger homestead which, in reality, comprised the farming unit. While a good bit was learned about the organization of households within homesteads, the approach did lead to a considerable extension of the questionnaire and to some complications in subsequent analysis. Clearly, there is a cost to gaining information on and understanding of household structures/organizations, in terms of the time needed for surveying and analysis, which is difficult to justify given the emphasis on obtaining short-term payoffs from on-farm research.

However, some on-farm researchers in some environments (e.g., Norman 1983, 12) are now suggesting that there is a dearth of relevant experimental station data that on-farm researchers can adapt to suit local farmers' circumstances and that, in these cases, "it is difficult to visualize major pay-offs to FSR in the next few years." Where the prospects for near-term pay-off from adaptive research are less good, there may be more of a case for extending the diagnostic work to incorporate household characteristic analysis and to gain a fuller understanding of the household environments within which farmers operate.

Evaluating New Technologies

Researchers are coming to recognize that technologies which increase productivity per unit of land are not the only ones that can be beneficial to small farmers. Technologies that do not increase area yields but make more efficient use of time or cash are often equally acceptable.

Technologies which save family labor time are particularly attractive to small family farm units. The rapid uptake by small farmers around the world of improved implements, herbicides and mechanization, as well as farmers' own labor-saving strategies, bear witness to this.

From a household economics perspective, utility is maximized by producing the desired set of goods with the least cost in terms of the ultimate resource: the time of household members. Given the many demands for family labor in farm and non-farm activities, market and non-market production, and work and leisure, household economics sees family labor as being at a premium, with the major objective being to employ it in alternative uses as efficiently as possible. This implies that households seek to maximize the subjective return to the labor of their members and that what tasks are performed and by whom depends on the opportunity cost of members' time.

The opportunity cost of labor time also often forms an important component in the evaluation of farm technologies by on-farm researchers. However, opportunity time costs are generally determined in terms of alternative farm activities or of wages that can be earned off the farm. (The cost of women's time during parts of the season when there is little crop work is generally assumed to be near to zero.)

Commenting on the unresponsiveness of farmers to advice on bush clearing in western Kenya which experimental results had shown to be productive, Tessema (1983, 24) says: "Many were unwilling to carry out the work because they say it is a hard and difficult task even though it does not conflict with other operations, as it can be done in the dry season when there is little other activity." Even in times of little farm activity, the demands on family labor are many and, as the above example illustrates, it is wrong to assume that when there is little farm work to do the opportunity cost to family labor is negligible.

Taking a household economics perspective will help to prevent researchers from falling into Tessema's trap, and will provide a basis for making some assessment of what value to place on family labor used outside farming and wage employment. The question researchers need

TABLE 4.4
Farm-Based Partial Budget Analysis

| | Return per Hectare Analysis | |
	Traditional	New/Technology
Yield kg/ha	1300	2400
Adjusted yield (−15 percent)	1100	2040
Gross benefit at ¢1/kg	1100	2040
Cost of fertilizer	—	192
Labor input (man days)	61	106
cost a ¢10/day	610	1060
Total variable costs	610	1252
Net benefit per hectare	490	788

Source: Bruce et al. (1980), Table 6.2.

to ask is what other tasks are being performed by the relevant household members at the time. Answering this question will probably be easier than going on to the next stage and estimating the subjective value of a unit of the member's time in that activity. What value do you put on an hour spent looking after children or collecting firewood or drinking beer with friends? The important point, though, is that the answer is certainly not "zero" just because the activity does not relate to farming.

Household studies can complement on-farm research and contribute to its effectiveness by: a) Highlighting the importance of non-farm non-wage activities in household production, and b) Generating rough guidelines on the values that might be placed on the use of labor time in household production activities.

Even where positive opportunity time costs are assumed, the farm-based and household economics approaches to evaluating farm technologies can give markedly different results. For example, Table 4.4 presents a typical partial budget analysis in which opportunity costs of labor are included and a reasonable return on capital is obtained when extra management time and fertilizer are applied.

Moving from the traditional to the new technology gives an increased net benefit (gross benefit less total variable costs) of 298 cedes. This additional net benefit is achieved at a cost of 642 cedes (1252-610), which implies a return to capital of 46 percent (298/642x100). On the

TABLE 4.5
Household Economics Time Efficiency Analysis

| | Costs per Ton Analysis | |
	Traditional	New/Technology
Time Costs/Ton		
Man-days required/ton[a]	55	52
time costs a ¢10/day	550	520
Cash costs/ton		
fertilizer cost/ton[b]	—	94
Total cost/ton	550	614

[a]Man-days per ha/adjusted yield per ha
[b]Fertilizer cost per ha/adjusted yield per ha

basis of this conventional analysis it is probably worth while moving to the new technology.

Compare this approach with the following analysis of the same data based on the household economics theory that farm households seek to minimize the costs of producing goods for their own consumption in order to maximize returns to family labor time. Table 4.5 presents the analysis of the data in Table 4.4 based on a comparison of the costs of producing each unit of the crop, rather than on the returns to capital invested per hectare.

With the new technology each ton can be produced with three fewer man-days of labor input, giving a saving of 30 cedes per ton. However, since the new technology requires an extra cash outlay of 94 cedes, it is 64 cedes more costly than the traditional technology per unit of produce. On a per-ton basis then, the traditional technology, which requires more labor and less cash, is the lower cost alternative (at the given opportunity cost of labor time).

For subsistence producers, whose priority objective is often to grow their own food requirements (either because it is expensive to purchase their needs or because reliable retail supplies do not exist), the cost of production analysis is probably more relevant than a computation of the returns to capital invested per hectare.

More important than the different answers given by each analysis, is the difference in the implications of each approach for changes in the value of time of household members (or household welfare). In the farm-based approach, the new technology becomes less attractive as the opportunity cost of time is increased since the new technology uses more labor per unit of the enterprise and net returns per hectare are reduced. In the household economics approach, the new technology becomes more attractive as the opportunity cost of time increases because less time is needed to produce each unit of the consumption good and the value of this time-saving is increased.

It seems logical that, where labor hiring is not prevalent and scarce family labor time must be used in a subsistence crop activity, increasing the values of members' time (or household welfare) is likely to encourage the use of a cash-expensive technology that reduces the labor required per unit of production, rather than discourage it, as the farm-based approach implies. An understanding of household circumstances, aims and objectives is crucial to the evaluation and design of appropriate technology for small farmers.

Summary

In this paper I have suggested that the two new philosophies of on-farm research and household economics have much in common theoretically but that household economics thinking is not generally incorporated into on-farm research methodology, because on-farm research has a limited, clear objective to generate appropriate farm technology in the near term based on the use and adaptation of existing technical information and a knowledge of farmers' circumstances. This objective can often be achieved by taking account of the natural and economic environment in which the farm operates without broadening the analysis beyond the boundaries of the farm to encompass the larger farm-household unit.

On-farm research findings, however, are beginning to indicate that on small farms the linkages between the farm and household are quite strong and that household factors will often have a significant influence on farm decisions. Incorporation of a household economics perspective in on-farm research methodology can improve the effectiveness of the approach and help researchers to perceive more clearly the implications of the two-way linkage that exists between farm income and household welfare.

This two-way relationship between household welfare and farm income has implications for macro-policies. As Goran Hyden has suggested in the first chapter of this book, African farm households operate in a socio-economic environment where there is universal land access, where there is no agricultural surplus labor and where migrants to urban areas retain strong rural links.

Universal access to land results in specialization within rather than between households. This means that farm households are often not solely or even primarily farmers.

Because there is a shortage of agricultural labor on the market, non-farm activities compete directly with other on-farm uses of family labor and farm production is often compromised.

Even where most income is obtained off the farm, households maintain a rural base for social and security reasons. Overall household welfare is maximized this way, though it implies reduced farm production owing to labor shortages. In his paper for this volume Hyden refers to this as premature urbanization. It may be premature from the macro-agricultural production point of view but in the socio-economic environment of Africa it maximizes welfare at the farm household level.

Notes

This paper draws on the general thesis developed in (and forms the basis of Chapter 13 in) the author's book *Agricultural Development in Southern Africa: A Household Economics Perspective on Africa's Food Crisis*, copyright © 1986 by James Currey, London and Heinemann, Portsmouth, New Hampshire. Permission to use this material was granted by the publisher.

1. The International Maize and Wheat Improvement Center. The views expressed in this paper are the author's and do not necessarily represent those of CIMMYT.

2. Complexity may also exist in terms of the range and mix of farm and non-farm activities carried out by small farm households. Such complexity may not be readily apparent in a farming context but may be very significant in the broader household context, where different members undertake a wide range of household production tasks.

3. This theoretical gap has been filled to some extent by the new household economics theory of consumer choice. See, for example, Low 1982(a), 1982(b) and 1982(c).

4. This is not an isolated case. Other studies in Swaziland (FMS 1978) and Zimbabwe (CIMMYT 1982) demonstrate the same differences between cattle owners and non-owners.

5

Intra-Household Processes and Farming Systems Research: Perspectives from Anthropology

Jane I. Guyer

The social science contribution within FSR has been envisaged as a filling out of the terse observation that "farmers, not fields, make decisions on technology" (Byerlee et al. 1982, 899). So far, there have been two major points in the FSR procedure where social scientists have an important role: (1) in outlining the social factors over which farmers have no short-run control, such as land tenure, and which therefore define the "recommendation domains" within a particular population, and (2) in elucidating the cultural factors which define farmers' goals and motivations.

Insofar as FSR draws on economic models, it tends to identify these "farmers" as individuals or households. The sheer difficulties experienced in predicting farmers' decisions in Africa demand that one step back a pace and ask the prior questions: "Who are these farmers? How, and with whom, do they made economic decisions?" It is here that the anthropological findings on intra-household relations and the gender division of labor may be crucial.

The first part of this paper outlines these findings and discusses their application to the problem of analyzing agricultural decision-making. In other words, it adds a third item to the social scientist's agenda within FSR. Noting the methodological problems this presents, the second part of the paper suggests that a rigorous means of assessing the interaction between agricultural and gender factors may depend on developing a complementary research endeavor, namely a study of the longer-term processes of agricultural change. The third part examines the practical, time-cost considerations involved in incorporating anthropological methods into rapid rural reconnaissance surveys.

The Household as a Decision-Making Unit

The identification of a decision-making unit is important in farming systems research (FSR) because the unit's socio-spatial boundaries become an approximate guide to the distinction between exogenous factors (external factors outside the control of the decision-maker) and endogenous factors (factors partly within the control of the decision-maker). Because FSR is concerned with production and consumption, the "household" has been its central unit of analysis. In theory, it can be studied with techniques developed for studying production and consumption decision-making elsewhere.

There are problems, however, with the "household" as a decision-making unit in the African context. As Polly Hill has suggested (1975), in Africa there is not only a division of labor by sex and age but also a broader division of economic spheres. Men and women—and often children—separately control productive resources, take partly independent decisions, manage personal incomes, assume different responsibilities and favor different investments. Their liens on each other's resources, labor and income are so complex that the outcome of "household" decisions is difficult to predict and even to describe systematically.

Descriptive Problems

There are many examples from anthropological literature on African residence, production and consumption patterns which do not "fit" the assumptions of a simple household model. Indeed, reservations have been expressed about the use of "household" as an analytical concept in anthropology and economic surveys for at least 35 years (Deane 1949; Fortes 1949). I shall outline some of the descriptive problems briefly but not dwell on them because, clearly, for economists, the decision-making model is an "as-if" model, not intended to comprise all complexities, and for anthropologists, the ethnographic complexity should be only a starting point and not a resting place.

The most graphic examples of descriptive problems come from areas with a matrilineal ideology of descent. In several Ghanaian family systems, in both rural and urban areas, the crucial functions of co-residence, production and consumption do not define the same group membership. As Fortes described the Ashanti (1949), a man and his wife may not live in the same house. Husbands and wives may remain in their own natal compounds after marriage and earn individual incomes in farming and trade. Wives may send food to their husbands every evening and receive contributions from them for the care and education of their children. In such cases, consumption units crosscut the boundaries of residential units, and neither corresponds to a cooperative unit for production.

While the problem is extreme in matrilineal societies, it is by no means limited to such societies. (See also Sanjek 1982.) In most rural areas of Africa, access to productive resources and consumption goods is determined by activating a hierarchy of rights: The right to land may be acquired through membership in a descent corporation; the right to a particular plot, through one's immediate parentage or, for women, through marriage; and the right to labor through a complex of inter-personal expectations and negotiations within the family, the kin network and the wider community. Each set of rights is qualified, or contextualized, by the others but is not determined by them.

This is also true of responsibilities: The obligation to defend a particular set of resources for the next generation may rest with someone different from the person responsible for feeding and clothing that generation on a day-to-day basis. Typically, the former is vested in a man, as representative of a larger corporate unit such as the compound or lineage, and the latter is vested in the children's mother.

In matrilineal societies such as the Ashanti, descriptive problems arise from overlapping memberships in production, consumption and accumulative groups or units. In other societies, such groups may be "nested" within one another. (For example, in polygynous households the component mother-child units may have certain kinds of relative autonomy.) A method developed by scholars in the French tradition of human geography has been helpful in these situations. A distinction is made between the enterprise as a work unit (*exploitation*) and the consumption unit (*groupe de consommation*), e.g., Binet 1956. For budget studies, the work unit, composed of persons who submit to a single decision-maker for major expenses, has been designated the *groupe budgetaire;* the consumption unit, people who habitually eat from the same table, as the *groupe alimentaire* (Winter 1970, 35). Other kinds of units can be added where relevant. For example, another kind of group may be the unit of investment in major collective enterprises such as fighting land tenure cases in court or purchasing heavy equipment (Gastellu 1977).

At a descriptive level, this brings consonance to ethnographic analysis and decision-making analysis; the one can be translated more easily into the other. On the other hand, this approach raises very difficult problems when it comes to analyzing the implications for production, consumption and investment for one another. For example, if the point of knowing about budgets is to determine the implications of income earning and income control for the allocation of different people's time, on the one hand, and investment choices, on the other, it is difficult to trace organic links among production, budgetary, consumption and investment units that have been separated analytically. One cannot assess the implications of sales from "subsistence" food crop farms unless there is a method that permits analysis of the choices of the "consumption unit" in relation to the choices of the "production" and "investment" units. These units are neither separate in membership nor coterminous but are, instead, some other alternative which is particularly recalcitrant to formulation into the kind of model needed for analysis of decision-making (see Harris 1981).

Another factor, the developmental cycles of domestic groups, also presents problems of definition and understanding. Here again, it is quite clear that any simple demographic, or Chayanovian, model will not apply to kinship systems in which divorce rates may be high (Bledsoe 1980), in which child fosterage is extremely common (E. Goody 1970) or in which separated family members participate in one another's economies over long distances (Abbott 1976). In such cases, the "natural" growth cycle of the family, with predictable patterns of change in worker/consumer ratios, is too radically redirected to be a useful model.

Even in societies where one can identify developmental cycles, the changing status of particular individuals in the political system may have greater importance than age itself. For example, Robertson and Huges (1978) interpret the interest of different Ugandan farmers in credit as a function of social status. I have attempted elsewhere to relate farming patterns to expenditure demands, particularly social and ritual responsibilities, among men in different positions (Guyer 1972).

Simplifications can be made in order to reduce the complexities but they involve solving some knotty conceptual problems, including two which will be discussed in more detail: (1) the ambiguity of terms such as "production," "investment" and "consumption" when used to designate decision-making units within or across household boundaries and (2) the inaccuracy of using relations among units where the critical mediating relationships are actually gender relations.

Conceptual Difficulties

Types of Unit. The functions identified for economic analysis, such as production or investment, cannot necessarily be unambiguously identified with any particular group because it depends what is being produced (for example, food crops or export crops) and what kind of investment is being made (housebuilding, children's education, etc.). One could define a particular function, such as payment of school fees for children, as unambiguously defining an "investment" unit but this unit may differ from the one which "invests" in agricultural equipment or bridewealth payment or any of the other functions which aim at long-term income generation and security.

The other alternative is to define whatever men take care of as "investment" and whatever wives and children are concerned with as "consumption." But this begs the entire question of who makes different kinds of decisions. In my own view, trying to make such definitions precise leads to an infinite regression of minutely specified types of unit and local particularities—something the household model is intended to prevent.

The Importance of Gender Relations. Second, the distinction between "production" and "consumption" units usually boils down to the fact that men and women have different cycles of rights, activities and responsibilities, a situation otherwise designated as "the division of labor by sex." The relationship between production and consumption groups is really the relationship between a man and his wife or wives, in the "nested group" situation, and between people and their kin (often brothers and sisters) in the "overlapping group" situation.

In the southern Cameroon cocoa belt, for example, the woman has the right and responsibility to provide staples for the family diet while the man earns his primary income from cocoa. With respect to cocoa production, the woman's labor is "exogenous" to the household head's decision-making. But the relationship between her activities and his activities is "endogenous" to the household defined in a general, socio-spatial fashion. The fact that this relationship involves negotiation has been explicitly recognized in policy discussions of cocoa production. There is enough land to expand cocoa but not enough labor, and successive reports have stressed the importance of increasing the labor input into cocoa. It has been suggested that a "social transformation of the woman into a potential worker in cocoa" be effected. In order to achieve this, the man is encouraged to remunerate his wife by, for example, "providing a tin roof for her kitchen" (Le Plaideur 1977, 190, 198). In the short run, this kind of transformation is inconceivable because food production is the means by which women control their own cycle of rights and responsibilities. But in the somewhat longer run, as the "consumption unit" assumes responsibility for a larger bundle of goods, or the "investment unit" attracts investments of labor or personal incomes, there may be areas for negotiation.

It is clearly more precise to regard the influences of production and consumption on each other as a function of gender relations than to perceive them as a relationship between "nested units." In Africa, it still matters precisely who has resources to allocate. Men and women have different resources—as well as different constraints on their choices, different responsibilities to meet with their incomes and different possibilities for spreading the risk of failure. If there is a single phrase which should be expunged from all writing on African farming, it is, "the peasant . . . he," not only because women provide such a huge proportion of agricultural labor in Africa but also because women are decision-makers.

Since for decision analysis one needs to define either units or relationships unambiguously, this raises the question of whether the gender division of labor is subject to clear principles. Until recently anthropologists and economists have held totally opposite views on the malleability of gender relations and the sexual division of labor. Anthropology has tended to depict either a kind of naturalism (women's work is associated with root crops, men's with cereals) or a complex cultural specificity. In either case, gender relations have been seen as persistent over time. At the other extreme, Cleave has implied that the whole configuration is subject to rational calculation for maximum household efficiency: "Traditional division of labor by function or crop, which may be seen as a form of disguised unemployment in traditional systems, is rapidly modified when the opportunity for new profitable employment, on or off-farm, appears" (1977, 165).

In my own view, both of these positions are vastly overstated. It is precisely the long historical directions of change and the continuous process of negotiation that we need to be studying (Guyer 1980; 1984). We need to understand what causes change in the division of labor, the terms of exchange between men and women, and the size and internal structure of the social groupings within which these are organized. Are there economic/agronomic causes? Are there economic/agronomic implications?

One apparent trend in the social organization of the division of labor may have profound implications for farming patterns, namely the decline in the marriage rate. Polly Hill argues (1978) that this is bound to have an effect on land use and cropping patterns because the complementarity of male and female labor is ruptured. Here again, one must pay careful attention to the shifting types of relationships of which "households" are composed. The breakdown in the 20th century of larger social units into something more like peasant households may seem "efficient" for a brief period but could turn out to signal a powerful trend, which continues to unfold, toward ever smaller, more fluid and more contractual units. Where there is a gender division of labor, rational personal solutions for short-run income earning and control and for long-term investment in farming may have important cumulative implications. For example, the reduction in seasonal peaks which Cleave (1974) sees as a general trend in African farming may be a function of the reallocation of labor within households, but it could also result from the changing composition of the household.

In the context of policy, these factors bear on the crucial question, "Who?" From whom should we gather information about what? Who should be included in a recommendation domain? Who "counts" when we evaluate effects? For example, it matters a great deal to any effort to change the total productivity of a particular crop to know whether a household head can mobilize the processing labor of his wife or the off-season labor of his sons. It matters critically to know the constraints under which women work if they essentially comprise the recommendation domain, as they would in many parts of Africa, with respect to staple food crops.

Alternatives to the Household Approach

Anthropology suggests, I believe, that the "household" as an analytical unit for formal study of decision-making processes—as distinct from a convenient term used for data-gathering—involves an almost infinite regression of conceptual and methodological problems. We must be very careful about concepts and models brought from elsewhere to a new round of intensive study of Africa. Household analysis derives from the Eur-Asian social context, where millenia of religious, legal and fiscal measures have given the household a corporate character (Goody 1976; 1983); in this context, households are, in law, units of land tenure, legal responsibility and taxation, backed by powerful ideological associations between house and social status. There are many areas of Africa where none of this exists, and where even the terminology for such units is vague, recent, of pidgin origin or more or less invented by colonial governments.

In analysis of decision-making, the main alternative to a household approach is an individual approach. The method of plotting out how individuals draw on resources and lay claim to income has much to recommend it. It can be used, for example, to bring out the constraints under which different categories of the population (divided by age, sex, socio-economic status, etc.) function. But it should not be used exclusively as it clearly lacks the means for tracing networks of interdependence and distribution, both within and beyond domestic units. In systems where the law and the market are not the only institutional frameworks within which people have access to resources, any study of individual choice must also specify the nature of the other institutions (Berry 1984).

The problems outlined above become more acute as the decision modelling increases in formality and as an emphasis on household decision making dominates the repertoire of methods. If innovation is the goal, whether in pest control, cropping patterns or investment strategies, one cannot afford to be rigid in methodology—to take a stance in which, because one's only tool is a hammer, every problem becomes a nail. The question is not whether a household decision-making method is or is not relevant, can or cannot be adapted, to Africa, but, rather, how the range of methods available in the social sciences can serve particular field and policy issues.

I do not believe that broadening the range of methods plunges us directly into a vague three-dimensional seamless web of "holism". It merely widens the range of conceptual frameworks to include ways of examining how people obtain resources with which to make production decisions and how this affects their production and consumption. The importance of such factors as the gender division of labor, the existence of constituent units in larger compounds and the interdependence of domestic units makes it very difficult to predict decisions and, above all, to predict aggregate patterns and trends without addressing these factors.

Given the narrow range of important issues that can be addressed with the household decision-making model and the questionable simplifications required to use it, other frameworks and other methods need to be developed for the analysis of agricultural change. If the central problem is taken to be longer-term processes, such as agricultural intensification, indigenous agricultural innovation, occupational diversification or increasing commoditization—as distinct from short-term decisions about technology adoption—then such factors as the gender division of labor and household structure become potentially clarifying explanatory factors and not the awkwardly obfuscating issues they appear to be. Understanding these processes is an important parallel endeavor to research on short-term technical bottlenecks.

Agricultural Change and Domestic Processes

The description of units, and of relations within units, has important limitations if our main interest is in dynamics. What we really want to know is how these units work under a variety of familiar and predictable conditions, how they have shifted in the recent past, whether current trends will continue if present conditions are intensified and how they might change under new circumstances. If we focus on the important processes, then intra-household relations and other aspects of the social system traditionally dealt with by anthropologists enter in a powerful rather than mystifying, way. This is illustrated by the following examples bearing on agronomic and economic issues.

Agricultural Intensification

There is a long-term trend in Africa toward more intensive use of the land as a result of population growth, the extension of cultivated areas for increased commercial cropping and the prevention of population mobility by social and political constraints. Even in regions with low population densities, people are modifying old agricultural patterns to accommodate commercial and sedentary production. Agricultural intensification is perhaps the single most important process, ecologically and economically, occurring in Africa today; yet it is poorly described and understood.

There are certain general models of intensification, such as Boserup's famous stages of agricultural growth (1965), but, as Richards (1983) and Norman (1982b) point out, local farming is a fine-tuning operation. Boserup offers few clues to the small shifts that may contain a problem and gives no attention to the many great failures in agricultural history or the inability of a population to come up with any kind of solution. This is a point made by Lagermann (1977) about Igbo farming: people see the problems but have no solutions powerful enough to deal with them. In the system in which I worked in southern Cameroon, understanding gender relations is crucial to understanding cropping patterns and the innovations made under increasing land pressure.

The two main field types (and several minor types) draw on male and female labor differently. Over the past hundred years, the system has come under various pressures including (1) population growth in sedentary villages, (2) cocoa production and (3) increased food production for the urban market of Yaoundé. In response to these pressures farmers could pursue many different courses of action: shortening the fallow on the old field system, altering the frequency of farming particular types of field, farming farther and farther from home, increasing crop densities, adding new field types or crops, fertilizing and/or specializing. There is a whole range of possible technical and social solutions here, and each one has different ecological, economic and social implications.

The actual pattern of change shows that, although crop associations and labor profiles have altered very little, the fields and intercropping patterns most associated with women—elaborated in quantitative ways by expansion and more frequent, intensive cultivation—have become the backbone of the food system. By contrast, a major field type associated with men in the past has been greatly diminished. Because each field type has involved different degrees of clearing the plot, different crops, different crop densities and different fallow periods, the gender factor obviously has ecological implications. Since the regional economy is under pressure to produce food for Yaoundé, there are also clear economic implications.

The questions asked about intensification are, therefore, about the gender factor: questions about men's and women's agricultural practices, social organization, work patterns and income control. For example, how do men participate in the food economy: by cultivating their own fields? with old crops or new crops? by increasing their input into women's fields? by hiring labor? by increased contributions for the purchase of food? How, and why, do women reallocate their labor: more fields? more crops in the same fields? different crops? less farming and more processing and marketing? increased purchase of food? of what kinds? If questions are posed in this way, then gender is seen to be an influence that shapes agro-ecological processes, not a relationship awkwardly grafted on to household analysis.

Sale and Purchase of Food

Food sales and purchases appear to be increasing in rural Africa. In an earlier period this might have been welcome. At present it looks more ominous. Increased market involvement has been an obvious, though somewhat disputed, goal of development economists (Johnston and Kilby 1975; but see McLoughlin 1970). But the relationship between production, market sales and market purchases is complex and interpretation has tended to veer to extremes: some hold that the generalization of commodity relations has disastrous welfare implications; others regard it as a panacea which may, at worst, involve a few sticky patches of adjustment. In fact, the reasons for greater market involvement and its implications for farming patterns and rural welfare levels are varied; this is another topic for which an understanding of intra-household relations may be critical.

The food sales process is structured by exchanges and transfers within families. A farmer cannot commit the family's diet to the market by specializing in a commercial crop unless there are understood guidelines for budgeting the cash income. Throughout Africa women are responsible for, and are critically concerned with, the means by which the family is provisioned. Haswell (1975) acutely noted the trepidation with which the women in Genieri (The Gambia) saw their husbands reallocate to groundnuts land and labor which had previously been devoted to millet.

It is a mistake to think of women's concern about diet as subsistence conservatism. Genieri women farmers took up an entirely new crop, rice, to mitigate the effects of their husband's investment in groundnuts. Other women have gone into trade, while still others have intensified and elaborated a tried-and-true system. The question is really one of control: In a self-provisioning system the woman's right to cooking ingredients may be backed by guarantees and sanctions. But how will distribution be organized when the income is in cash, in her husband's pocket, rather than in grain, in a highly visible and accessible granary?

The general issue here relates to the structure of risk distribution. Risks are not just taken, or avoided: they have costs, which are passed on in predictable ways. Women's ability to pass on the costs of risks is generally more limited than men's; they are not more risk-averse, in some abstract sense, but they may need different contingency plans. These, in turn, may affect women's willingness to invest their own resources in an innovation for which the absolute gain might be considerable but their own personal gain unpredictable (Conti 1979).

Implications for FSR

Farming systems researchers do not need to understand all the nuances of the implicit and explicit contracts that make up family life in different kinship systems, but they must assess the costs, rewards and risks of innovation at the points where they will be most felt rather than from a generalized vision of "farm households."

In short, gender and intra-household relations become intrinsic to research design in relation to certain problems. It is not a question of grafting on a new factor, but of having recourse to a whole other framework of analysis, one which holds fewer factors constant and, as a result, can address long-term change.

The extent to which gender and intra-household relations can be included in rapid rural reconnaissance surveys, advocated by FSR researchers, is not altogether clear. A basic map of production, consumption and investment units, and of the division of labor by sex and age with respect to various crops and off-farm occupations, would seem indispensable. But if FSR remains narrowly focused, and if macro-analysis remains focused at the level of the state, then there is a vast middle ground, composed of regional systems of resource access and the directions in which they are changing which remains to be studied. Consideration of gender and intra-household processes is most important at this level of analysis.

Values of Methods from Anthropology

The concerns discussed in this paper may present a problem when the goal is "to develop efficient research methodologies" (Bylerlee, Harrington, and Winkelmann 1982, 903). There is some feeling that anthropological methods require long-term commitment and a largely open-ended methodology and that subjects like intra-household processes may be too complex to understand quickly—or even too sensitive for inquiry. For example, Norman examines the problem of "the time that would be required in deriving social impact evaluations" and suggests that "socio-cultural constraints should not generally be broken" (1982b, 7, 3). It is certainly true that full-scale theoretical work takes time and that modes of inquiry may be sensitive. On the other hand, anthropological work can offer certain important methodological insights.

The anthropological practice of learning key indigenous concepts quickly and of using these in interviews is an efficient and time-saving method of inquiry, which does not require fluency in the language as a whole. Indigenous terms for different kinds of loans or credit, soil types, seasons, measuring baskets, etc., can enormously increase the accuracy of communication and understanding and do not necessarily take long to learn. Surveys of crop combinations, for example, can be a clumsy guide to field types and their associated labor patterns if these have a name in the local language. For rapid survey purposes, it may be relatively accurate to use local measures of field size, if such exist.

Without a minimum of indigenous terminology, one can completely misunderstand quite important distinctions that will never appear in translation into English including, for example, distinctions among different types of fallow land. Conversely, distinctions that researchers make may be quite unclear in translation into an African language; the term for "year" in the Beti language is the same as the term for "season," hence the importance of specifying the different seasons by name.

Collinson has argued for more open-ended methods to increase the efficiency of the rapid survey approach. There is a good bit of room for systematic study and criticism of methods, keeping in mind anthropological work on intra-household processes.

Knowing that women have incomes means thinking through ways of focusing questions about these incomes and how they relate to the incomes of men (Guyer 1983 ms.). If one wants to know about control of major investments, for example, it may be far more efficient to develop methods for studying rotating credit contributions and uses of the purse, by sex, than to do household budget surveys.

Knowing that women have choices means thinking through the methodologies for studying how "household" labor is mobilized. The daily and seasonal routines of household members may be much more important than time allocation in the absolute sense.

Knowing that risks can be shared unequally means developing ways to trace the consequences beyond the initial stage through to the implications as perceived by different parties to the decision. Certainly, these questions relate to complex social processes but, given the knowledge already available, it should be possible to devise a series of research questions and methods which would take less time in the field than the initial data collection on which they are based.

Finally, the comparative context is critical to the formulation of important questions. The varying directions of change—whether intensification, commoditization or diversification—are only comprehensible within a comparative frame. In fact, it was such a frame that provoked scholars to develop new approaches to understanding African patterns of change in the first place.

6

Intra-Household Bargaining in Response to the Introduction of New Crops: A Case Study from North Cameroon

Christine W. Jones

A central tenet of farming systems research (FSR) is that households have multiple objectives and that these objectives are most often specific to individuals according to their structural position within the household.[1] Household members are likely to have conflicting preferences in regard to the intra-household distribution of effort and reward. Yet FSR never explicitly considers the problem of how conflicts among different households members' objectives are reconciled. Unless there is a "household dictator," such conflicts can only be resolved through some process of bargaining and negotiation.[2] As T. W. Schultz recognized a decade ago: "The assumption that the family integrates the welfare of its members into an internally consistent family-utility function attributes a role to the family that undoubtedly exceeds its capacity as a social institution" (1974, 11).

The implicit assumption of FSR, namely that conflicts among household members' preferences are resolved through the existence of "social norms," obscures the contractual basis of the household. In fact, "social norms" are the result of a bargaining process taking place between members of a household. While social norms may be used by various household members in their struggle to define the boundaries in which recontracting takes place, they are neither static nor a constraint completely exogenous to the household. The incorporation of new agricultural technologies into a farming system is likely to involve some recontracting within the household. As the following case study will show, joint rationality at the level of the household does not always prevail and thus allocative efficiency does not always obtain. Furthermore, how the gains from the new technology are shared among household members affects individual household members' welfare. To the extent, therefore, that FSR is explicitly concerned with identifying agricultural technologies (or policy interventions) that will increase the productive efficiency of the system and improve individual welfare, it must examine the implications of changes in intra-household contractual arrangements from the standpoint of both efficiency and equity.

The Mobilization of Women's Labor for Rice Production in Cameroon

The adoption of irrigated rice production in Cameroon, which required a major reallocation of household labor, resulted in a significant increase in household income. However, an evaluation of the project undertaken by the donor agency that financed the project asserted that women were unwilling to participate in rice production because the proceeds were controlled by their husbands largely for the husbands' own benefit. Field research was undertaken in Cameroon to test this hypothesis. The following case study examines the relation between women's labor allocation in their husband's rice fields and the intra-household distribution of the proceeds from irrigated rice production.[3]

The Setting

The formal survey work on which this paper is based was carried out in two villages, Vele and Widigue, located within the perimeter of the SEMRY project area. The SEMRY project area extends northward from the town of Yagoua along the western bank of the Logone River, which forms Cameroon's border with Chad. Compounds are dispersed along the two unpaved roads that fan out northward from Yagoua along the eastern and western sides of the project perimeter.

Almost without exception, every compound in the villages surveyed cultivates red sorghum, the mainstay of the local diet. On the heavy clay soils of the project area and with the blessing of the rains, which average about 800 mm per year in the single rainy season (from May to October), farmers can achieve fairly high yields—about 1000 kg/ha.[4] In the last 25 years, farmers have also adopted a special variety of sorghum (*dongologna*) which is transplanted on flood recession fields at the end of the rainy season and harvested just before the hot season begins in March. For approximately the last eight years, farmers in the two villages surveyed have also had the opportunity to cultivate rice.[5] Paddy yields are quite high—about 4.3t/ha in the rainy season and about 5.5t/ha in the dry season.

The villages in the project area are ethnically quite homogeneous; virtually all the farmers in the southernmost three-quarters of the project area identify themselves as Massa. Polygny is the ideal for most Massa men. Not all achieve it, however, since the bridewealth payment is quite high—usually 10 head of cattle, the equivalent of about 24 seasons of sorghum cultivation.[6] As a result of the high bridewealth payment, Massa women are married at a very young age and reside virilocally (with their husbands). Upon her husband's death, a woman is usually inherited by one of her husband's junior agnates (relative through male descent). It is rare, therefore, for a woman to become a compound head. In Vele in 1981, for example, only 2 percent of the compounds were headed by women. About half the compounds in Vele, as in other villages, are composed of two or more households. ("Household" is used in this paper to designate the conjugal unit of husband, wife, or wives, and unmarried children. It should be noted, however, that there is no word in the Massa language which denotes the conjugal unit.)

The Organization of Sorghum Production

Rights in land are held by small territorially-based descent groups. The compound head controls the distribution of the land that surrounds the compound. This is usually divided into one large field, worked collectively by the junior men women of the compound. If they want, individuals can generally obtain additional sorghum land to cultivate. For example, they may clear "bush" fields for their own use. Women are also sometimes given a field by their natal families, which they periodically return home to cultivate through the rainy season. It is becoming increasingly difficult for people from the villages along the eastern perimeter to extensify their sorghum cultivation because they are hemmed in by the Logone River on one side and the rice fields on the other. Despite the emerging sorghum land constraint, however, a land rental or sales market has yet to develop.

With the exception of the collective field, to which every compound member is expected to contribute several days' work of planting, weeding, and harvesting, sorghum fields are usually cultivated on an individual basis. Rarely does a man cultivate with his wife. Each individual works his or her own sorghum fields, with little exchange of labor. Of the time spent by women on cultivating sorghum, 95 percent was on their own fields. It is clear that women have a minimal obligation to work on their husbands' field(s) or on the collective field, in contrast to many other semi-arid farming systems in West Africa (Norman et al. 1981). (Unmarried men, however, generally do cultivate with the compound head or their father, although there are exceptions.)

Most married women have their own granary in which they store the sorghum harvested from their individual fields. Each woman cooks for herself and her children every day; co-wives alternate the task of cooking for their husband. A woman's sorghum is eaten first. When her supply is exhausted, the husband's supply is used next. The sorghum harvested from the collective field is eaten last and is usually parcelled out among the women of the compound every few days during the "hungry season" immediately preceding the following year's harvest. Thus, the group eating from a common pot, i.e., a single granary, varies throughout the year.

The Organization of Rice Production

The organization of rice production differs significantly from sorghum production. Since 1971, rice production has been controlled by a semi-autonomous government authority, SEMRY, which oversees the management of about 5,400 hectares of pump-irrigated fields. In 1981, as in other years, about a third of the area went uncultivated owing to lack of farmer interest.

SEMRY controls the allocation of the rice fields to farmers, who sign up each year with SEMRY. They agree to reimburse SEMRY in kind at the time of sale of their paddy (unhulled rice) for the services provided by SEMRY; these services include mechanized plowing, seedlings, fertilizer, herbicide, water, extension services and sacks. The charge for SEMRY's services is 55,000 CFA per *piquet*, or half-hectare, the basis unit of cultivation. At the current producer price of 55 CFA in 1981, the fixed charge amounts to 1000 kg of paddy, almost half the mean yield (2.2t) per *piquet*. In principle, farmers are required to sell all but 10 percent of their paddy to SEMRY; in practice, however, households retain about 17 percent for home consumption, and on occasion, for sale on the parallel market.

At present, SEMRY controls the dates during which seedlings can be transplanted, which varieties are cultivated, the level of fertilizer use, the allocation of land, the water supply and the producer price of paddy. The only aspect of rice cultivation that SEMRY does not control, somewhat to its dismay, is the decision about how much and whose labor is allocated to rice production.

Unlike sorghum cultivation, there were no instances in which rice fields were worked collectively by a multi-household compound. Although one compound member occasionally comes to the aid of another, sometimes for a cash wage, the compound head cannot mobilize the labor of any compound member for rice production except the labor of those in his or her immediate conjugal household. In further contrast to sorghum fields, which are generally individually worked, most rice fields are cultivated jointly by members of a conjugal household, irrespective of who actually registers for the field with SEMRY. Women are permitted to and, in fact, do register for fields in their own names; about 20 percent of the women in Vele had a rice field in their own name.

The woman is expected, however, to turn over all the income from her field to her husband even if the field is registered in her name and she actually takes possession of the money from sale of the household's paddy to SEMRY. It would be difficult for her to conceal from her husband how much money she received for the sale. Farmers know approximately how much a sack of paddy is worth, and, in addition, every producer is given a slip on which the quantity sold and the income received are recorded. It should be noted here that women have traditionally not enjoyed rights to the disposition of whatever income they earned beyond what was needed for household subsistence (de Garine 1964). For example, a husband has customarily had rights to the dry season tobacco (or income from tobacco) grown by his wife and has used this to facilitate bridewealth and cattle loan transactions (Dumas 1983).

As has been observed elsewhere in Africa, (Etienne 1977; Dey 1981; Guyer 1981), men and women have conflicting interests regarding the use of household income. Ultimately, Massa men seek to accumulate enough income to purchase livestock to use for bridewealth transactions or to make prestigious loans of cattle (Dumas 1983; de Garine 1964). While women often benefit from men's purchases, at the margin they would prefer that more of the income be used to purchase the consumer goods that have become increasingly available and socially necessary in the last decade or two. What husbands and wives disagree about is not the right of a husband to the product of his wife's labor, in the abstract, but, rather, how much of the income from the product should be returned to the woman for her "discretionary" needs after household subsistence needs are met.

One concludes that, at the very least, a woman would not be willing to work for her husband on rice production unless she was compensated at a rate equal to the opportunity cost of her time on sorghum production. This hypothesis is addressed in the next section, which considers the contractual arrangements under which women's labor is mobilized for rice production.

The Remuneration of Women's Rice Cultivation Labor

Following the paddy harvest, men reserve a certain number of sacks of paddy for home consumption which they turn over to their wives for safe-keeping. In effect, the paddy retained for home consumption compensates for the sorghum production that both husband and wife forgo in favor of rice production. In addition, men also give their wives a lump sum in cash following the sale of paddy. Women perceive this money and paddy to be compensation for their rice cultivation labor. It is given to them, they say, "in return for their sweat." The married women in my survey received an average of 7,700 CFA in cash and about 9,200 CFA worth of paddy (essentially half of the value of the paddy retained by the household), or 16,900 CFA in total. Valued at the market wage rates (see below), a woman's labor contribution is worth about 31,200 CFA so her husband retains direct control over about 14,300 CFA produced by her labor in addition to the product of his own labor.

If a woman receives what she considers to be an insultingly small sum of money, or no money at all, she is likely to become quite angry with her husband and most unenthusiastic about participating in rice production the following year. Husbands are quite aware that their wives' continued participation depends on their own "generosity."

Of the 31 married women in the sample from Vele and Widigue whose husbands controlled the distribution of income from rice production, only three women did not receive any cash at all. In one case, the husband had received no cash from the sale of paddy since the harvest was very poor. In the other two cases, however, the women were very angry at not receiving any cash. One woman's husband offered her 1,000 CFA, which she refused to take. A fight ensued. I visited the other woman several days after the rice harvest. At that time she was waiting for her husband to decide how much money he was going to give her. I went again to see her about two weeks later and found that she was at her parents' compound, recuperating from a severe beating by her husband. Her co-wife explained that their husband had beaten her because she hadn't prepared his food for two days. Refusing to prepare food is one of the most effective ways women make known their displeasure with their husbands. The fact that almost all women did receive cash (except in the case where there were extenuating circumstances), and that there was considerable conflict in the two cases where they did not, indicates that women have some claim on the money which is earned from rice cultivation.

The following regression is estimated to establish that there is a significant relationship between the amount of compensation women received from their husbands and the number of days women worked on their husbands' rice fields:[7]

(1.1)   Compensation = $-1922 + 358$ (DAYS)
        (t-ratios)   (0.82)   (8.21)
        $R^2 = 0.70$, F = 67.36

The rate at which they are compensated by their husbands, 358 CFA per day, is significantly less than the average returns to labor from rice cultivation, which are about 600 CFA/day[8] and is also significantly less than the average wage of 600 CFA/day which women would have received had they been compensated for their labor on rice production at the market wage rates. The average wage rates paid to Vele women for transplanting, weeding and harvesting were 805 CFA/day (n=55), 523 CFA/day (n=26), and 501 CFA/day (n=67), respectively. Households generally hire labor to replace ill household members when they want to finish a task quickly or when they find they cannot complete an activity. However, as one would expect in a land surplus area, hired labor comprises only about 10 percent of the total labor input, of which about 90 percent is female.[9]

One might wonder why women continue to work for their husbands if they are compensated at a rate much lower than what they could earn working as hired labor. The answer is that, in principle, married women are expected to work on their husbands' fields if they are not working on their own. If they refuse to work on their husbands' fields, they risk a beating. Thus, most women work as hired labor no more than several days out of the entire agricultural season, most often when their need for cash, usually to purchase food, is urgent.

However, several of the married women worked more than several days as hired labor. Five of the 15 married women in Vele who worked as hired labor accounted for 67 percent of the total number of days worked by the group of 24 married women whose husbands controlled the disposition of the income from rice production. All five women received less than the average rate of compensation from their husbands. The woman who worked the most days as hired labor (22 percent of the total days women worked as hired labor) was the one who received no cash from her husband at the end of the harvest and was later severely beaten by him.

It is possible that husbands reduce the amount of income they give their wives after the rice harvest in order to express their displeasure with their wives' decision to work as hired labor instead of working for their husband. However, it is also possible that the causality goes in the opposite direction: women who spend more than several days working as hired labor may do so in order to express their displeasure with the amount of compensation they have received in the past from their husband. In fact, several women told me that if a woman is not adequately compensated for her labor by her husband, then she will spend more time working as hired labor the following year. (Some women who are under-compensated by their husbands may also hire out because they need to work in order to make ends meet.) When women do hire out, they may stagger the days that they work as hired labor, or work in the harvesting season, to avoid provoking their husband. The woman who worked the most days as hired labor spent only several days at hired labor during the transplanting and weeding period—even though she spent very little time in that period on transplanting and weeding her husband's rice field. Most of the days that she worked as hired labor were during the harvesting period, when the harvesting of her household rice field was accomplished quickly since little transplanting had been done.

Opportunity Cost of Women's Labor

Unless they are willing to provoke a serious conflict, women really have little choice but to work for their husbands if they want to profit from the higher returns to labor afforded by rice cultivation. The issue is whether women are better off working for their husbands than they are working on their own income-generating activities. One can begin to answer this question by determining whether the amount of compensation they receive from their husbands for their labor on rice cultivation is greater than the income they forgo from sorghum production and other income-generating activities on account of rice production.

The opportunity cost of women's labor on rice cultivation varies throughout the agricultural season, according to whether it competes with sorghum production for labor. Rice transplanting competes with sorghum planting and, to a much greater extent, with sorghum weeding. It is difficult to estimate the marginal returns to labor for sorghum planting and weeding because there is no hired labor market in sorghum in July and August in the villages that are heavily involved in rice cultivation. This would seem to indicate that the returns to sorghum planting and weeding labor are less than the 800 CFA per day earned by rice transplanting. In fact, in villages that are located at some distance from the rice fields, where labor is occasionally hired for sorghum planting or weeding, the wage rate falls in the range of 450-550 CFA/day.[10] The average returns to sorghum labor also fall in this range.[11]

However, rice weeding and harvesting do not compete with the sorghum harvest for labor. Thus, if women did not weed or harvest their husband's rice fields, they would otherwise most likely be earning income from beer-brewing, fabrication of clay pots, petty commerce, etc. A survey of women's earnings in various periods throughout the year indicates that women rarely earn more than the equivalent of about 100 CFA/day even in relatively slack agricultural periods. Thus, 100 CFA/day is assumed to be a reasonable approximation of the opportunity cost of women's nonagricultural labor.[12]

To estimate how much additional income Vele women[13] actually earned by working on their husbands' rice fields instead of pursuing their own income-generating activities, the number of days women spent transplanting, weeding and harvesting their husbands' rice fields, 16.6, 13.3 and 21.8 days respectively, are multiplied by the opportunity cost of that labor, 550, 100 and 100 CFA/day, to obtain 12,640 CFA. Vele women received on average 16,900 CFA from their husbands. Thus, women received 4,260 CFA more by working on their husbands' fields than if they had engaged in their own income-generating activities.[14] This should be contrasted to the 14,300 CFA difference between the value of women's labor and the value of the cash and paddy they received from their husbands. It is clear that women gained from working on their husbands' fields even though they captured less than a quarter of the net increase in household income generated by their labor.

The Intra-Household Responsibility for Food Provision

As indicated above, women are compensated for their labor on rice production at a rate which is greater than the opportunity cost of their time. If, however, they must use the cash they receive to purchase food that their husbands would otherwise have provided or purchased before rice cultivation was adopted, then the real value of their compensation is reduced. It has been alleged that cash crop production puts a greater burden on women to provide food.[15] Essentially, the argument is that men withdraw their labor from food production and use the income they receive from cash crop production for nonfood expenditures. In the case of the Massa, rice cultivation does not appear to have placed an increased burden on wives to provide either grain for the cereal dish or ingredients for the accompanying sauce. A comparison of nonrice- and rice-cultivating households in Widigue indicates that the quantity of sorghum which households forwent on account of rice is more than compensated for, in grain equivalents, by the quantity of paddy retained.[16] As for sauce ingredients, women have customarily been responsible for providing or purchasing the fish or leaves that are used to make a sauce. Men, however, do provide sauce ingredients on occasion. A comparison of the purchases of sauce ingredients by households headed by widows and those headed by men indicates that the difference in expenditures on sauce ingredients between the two sets of households is not statistically significant. (See Jones 1983, 83).

It thus appears that the cash women receive from their husbands represents a real increase in their income in that they have more money available to spend on consumer goods without forgoing expenditures on food. Indeed, about 65 percent of the cash women received was spent on "big ticket" consumption goods—mostly cloth or shoes, and, in some cases, enamelware. As women themselves say, rice production has provided them with the opportunity to buy such items. Furthermore, it is likely that women indirectly benefit from the purchases made by their husbands make with the income from paddy sales. In short, women appear to have benefited from rice cultivation even if they have not directly controlled the disposition of the product of their labor.

Allocative Efficiency

Given the rate at which they are compensated for their labor, women should have sufficient incentive to forgo their sorghum production and other income-generating activities once they have produced some minimum quantity of sorghum. However, a comparison of the labor allocation patterns of married women and women who cultivate on their own account suggests otherwise. The comparison is based on a sample of 36 women from Vele, including 12 who hired their own labor and controlled the distribution of the proceeds received from the sale of their paddy.[17] Of these 12, seven were widows who cultivated their own *piquets*. The other five were women who had their own *piquets* and whose husbands were too sick or too old to cultivate rice. The other 24 were married women whose husbands controlled the distribution of the income derived from the sale of the paddy, which was cultivated jointly by the household. These two groups of women will be referred to as "independent" and "married" women, although the group of independent women does contain several married women.

Table 6.1 compares the labor inputs of married and independent women to sorghum and rice cultivation throughout the rainy season. As Table 6.1 shows, there is a major difference between the groups in the amounts of time allocated to sorghum and rice production. This becomes pronounced in August, during the latter half of the transplanting period, when married women spent far less time transplanting rice and far more time on the second weeding of their sorghum fields than independent women. Married women continued to spend less time on rice and more time on sorghum than independent women throughout the rest of the season. This difference in the amount of time the two groups spent on rice cultivation is reflected in the amount of land they transplanted: independent women's households cultivated .47 ha per worker, whereas married women's households cultivated only .31 ha per worker.[18]

Several factors might account for the difference in the labor allocation patterns of the two groups. The number of children a woman has to feed might influence how much time she allocates to sorghum and how much to rice. Because sorghum is rainfed, yields vary and prices for

TABLE 6.1

Days Worked by Vele Independent Women and Married Women, 1981

All fields	5/15 to 6/22	6/23 to 7/14	7/15 to 7/31	8/1 to 8/27	8/28 to 10/2	10/3 to 11/2	11/3 to 12/31	Total
SORGHUM								
Planting								
Independent	4.6	7.7						12.3
Married	5.8	8.6	.2					14.6
	(.55)	(.39)	(.22)					(.36)
Weeding								
Independent		1.8	3.6	2.2				7.6
Married		1.9	4.0	5.1				11.0
		(.87)	(.70)	(.04)				(.19)
Attach & Harv.								
Independent					1.3	2.1		3.4
Married					2.1	3.8		5.9
					(.21)	(.04)		(.04)
Total Sorghum								
Independent	4.6	9.5	3.6	2.2	1.3	2.1		23.4
Married	5.8	10.5	4.2	5.1	2.1	3.8		31.5
	(.55)	(.47)	(.58)	(.04)	(.21)	(.04)		(.14)
RAINY SEASON RICE								
Transplanting								
Independent		2.9	8.4	13.4	.8			25.5
Married		2.4	7.0	8.1	.7			18.2
		(.57)	(.31)	(.01)	(.84)			(.03)
Weeding								
Independent				2.0	15.5	.9		18.4
Married				2.3	11.8	.2		14.3
				(.75)	(.08)	(.17)		(.04)
Harv. & Thresh								
Independent						1.8	29.0	30.8
Married						2.0	25.0	27.0
						(.83)	(.06)	(.08)
Total R. S. Rice								
Independent		2.0	8.4	15.4	16.3	2.7	29.0	74.7
Married		2.4	7.0	10.4	12.5	2.1	25.0	59.4
TOTAL ALL CROPS								
Independent	17.1	12.4	12.0	17.8	19.1	7.5	29.1	114.9
Married	16.7	13.0	11.2	15.5	15.9	7.4	25.3	104.8
	(.78)	(.70)	(.44)	(.08)	(.08)	(.92)	(.06)	(.06)

Note: Figures in parentheses are the probabilities associated with two-tailed t-tests.

sorghum surplus fluctuate. The amount of time a woman spends cultivating sorghum might reflect a desire to minimize her exposure to price variation in the sorghum market and to grow only enough sorghum to feed her children.

Another factor that might account for differences in the labor allocation pattern of the two groups is differential access to land. However, the difference in the amount of sorghum land cultivated by the two groups is not significant: the mean sorghum area cultivated by independent women was .19 ha, compared to the .18 ha cultivated by married women. Even when the number of children and size of sorghum fields are controlled for, a series of regressions shows that the differences in labor allocation patterns observed in Table 6.1 remain significant.[19] These differences do not seem to have affected paddy yields: independent women's households received 4270 kg/ha, while married women's households received 4330 kg/ha (t = .16).[20]

Married women's underallocation of time to transplanting (in comparison with time allocated by the independent women) cost their households a significant amount of income. One method of calculating the loss in income from women's underallocation of labor to rice production is to take the difference between the returns to the additional time (labor) spent by the independent women on rice cultivation and the opportunity cost of that time, assuming that rice cultivation is not an option. The additional time spent by independent women, as compared to married women, was 7.3 days transplanting, 4.1 days weeding and 4.1 days harvesting (on all fields). In total they spent 15.5 more days cultivating rice than married women.[21] If the labor is valued at the hired wage rate, then independent women generated about 10,075 CFA more than married women. However, married women spent 5.9 days more cultivating sorghum during the rice cultivation period, for a return of 3,245 CFA if each day is valued at 550 CFA.

In total, then, independent women spent 9.6 days more on agricultural labor than married women. However, we cannot ignore the possibility that married women engaged in nonagricultural income-generating activities during these 9.6 days. If they did, they would have earned 960 CFA, assuming that the returns to their labor were 100 CFA/day. In total, then, independent women earned 10,075 − (3,245 + 960) = 5,870 CFA more than married women. This is not a trivial loss of income—it represents about 6 percent of household income from rainy season sorghum and rice production, or about 12 percent of the returns to women's rainy season agricultural labor.[22]

What needs to be explained is why married women's households are less allocatively efficient than independent women's households. One hypothesis is suggested by dividing the married women into two groups on the basis of whether their households cultivated as much rice land per active household worker as the group of independent women's households. As the following regression shows, married women whose households cultivated as much rice land as the group of widows (and who spent the same amount of time cultivating rice) received a higher rate of compensation from their husbands than those whose households cultivated half as much rice land on average:[23]

(1.2) Compensation = $-1922 + 262$ (DAYS) $+ 65$ (DUMMY)
      (t-ratios)   (0.62)   (4.27)   (2.11)
      $R^2 = 0.74$, $F = 39.91$

(Where DUMMY is a dummy variable for the number of days worked by women whose household cultivated as much rice land as the widowed groups). The difference between their rates of compensation suggests that if married women received a higher rate of compensation, they would allocate more labor to rice production.

This raises the question of why husbands do not offer their wives a higher rate of compensation to elicit additional labor. As long as the rate is set below the marginal value product of their wives' labor, husbands would benefit. There is a specific rate of compensation that would maximize the husband's profit, but husbands cannot set this rate since they are not monopsonists, i.e. the only possible "buyers" of their wives' labor. Although women have little choice but to "sell" their labor to their husbands, in order to profit from the higher returns to labor offered by rice cultivation, a wife's labor is basically the only source of labor available to her husband. He can "buy" her labor or no labor at all, which makes her, in effect, a monopolistic supplier of labor. This is the classic bilateral monopsony situation of a single seller of a factor of production confronting a single buyer. In this case, the bilateral monopsony is created and maintained by the social institution of marriage and by associated sanctions available to both husband and wife.

Bargaining theory was developed to predict the "price" at which the factor would be sold in a bilateral monopsony situation. Bargaining theory assumes, however, that "joint rationality" prevails where joint rationality means that the household operates on its production possibility frontier.

Joint rationality does not appear to prevail in the majority of married Massa women's households since they could produce more income for the household by reallocating the same amount of labor to rice as they spend on sorghum cultivation. It has been implicitly assumed that the more allocatively efficient and the less allocatively efficient households have the same production possibility frontier and the same attitude towards risk. If this assumption is not correct, then differences in the labor allocation patterns of women in the two groups of households would be consistent with allocative efficiency. While such a possibility cannot be ruled out, it is important to recognize that when new agricultural technologies are introduced, allocative efficiency is not instantaneously attained. Bargaining between husband and wife over the division of effort and reward is likely to take place over many seasons of rice cultivation. Non-cooperative mixed interest games are not automatically or immediately transformed into cooperative ones.

In the case of the Massa, the introduction of rice production seems to have given rise to a new institutional arrangement—that of a woman being compensated for her labor by her husband. In the past husbands were obliged to provide their wives with certain goods but the "reward" was not directly linked to the amount of effort expended by the wife. In the case of rice cultivation, however, it is not only the rate of compensation and type of contractual agreement that are being negotiated but also the meaning of the contractual arrangement itself. Women are bargaining not only over the level of the "wage" that they are paid but also over their right to be paid a certain amount based on the level of their labor input. In effect, they are challenging the husband's right to dispose of the product of his wife's labor, a right which was recognized heretofore by the transfer of bridewealth cattle. To fully understand the intra-household bargaining process, one must analyze both the content (i.e., the contractual terms) and the meaning of the contractual arrangement that is under negotiation.

Variations in Intra-Household Contractual Arrangements

The case study presented above suggests that the amount of compensation women receive is a function of their labor input. They seem to be receiving what is in effect a wage, even though it is not explicitly identified as such. Secluded Hausa women also receive from their husbands what seems to be a wage:

> Just as the economic relationship between fathers and sons (and between brothers) often involves cash transactions identical to those between non-kin, so it is between husband and wives: thus, to take two examples, fathers pay their married sons in *gandu* for evening work on the farms, this being outside the range of their customary duties, and a husband will pay his wife at (or near) the standard rate across different types of farming systems. We know very little about the extent of variation in either the type of contractual arrangement for 'threshing' groundnuts, her

obligations being confined to domestic duties, mainly cooking. (Hill 1969, 398).

Other researchers have also noted that women are compensated for their labor by their husband (Guyer 1980; Etinne 1977; Hill 1978; Dey 1981). However, they did not collect data which would have enabled them to determine whether the compensation received was related to the flow of labor supplied to the enterprise controlled by the husband and to the opportunity cost of the wife's work. At this point, there has been very little empirical work that would permit a systematic comparison of intra-household contractual arrangements or the terms of different arrangements across and within farming systems. We know very little about the dynamics of recontracting—type, terms and speed of adjustment—when new agricultural technologies are introduced into a system. But without such information, farming systems researchers cannot make informed judgments about the viability of new technologies and their impact on individual farmer welfare.

The research agenda implied by these informational needs is, admittedly, an ambitious undertaking. But there is no reason to assume that social interactions between members of the same household will be any more complex than the interactions[24] explicitly recognized by the farming systems approach to research.

Notes

1. See the discussion in Norman et al. (1982) and also in Norman et al. (1981), especially Chapter 9.
2. Arrow (1951) shows that individual preferences cannot be mapped into a social preference ordering that satisfies the conditions of unrestricted domain, transitivity, Pareto optimality and independence of irrelevant alternatives unless the condition of nondictatorship is dropped. If the condition of nondictatorship is maintained, then the preferences of household members can only be combined into a household social welfare function through some process of negotiation that weights individual members' utility functions. A Nash-bargained household social welfare function does not satisfy the usual properties (e.g., negative own-substitution effects) associated with the utility function of an individual utility-maximizer. See McElroy and Horney (1982) and Jones (1983) for a discussion of Nash-bargained household utility functions.
3. The fieldwork on which this study is based was carried out in the Yagoua area from December 1980 through January 1982. It was done in conjunction with the Social Sciences Research and Training project (631-0007) financed by the U.S. Agency for International Development under USAID contract AID/afr-c-1610 with Tufts University. Several farm management surveys (Sisson and Ahlers 1981; Bikoi 1982) were carried out in conjunction with the project. Data

presented in the text are based on those surveys or my own fieldwork and on surveys which are described in Jones (1983). Labor allocation data were collected on a two-day recall basis over the entire rainy season cropping cycle for 60 women. For a description of the surveys and results, see Jones (1983).

4. According to the 1980 and 1981 farm management surveys (Sisson and Ahlers 1981; Bikoi 1982), the average sorghum yield in Widigue was 988 kg/ha in 1980 and 806 kg/ha in 1981. In Vounaloum, a village bordering along the Logone about 10 km upriver from Vele, reported yields were 360 kg/ha in 1980 and 1034 kg/ha in 1981. Sorghum yields in Vele were apparently exceptionally good in 1981—1616 kg/ha. While it is certainly not inconceivable that some Vele farmers obtained sorghum yields of that magnitude, a comparison with the yields obtained in Vounaloum, which is quite similar to Vele both in soil type and labor allocation patterns, suggests that the average yields reported for Vele may be overstated.

5. Irrigated rice cultivation in the Yagoua area began in the 1950s under the direction of the colonial government. The irrigation system was rehabilitated and expanded in the early 1970s under the auspices of a World Bank-financed project. Many of the farmers in the two villages surveyed did not participate in rice cultivation in the earlier years.

6. This assumes that a man cultivates .34 ha of sorghum (the field size cultivated individually by a nonrice female farmer in Widigue) and receives a yield of 1 t/ha.

7. This regression was estimated for 31 women whose husbands controlled the disposition of income from rice production: 22 women from Vele and 9 from Widigue.

8. The average returns from rice production are calculated using data from the farm management survey (Bikoi 1982). Net returns to rice production are calculated to be 111,000 CFA. The average labor input per hectare, converted to the standardized day (see Jones 1983, 26–27), 185 days/ha. This is in line with the 164 days/ha that independent women spent on their own rice fields, allowing for an additional 12 percent hired and exchange labor input found by the farm management survey. Dividing average net returns per hectare by average labor input per hectare shows an average return of 600 CFA/day. A similar calculation for Widigue gives an average return of 584 CFA/day.

9. This figure is based on a preliminary analysis of the farming management survey date obtained by Bikoi (1982).

10. Labor is hired for sorghum cultivation only in villages which are at some distance from the rice fields. Wage rates were obtained by asking the few farmers who hired labor for sorghum planting or weeding in these villages the rate they paid.

11. Average returns to sorghum labor are based on the following assumptions. Sorghum yields are estimated at 1616 kg/ha for Vele and at 806 kg/ha Widigue. (The yields were calculated by filling to capacity the container used to transport grain from the field to the compound, multiplying the weight of the filled container by the number of times the container was filled, and then applying a conversion rate to obtain the quantity of threshed grain.) The cost of hired

and exchange labor and seeds is 4000 CFA/ha. Labor inputs are 175 days/ha for Vele and 133 days/ha for Widigue. The post-harvest sorghum price is 74 CFA/kg. Yields and input costs are based on farm management survey data (Bikoi 1982), labor times on women's labor allocation survey data and sorghum price data on weekly weighings of sorghum in local markets. Calculated on the basis of these data, average returns to sorghum labor are 660 CFA/day for Vele and 418 CFA/day for Widigue. Since evidence from other villages suggests that yields of 1.6 t/ha are unreasonably high, yields of 1.4 and 1.2 t/ha are assumed (which are still on the high side). Returns to Vele women's sorghum labor would then be 569 CFA/day and 485 CFA/day respectively. For the purpose of the calculations presented in this chapter, returns to Vele women's sorghum labor are assumed to be 550 CFA/day and to Widigue women's labor, 500 CFA/day.

12. Vele women derive most of their income from sales of grain, sales of sorghum beer and wages from rice cultivation labor. The opportunity cost of women's nonagricultural rainy season labor is determined, therefore, by the returns to their labor from sorghum beer-brewing. In August, sales of sorghum beer by independent women (i.e., widows and other women who control the disposition of income from rice production) averaged 356 CFA over a two-week period, while married women's amounted to 265 CFA. In November, at the height of the harvesting season, independent women sold 77 CFA of sorghum beer, compared to paltry 44 CFA sold by married women. In contrast, there was a pronounced increase in the sales of both groups after the rice harvest: independent women sold 862 CFA and married women 500 CFA.

The greater quantity of sorghum beer sold after the harvest reflects increased demand for sorghum beer, because of the influx of cash, and the slack demands on women's agricultural labor. It may also reflect the fact that women have more cash to purchase sorghum to brew beer; almost without exception, women purchase the sorghum used to brew beer even if they have a surplus of grain. The interest rate of 50 percent (for any time period) is a powerful disincentive to borrowing money. In addition, brewing sorghum beer takes several consecutive days of labor, which makes it more difficult to brew beer during the peak agricultural season. Married women did not spend more days on sorghum beer production than independent women, even though they theoretically had more time available since they spent less time in total on agricultural labor than independent women. Thus, it would be reasonable to take the opportunity cost of the married women's (nonagricultural) time during the rice cultivation season as "zero." If they did not work on rice weeding or harvesting at all, they might be able to expand their production of sorghum beer somewhat, although there would hardly be sufficient demand to support full-time beer-brewing. Net profits per day of sale in August and November were about 500 CFA, for about three days of work. 100 CFA/day has been adopted therefore as the average opportunity cost of women's nonagricultural labor to reflect the limited opportunities women would have to brew beer on a full-time basis.

13. The estimation of the amount of income forgone is restricted to Vele women because the Widigue women spent less time weeding rice than Vele women because of their greater involvement in *dongolonga* cultivation. A calculation for the nine married women in the Widigue sample gives similar results.

14. If the opportunity cost of Vele women's sorghum planting, first weeding and second weeding labor is assumed to be 660 CFA/day (see note 8), the opportunity cost of women's labor in total would be 14,470. The net gain is still positive.

15. See Whitehead (1981), Dey (1981), and Dwyer (1983).

16. Unlike Vele, which is located much nearer the rice fields, there are a number of compounds in Widigue that do not cultivate rice (or cotton, another option in Widigue). Thus, there is no means of making an intra-village comparison in Vele to determine the amount of sorghum forgone by rice-cultivating households. Since sorghum land is more readily available in Widigue than Vele, households tend to extensify their sorghum cultivation to a greater degree in Widigue than Vele, one indication of which is the lower labor input per hectare in Widigue. Hence, an estimation of the sorghum production forgone by Vele cultivators, using Widigue non-rice cultivating women as a reference point for the comparison, would be misleading.

17. The comparison was confined to women from Vele for the reasons given in note 2, page 19. Also, there were very few women in Widigue who controlled the distribution of income from rice production.

18. Preliminary analysis of evidence from the 1981 farm management survey (Bikoi 1982).

19. See Jones (1983, 88–91) for the regressions.

20. Married women's households cultivate less rice land per active worker than independent women's households. Thus, one would not expect to see a difference in yields between the two groups of households on account of the differences in labor time of the two groups of women.

21. Married women spent 6.9 days more cultivating rainy season sorghum in the rice cultivation period (June 23–December 31), but independent women spent 1.0 days more cultivating dry season sorghum. Independent women also spent an additional 0.3 (0.4 days in total) days more than married women harvesting rice for their own use from SEMRY's nurseries (not an activity approved by SEMRY); this labor time is not entered in the harvesting data presented in Table 6.1, since it was done during the household rice weeding period.

22. If the returns to sorghum labor average 660 CFA/day, the difference in independent and married women's incomes would drop to 5,220 CFA. Valuing married women's household sorghum labor at 550 CFA/day and their household rice labor at 600 CFA/day per rice, married women's household rainy season rice and sorghum labor is worth 47,275 CFA. (Sorghum: 30.1 days $\times$ 550 CFA/day = 16,555 CFA; rice: 51.2 days $\times$ 600 CFA/day = 30,720 CFA). It is assumed for the purposes of calculating household income that men spend the same amount of time as women cultivating rice and sorghum. This agrees with evidence available on men's labor allocation.

23. The sample of 31 women used to estimate regression (1.1) was divided into two groups on the basis of whether their household cultivated .75 *piquet* or more per household worker. Thirteen of the households fell into this category, averaging .95 *piquet*/household worker, while the remaining 18 averaged .47

piquet/household worker. (The group of independent women cultivated .94 *piquet*.) About 31 percent of the married women in Vele cultivated .75 or more *piquets* per household worker; 25 percent cultivated 1.0 or more *piquets* per household worker. The Vele women who cultivated .75 *piquet* or more per household worker were compensated at the mean rate of 363 CFA/day, while the group of women who cultivated less than .75 *piquet* per household worker received only 302 CFA/day from their husbands.

24. Byerlee et al. (1982, 898) argue that complexity results from: "(a) direct physical interactions betwen production activities generated by inter-cropping and crop rotation practices, (b) competition and complementary resource use between different production activities, and (c) the multiple objective function of the farm household."

7

The Effects of Social and Economic Changes on the Role and Status of Women in Sub-Saharan Africa

Marie Angélique Savané

This paper[1] summarizes findings of a larger study still in progress on the effects of social and economic changes on the role and status of women in sub-Saharan Africa carried out under the auspices of the United Nations Research Institute for Social Development (UNRISD). The study was intended initially to cover six countries: Ivory Coast, Senegal and Upper Volta (now Burkina Faso) in West Africa and Mozambique, Swaziland and Tanzania in East and southern Africa. Because of insufficient funds,[2] the study has been undertaken to date in only three countries. It was begun in 1979 in Senegal, in 1980 in Burkina Faso and in 1981 in the Ivory Coast. National research efforts were based in the Ministry of Women's Affairs in the Ivory Coast, the National Center for Scientific and Technical Research (CNRST) in Burkina Faso and the Senegalese Center for Scientific and Technical Research (ISRA) in Senegal.

Case studies in each country focused on a different theme:

- The impact on women of the plantation export economy (Ivory Coast).
- The impact of male migration (Burkina Faso).
- The impact of agricultural modernization (Senegal).

Conceptual Framework

From a conceptual viewpoint, the study represented a departure from previous research on women in Africa. It was intended not merely to describe the existing division of labor between men and women at a particular point in time but also to explain how this gender-based

124

division resulted from processes affecting the conditions of production and consequent patterns of social stratification. The researchers hoped that it would be possible from this to determine the impacts of development policies on women and to prescribe actions that might rectify inequities or change adverse conditions.

Study Context

Different parts of Africa have been incorporated into the international market economy in different ways: some countries have joined the international system as producers of raw materials for export, others as providers of cheap labor and virtually all as markets for manufactured goods from the industrialized nations. The different forms of integration have resulted in unequal development among the different regions; among social groups, and, within social groups, between men and women. To understand the role and status of women in development, it is necessary to understand how social groups have been incorporated in the market economy; the social stratification that has resulted, and, within this framework, what specific responsibilities are assigned to men and women. This is important because the division of labor by gender, as a household strategy, is a response to the changing conditions of production. It is not static nor determined by biological or cultural factors alone; rather, it is primarily an economic variable that evolves spatially and over time. A change in the gender division of labor, therefore, constitutes an expression and manifestation of the position of women in both social production and human reproduction. Gender divisions also vary by social class. As a result, not all women are affected in the same way by economic change. Though women's participation in production is necessary for them to acquire status, i.e., a position of power within the family or society, it is no guarantee of such status.

From this general framework, two hypotheses were formulated as a basis for research:

1. That the process and ways in which many developing countries, including the countries of sub-Saharan Africa, have been integrated into the world market have created profound changes in traditional social institutions which affect men and women differently and that, in general, these differences are closely linked to the new class relationships emerging in specific contexts.
2. That development policies and programs, even those intended to aid women, have frequently worked to women's disadvantage, depending on the specific context and on the social class to which the woman belongs.

These hypotheses were tested through analysis of biographic data, questionnaires, interviews and observations of the sample populations covering such subjects as (1) changes in agricultural production; (2) family structure, fertility and traditions; (3) income and financial obligations; and (4) women's perceptions of changes. The findings from three countries are outlined below.

Agricultural Production and the Divison of Labor
Between Men and Women

Biographic data and completed questionnaires confirmed our first hypothesis, that the gender-based division of labor is a dynamic variable which changes according to the requirements of profitability in the central industrialized nations and in the peripheral developing countries.

Senegal

In Senegal, a Sahelian-Sudanese country with one rainy season a year, the study was carried out within the so-called "experimental units"[3] located in the Siné-Saloum region, also known as the Groundnut Basin. Smallholder cultivation of cereals is the main regional activity. Work and leisure periods are defined within the year by a productive (rainy) season and a dead (dry) season. The development of export crop production, mainly groundnuts (peanuts) and cotton, has increased the workload of farmers during the rainy season since households must produce both subsistence crops (millet, sorghum and maize) and export crops in order to meet their new obligations (taxes) and purchase imports and manufactured goods.

In the absence of advanced technology, it has been necessary to increase labor inputs. As a result, women, who were previously excluded from millet cultivation, now participate in various cultivation tasks, including sowing, weeding, clearing the fields, guard duty, harvesting and transporting produce from the fields. In addition, women work on their own plots, gather produce and perform household chores. They also grow groundnuts for consumption and sale.

With the coming of independence, the Senegalese government promoted the development of export crops as a means of financing development programs. This affects households since the land allocated for cash crop production has been increased, to the detriment of food crop production. Women will be increasingly affected as the demand for female labor grows, not only to supplement male labor but also to replace absent male migrant workers. Married women are increasingly obliged to purchase certain products and food supplies. Overburdened by what has become "compulsory" labor, women must reduce the time they spend on their own fields. In combination with the other factors described above, this cuts into their productivity and revenues.

In the Senegalese sample area, some women were excluded from agricultural work when tasks were mechanized and wealthy farmers could afford to hire seasonal labor. As a result, women from well-to-do households spend less time on agricultural work and also derive certain additional benefits from the process, e.g., the use of fertilizer and machines on their own fields (even if the mechanized tasks are not carried out so carefully as on the men's fields). On the medium-sized plantations, the work done by women is generally not mechanized, which means that their work in the fields has increased with expansion of the land under cultivation, allowing less time for work on their own fields. Among smallholder farms, the situation of women has not changed appreciably. In every case, however, women's labor continues to be paramount in harvesting and transporting agricultural produce.

Within the farm family, there have been some positive changes, including the introduction of such labor-saving devices as threshing machines, mills, well-pulleys, carts, etc. These benefit women—or, at least, the women whose households can afford them. On the other hand, with the increased use of animals for traction, water usage has increased and women must spend more time drawing water from wells.

Burkina Faso

Because Burkina Faso has very limited mineral and agricultural resources, it has been incorporated into the international division of labor as a provider of cheap labor for the coastal economies of Africa, principally the Ivory Coast and Ghana, which are growing rapidly.

The study covered three migration zones: a departure zone for migrant workers, a reception zone for spontaneous rural-rural migrants and a resettlement zone for organized migrants working in the Amenagement des Vallées Volta (AVV), a project to produce cotton and cereals.

In the departure zone, women provided 40 percent of the labor on family farms while, at the same time, cultivating cereals, groundnuts and vegetables on their own plots to provide food for their households. Rising migration rates have led to an increased role for women in cereal production since many women cultivate cereals on fallow lands in order to build up their personal stocks in anticipation of hard times to come. Because women must substitute for absent male migrant workers, they are overburdened by their work in producing cereals, from which they were formerly excluded, and no longer have sufficient time for the other activities, such as artisan crafts, market gardening and food processing, which previously contributed to the family budget. To the extent that monies received from absent migrant workers are not enough to cover the family's food needs, women in the departure zone have become in effect household heads, since they not only provide household labor but also supplement the male work force in areas of heavy migration and bear increased responsibilities as food providers. In no cases were women found to migrate from this zone.

In the reception zone for spontaneous migrants, women were documented as participating in all agricultural activities on the family farm except for clearing the fields and cutting millet stalks. Women are solely responsible for transporting the harvest. In general, these women also tend their own plots, on which they grow sorghum, millet, groundnuts, rice, greens and vegetables. Women work alone on their fields or with assistance from their children. They have no contact with technical extension staff, but some use fertilizer or obtain seeds through their husbands. Because women in this zone do not produce cotton, the principal cash crop, their income is small since their only source of revenue is the sale of surplus food crops.

In the resettlement zone for organized migrants to the AVV scheme, women, like all other household members, provide labor. The activity index calculated by AVV is 0.75 for women aged 15 to 55 years; for men in the same age group, the index is 1.00. But this calculation reflects only the work that women do in the AVV area. It does not include women's domestic chores (preparing meals, drawing water, collecting wood) or the work women do on their own fields. Women must use their "free time" for such work in order to balance the family budget and provide food for their families. Because of the increase in their workload caused by participation in the AVV scheme, women can no longer practice small-livestock raising, which was a traditional activity, although they continue to water the household's sheep and goats and may take them out to pasture or herd them into pens when children are not available for these chores. Although women constitute 53 percent of the workers on family fields in the AVV scheme and work very hard, they earn very little, mainly because they are not paid directly but are given "gifts" in exchange for their labor. Moreover, because they don't have enough time to cultivate their own fields, their income is lower than that of women in the departure zone or in the reception zone for spontaneous migrants.

Ivory Coast

The third study was carried out in the southeastern and northern parts of the Ivory Coast. The widespread adoption of cash crops (coffee and cocoa) in the southeastern forest zone has clearly led to a new division of labor. There is a very short period between the productive and unproductive seasons on the plantations, and labor is divided according to sex and crop. Men work on the plantations that produce cash crops, while women concentrate on subsistence farming (plantains, bananas, cassava, coco yam, yams, etc.). But women may carry out certain tasks on the cash-crop fields if enough male migrant workers are not available.

In the north,[4] where there is heavy migration of male workers to the south, the introduction of cotton and the relatively recent modernization of cultivation techniques have led to a specialization of labor by sex and type of activity. Women see their agricultural workload increasing since production is based entirely on family labor; women share some of the tasks involved in growing cotton while, at the same time, cultivating rice, groundnuts and maize on fields allocated to them by men.[5]

Negative Impacts on Women
of Agricultural Modernization

The second hypothesis tested was that agricultural development has worked to women's disadvantage, at least under some circumstances. In general, the study found that the modernization of agriculture involving the production of cash crops—characterized by a tightly controlled technical structure and the use of new production factors such as fertilizer—has indeed brought about new kinds of specialization in agricultural labor and that it has often had negative effects on certain women. Contrary to the exaggerated generalizations that have recently characterized debates over "women and development," however, it has not adversely affected all women. While some women have been affected adversely, this has not occurred because Europeans "misunderstood" the relationships involved in production or because African planners "forget" women. Rather, adverse effects have resulted from the intro-duction of capital into agriculture, which has been reorganized to suit the requirements of capital. Rural households, of which women are a part, have responded according to their role in production. Because of their subordination to the patriarchal system, women are not directly associated with capital; their husbands serve as middlemen, and women either benefit from modernization or suffer its negative impacts on their workload and income, depending on their husbands' standing.

The study shows that labor has been divided differently and that women are affected according to their social standing and according to the type of technological innovation that has been introduced. Findings suggest the following typology:

1. Where modernization requires intensive labor use and where social differentiation is not pronounced, there has been an increase in the volume of work performed by women in the family fields. This is true in Burkina Faso among women in both the departure zone and the reception zone for spontaneous migrants. In these zones, women have no access to cotton-growing, the principal economic enterprise, although they grow cereals and vegetables on their own fields, keep some livestock and derive some income from handicrafts. In the organized resettlement areas of the AVV, women not only raise cereals on the family plot but also work in cotton. This is also the case in the Ivory Coast, where family labor is essential to cotton production. In the two last cases, the rigidity of the technical approach and the extent of the areas to be cultivated necessitate women's involvement in all phases of production. Overburdened with work, women have little time to spend on the family's land, and their income drops, often to a ridiculously low level.

2. Where modernization requires intensive labor use and where there is substantial social differentiation in terms of access to land, the large plantation owners have employed foreign labor. (This is true in the southeastern part of the Ivory Coast, where owners employ Mossi workers from Burkina Faso.) Women grow subsistence crops and can sell the surplus. Middle-sized plantation owners, who cannot pay for the number of foreign workers they require, generally hire some workers and rely on women for some specific tasks; this cuts into the time that women can spend on food crop production. To cope with these demands, women may replace yams, which require a lot of care, with plantains, which requires less time. In instances where a planter has only limited land and cannot pay any foreign workers, he relies on family labor, especially women. These women also may adjust by growing manioc and plantains, which require relatively little care.

3. In countries like Senegal, where modernization requires maximum use of production factors and where women grow cash crops on their own plots, several situations have evolved: 1) On wealthy plantations, all work is mechanized and women's fields may benefit from the use of new production factors. Women work fewer hours and their income rises. 2) On plantations where only some of the agricultural work is mechanized, women continue to perform manual tasks, such as hoeing, weeding and clearing the land. Because the family's holdings have become larger, they spend more time than before on agricultural work. This may affect the amount of time they can spend on their own fields and, in turn, their productivity and income.[6]

The findings outlined above indicate that agricultural modernization has brought about the problem of capital-introduction into agriculture and consequent social stratification. Some women benefit both in terms of higher income and by virtue of reduced workload, in the fields and domestically. These gains depend, however, on the positions their husbands occupy in the social structure since it is essentially through their husbands that women can accumulate capital and invest in such areas as trade, livestock and transport; gain access to credit, or purchase land. The majority of women remain dependent for revenue on the sale of surplus food crops they produce—despite their heavy workload—on plots allocated to them by men and/or on other remunerative activities. The income that women earn from food crop sales or other activities is spent on the costs of maintaining their families.

Conclusion

It is obvious that programs to assist women, or integrated projects, should take into account these findings in order (1) to identify the women who need extension services and (2) to design projects that will not be detrimental to the poorest women. One goal of involving women in agricultural production should be to increase their income and reduce their workload so that they may enjoy more leisure time and better health. The findings also demonstrate that certain demands, such as women's ownership of land or access to credit, are still "wishful thinking" for most women, who cannot give adequate guarantees either in money or through their husbands.

It should be possible to formulate concrete projects on the basis of study findings. In regard to food production especially, the study has demonstrated areas—food production, food processing and transportation—where women are playing a vital role, a role that must be taken into account in attempts to solve the problem of food self-sufficiency.

Despite the profound changes that are affecting the structure of production and social relations, it must be said, however, that the status of women in Africa remains basically unchanged. Women are illiterate or barely schooled, constrained by innumerable traditions, and destined to bear many children because of their ignorance of modern contraceptive methods. They do not really seek to change their place in society. There are clearly many steps to be taken in all these different areas.

Notes

1. Translated from French.
2. Support was received, however, from the government of the Netherlands, The Ford Foundation and the United Nations Fund for Population Activities (UNFPA).

3. Units established as part of an experimental program of cultural modernization begun more than 12 years ago.

4. The study was carried out in the Boundiali region, a savannah zone located in the extreme north close to the Mali border. The climate is tropical, with two main seasons: one dry, from November to May, and one rainy, from June to October. The region has not been affected by the growth of the export-oriented plantation economy that characterizes the southeastern area, but in recent years parastatal companies have tried to introduce industrial-type plantations. To encourage cotton cultivation, cleared tracts of land and farming equipment have been made available to households.

5. Because of the patriarchal authority structure prevailing in the region, women have no access to land except through their husbands. The land allocated to women is solely for growing food crops, with cotton-growing being reserved to men. Since the agricultural extension service is concerned exclusively with cotton, beneficiaries of the service were found to be exclusively male.

6. In the Boundiali region of northern Ivory Coast, new labor requirements for cotton production are creating labor bottlenecks for food crop production.

8

Household Management in Botswana: Cattle, Crops, and Wage Labor

Pauline E. Peters

Introduction

In the rural economies of southern Africa, people's strategies for gaining their livelihood characteristically depend on combining crop production, stock raising and off-farm employment, including wage labor. Strategies vary both within and between countries, and productive activities exist in different combinations. These variations provide challenges at different levels of analysis. At the micro end, an anthropologist studying a small group of people or a farming systems researcher working with a small group of farmers may find it difficult to grasp the extent and significance of the variations. Evidence drawn from recent research in Botswana raises questions about some analytical distinctions that have been made by FSR, especially those involving "the farming household" or "farm family" and the appropriate units and boundaries for research, analysis and action.

It is becoming very clear that the patterns of diversified income strategies in Botswana are dependent on inter-household linkages and intra-household strategies. Access to draft power and male labor are the key constraints on time plow-planting, essential in a harsh, unpredictable natural environment. Access to draft power is affected by the unequal distribution of cattle-holding and income, and the availability of male labor is affected by the high rates of male labor migration. Inter-household linkages are crucial to assuring access to both types of resources. At the same time, female labor is a significant factor in households' successful income strategies. FSR must understand intra-household relations as well as linkages between households.

Tswana Strategies of Livelihood:
The Aggregate Picture

The two most salient characteristics of the Tswana rural sector are the diversified nature of households' income strategies and the wide variation in households' wealth and income.

Income Strategies

Data from an agricultural survey in 1980 on the production mixes of Tswana rural families show that "the vast majority of farms, 75%, engaged in some form of 'mixed' farming (i.e, they raised two or more types of agricultural products" (Litschauer and Kelly 1981, 4). A major distinction is drawn between those who raised cattle (72%), an activity usually combined with crop production and rearing small stock, and those who did not (28%). This latter category divided more or less equally into two, those growing only crops and those raising livestock (apart from cattle) either with or without crop production. Of the larger cattle-keeping group, 12% did not grow crops, whereas 60% did so (*Ibid*).

To understand the significance of this production mix for family livelihood and for agricultural research and policy, other factors must be considered. First is the state of arable production. The two major grain crops grown, and also the most important food grains, are sorghum and maize. (Some millet is also grown.) Yields per hectare in Botswana "are among the lowest in the world, the average for cereals being 250 kg. per hectare over the past 10 years" (Alverson 1982, 6).[1]

Alverson goes on to point out that half of the households engaged in farming in 1980 cultivated less than 3 ha. of land and only 10 percent cultivated more than 7 ha. Yet, taking the average yield of grains and an average household size of seven to eight members, more than 8 ha. must be cultivated to meet the household's food needs for a year. A tiny minority achieve this.

In contrast with the low returns from food crop production, stock raising—especially cattle-keeping—is far more likely to provide income for Tswana families. The relatively good marketing system for beef cattle and the high (above world) price made available to beef producers by Botswana's preferential access to the EEC market are responsible for a general preference for cattle. As Litschauer and Kelly conclude, even though crop production is important for many Tswana families, "the cattle industry is the most important part of agriculture from a total farm income viewpoint." They further conclude that marginally to increase cattle offtake "would have a greater impact on total farm income than one [increasing] the levels of crop production" (Litschauer and Kelly 1981, ii).

But this conclusion must immediately confront the fact that cattle holding is highly skewed in Botswana, as in other countries in southern Africa. Hence, if the aim is not only to increase levels of productivity and gross national income but also to reduce, or at least not exacerbate, the skewed distribution of income, improvements must somehow be sought both in arable production and in stock raising (Ibid.).

There is yet another factor to be considered, namely, wage labor or off-farm employment. A series of publications, using data from both large-scale surveys and intensive investigation of small populations, has documented the critical importance of wage labor for the majority of Tswana families across a wide range of total income. The Rural Income Distribution Survey (RIDS) found that two-thirds of the households surveyed in 1974-75 received over 40 percent of their total income from off-farm employment (RIDS 1976). Brown makes the point, based on RIDS data, that "the poorer 50 percent of households counted on money transfers and employment as their primary source of income, despite the fact that the 1974 harvest was very good." (1983, 370). The more recent National Migration Study of 1979 documented the fact that "the majority of rural dwelling units had a wage-employed member [for varying periods] during the year" (Behnke and Kerven 1983, 10, my insert), a situation that led David Cooper (1979, 1980) to consider that "worker-farmer" was a more appropriate label than "farmer" for most inhabitants of the rural areas of Botswana. (Given the extensive transfers of income and people between urban and rural areas, this label is also more appropriate for many families residing in the urban areas.) Basing his comments on findings from the RIDS and from farm management surveys, Alverson also showed in 1979 that, in comparison with potential earnings in the South African mines, the "opportunity cost" of current cereals farming in Botswana was very high. He concluded that "in the absence of regular transfers of wage-based income, or the significant sale of stock per annum, very few if any Botswana farmers can expect to pay for [any introduced] improved methods by sale of increased yields" (1979, 40-1).

Behnke and Kerven have commented on the significance for farming systems research of this diversified effort by most Tswana households. They insist that FSR must take account of the fact that arable production "may not be the major concern for many farming families in Botswana" since these families "are concerned with stabilizing and increasing their entire income, much of which may come from nonfarm employment" (1983, 10). Farming systems researchers may be concerned with showing that subsystems in agricultural production are part of "the whole farm" system. In Botswana, the pattern of diversification suggests that "the whole farm" is itself a subsystem of a larger whole.

Measuring Variation in Production Mixes and Income

Farming systems researchers in the Tswana rural sector should also be concerned with the extent of variation in households' production mixes and in their levels and sources of income. Two main methods have been used to capture the range of variation: one approach has been to divide the population into categories of resource endowment, taking ownership of cattle as the single most powerful indicator of relative position. Another method is to show how different types of households are distributed along the range of variation. These two methods of assessing variation within a population are analytically linked. The former (distributional) analysis sets out the categories of key distributions, the latter (structural) analysis focuses on the "real" social units comprising Tswana populations. Moreover, both methods must, first, establish variations within a population and, second, elaborate on the determinants, or generative dynamic, of the variation.

Like any other research endeavor, farming systems research has to identify the key social groups in a population (compound, household, cooperative, etc.); distinguish these from significant socio-economic categories (the rich, the cattleless, the old, women, etc.); and show how they relate. In short, one must decipher how social groups and categories are generated, or "sedimented," by social processes and how the developmental or life cycles of households intersect with historical processes (Murray 1981; Peters 1983b; and Spiegel 1980). As indicated below, these distinctions have significance for the body of knowledge developed by FSR as well as for determining appropriate recommendation domains and effective technologies.

The Household as a Key Unit of Analysis

The basic unit of analysis in recent farming systems research has been the "farming household." The "farming household," a concept similar to the model of "the peasant household" in peasant studies and economic history in Europe and Latin America, is perceived as the major decision-making unit. A major rationale for taking the "farming household" as the primary unit of decision-making—and, hence, the appropriate unit of analysis for investigating farming patterns and how farmers gain a livelihood—is that there is "considerable overlap between the unit of production and the unit of consumption . . . in developing countries" (Norman 1982, 1). In practice, the term, "farming household" is used interchangeably with the "farm family" or even equated with the "farmer" (Gilbert et al. 1980).

Mounting evidence from many sources now suggests that there are numerous problems with taking the "farming household" as the primary sampling unit. For one thing, the research record indicates that, while there is far more overlap between consumption and production in African rural family units than in families in Western industrial nations, there is far less overlap than allowed for by the model of the "farming household." (Among the Serer, for example, husbands and wives belong to the same unit of production but to different units of consumption. This is only one example out of many.) Moreover, different categories of members within the farming household often have different, sometimes competing, goals.

In noting this, however, one must recognize two points: the first is that the current emphasis on the farming household, or family, responds to an earlier focus in agricultural research on the individual farmer; in its recognition that the farmer is a member of a social unit and that this unit has multiple activities and goals, this emphasis represents a significant analytical and methodological advance. The second point to note is that, although researchers may recognize that households are not unitary, neatly bounded units, they do not then translate this perception into any modification of the household model or, it seems, into methods that take full account of either the multiplicity of aims within the household or the existence of linkages among separate households. Too often, statements acknowledging that intra- and inter-household relations modify the household model are relegated to footnotes and are not incorporated into the analytical framework. (See, for instance, Gilbert et al. 1980, 6, note 1; 13, note 1; and 42, note 2; Norman, Simmons et al. 1982, 28.)

A major analytical distinction is made by key farming systems theorists between endogenous and exogenous factors. This relates directly to the premise of the farming household. Factors are designated "endogenous" because they are considered to be within the control of individual farming households; endogenous factors include the basic factors of production such as land, labor, capital, management skills and information. "Exogenous" factors are those considered to be largely outside the control of the farming household and include the whole structure of local and supra-local institutions, social relations, systems of belief, norms and so forth.

Some FSR theorists have pointed out that, in the long run, members of a particular society determine the social milieu, i.e., the factors defined as "exogenous," but others maintain the endogenous-exogenous distinction remains valid because the aim of FSR is to achieve certain positive changes in the short run (Baker et al. 1983, 7). This seems unexceptionable. But another objection is more to the point.

Investigations of numerous systems of rural production in Africa have demonstrated that viable production by individual farm households depends on their being embedded in supra-household networks. These supra-household linkages may take the form of mutual aid or have the character of patron-client relations. Whatever the form, it is clear that access to key resources or to basic factors of production lies outside the household as often as it lies within it—even in the short run. Although there are variations important to research and intervention, this pattern is currently widespread throughout Africa. (See the numerous citations in Guyer 1980.) Given this evidence, one is forced to conclude that the endogenous-exogenous distinction, as currently formulated, is inappropriate for proper understanding of most African rural economies.

It is also worth pointing out that the endogenous-exogenous distinction is based on the concept of a relatively autonomous farming household. Like the European "peasant household," the African household has been assumed to control its members and corporate resources and to have considerable autonomy of action from similar units. But the current realities of production, consumption and investment in most African countries, including Botswana, are such that individual households do not have full control over their access to land, tools or draft power; they acquire access to necessary factors only by being part of larger, supra-household groups or networks. Moreover, households' diversified strategies are dependent on their internal composition. In short, it is essential in African farming systems research to understand both inter- and intra-household relations.

A View from the Household:
The Disaggregated Picture of Diversification

Inter-Household Linkages: Interdependence in a
System of Plow Agriculture

This section summarizes research findings on inter-household linkages and intra-household relations in Botswana. In years of sufficient rainfall, a large majority of Botswana's people engage in crop production. Of those producing crops, 90 percent broadcast seed by hand and then plow, according to the Botswana Agricultural Statistics Survey. Most plows are drawn by oxen, other cattle or donkeys, as well as by tractor; the extent of tractor use varies substantially by region and by type of producer. All accounts of this pattern of plow arable production stress that the two critical constraints are draft power and labor. It has also become clear that neither of these is homogeneous and, further, that they are frequently interdependent.

Botswana's semi-arid environment is harsh, with low unpredictable rainfall and frequent droughts. Rain is "spotty," with consequent variability in growing conditions over small areas. On the other hand, sudden heavy downpours or freak, but not uncommon, hail storms can destroy and wash away new plants. Difficulties with different soil types, various pests and the often devastating effects of flocks of small birds (*thaga*), which feed on ripening sorghum, provide further problems for Tswana farmers.

The unpredictability of the rainfall patterns makes the timing of plow-planting absolutely critical. This has long been recognized by observers and is a concern articulated by the Tswana themselves. A recent account neatly summarizes the problem: "The timeliness of planting in relation to soil moisture, ideally into a wet seedbed approximately two days after a rain of over 25 mm, greatly affects yield"; inappropriate timing of planting can affect per hectare yield by as much as two tons (Lightfoot 1982, 57).

The primary obstacle to farmers' achieving timely plowing is their difficulty in gaining access to draft animals. This social fact is graphically demonstrated by the highly skewed distribution of cattle holding in Botswana. Between one third and 40 percent of Tswana households do not own their own cattle, and most cattle herds owned are small. It has been estimated that approximately 30 head are required for the minimum span of four draft oxen (Carl Bro. Int., 1982). The Agricultural Statistics of 1980 estimated that 73 percent of farming households have fewer than 30 head at their disposal, which means that most farmers must find other means of obtaining sufficient draft power (Lightfoot *ibid.*). Studies indicate that control of cattle, or having "demand-rights of access" to cattle as distinct from "the privilege" of using them (Alverson 1979, 1982),[2] varies directly with the acreage plowed. For example, 28 percent of farming households have no demand-rights to cattle, 17 percent have such rights to one to 10 cattle, and 17 percent to 11 to 20. In 1980, households with no demand-rights planted an average of 1.7 ha., those with one to 10 cattle planted 2.6 ha., and those with 11 to 40 head planted 3.8 ha. (Alverson 1982, 6–7). Lack of cattle, as Lightfoot and others stress, also delays plow-planting and reduces yields.

Information on how households acquire access to draft cattle has been accumulating in recent years. Although much still remains to be understood, it is very clear that, for the large majority, access to sufficient and timely plowing is acquired through a farming household's links to other households. These links may include kinship, affinity, co-residence, friendship or patron-client relations. While the particular exchanges vary in form, a common outcome is that individuals or households at the end of a "queue of access" to particular draft teams are vulnerable to the risks resulting from failure to achieve timely planting. The implications of inequitable cattle distribution for exacerbating existing inequities have been documented by many observers (Alverson, Cooper, Kerven, Gulbrandsen).

Households at the end of the queue for draft power are likely to be kept there not only by the conditions of production but also by labor supply factors. Many exchanges for draft power involve the offer of a household member's labor in return for the use of draft. As a result, cattleless farming households run the risk not only of failing to acquire draft animals early enough to plant at the "best" times but also of having to provide labor during the crop cycle on the lender's fields at the expense of their own fields. Poorer households may be unable to break out of a cycle of low output and income in part because they lack adequate access to draft and in part because, to borrow draft, they are forced to spend less time on their own fields than they would wish or than is necessary.

The diversifying strategies which Tswana families follow to multiply potential income sources and spread risk involve not only agricultural activities but also off-farm work. Most Tswana families have at least one member absent in wage labor for part of the year—in South Africa, in the urban centers of Botswana, in smaller settlements or in the lands and cattlepost areas of the country. The aim of these individuals and families is, of course, to increase income and hence livelihood. At the same time, because most families prefer to spend as little cash on food as possible, they seek to produce grain and other foods on their own fields. Yet their ability to produce these foods—and, to a varying extent, crops for sale—is often undermined by the absence in wage labor of one or more members of the family. They are in a classic Catch-22 situation.

Education also removes children and teenagers and thus further drains the family's labor supply. While the absence of adult men is felt most in relation to plowing, bush-fencing and, to a lesser extent, harvesting, children 10 years and older are critically important for "bird scaring," when the ripening sorghum heads are vulnerable to the depredations of many birds, and possibly—though this has not been well documented—for better, more thorough and timely weeding. Nevertheless, education, as a means of attaining a job and income, remains a key strategy in Africa for maintaining and increasing the general welfare of individuals, families and lineage or extended groups.

When cattle raising is added to crop production and to wage or self-employment, we have the full gamut of diversified production in Botswana. Cattle represent for Tswana not only a source of draft power but also a leading source of income, store of wealth and channel for investment. The specific strategies and particular mix of strategies followed with livestock vary according to the size of their herds and their other economic options. But in many of the patterns of stock raising documented for Botswana, inter-household exchanges are significant. Important supra-household networks include not only those that channel draft animals but also networks that care for stock over time. Many wage workers seek to use part of their earnings to start, maintain or increase a cattle herd. But if an adult man is engaged in wage work away from his home, who is to look after the cattle? The answer is complex but the diverse solutions very often entail inter-household exchanges. For example, fathers and sons or sets of brothers take turns to leave as labor migrants, thus ensuring that there is always an adult man left to care for the cattle. Other cases involve similar inter-household strategies between a man and his mother's brother.

A critical finding of research that has not been taken into sufficient account by agricultural or farming systems researchers is that the conditions of diversified production in Africa often lead to the creation of larger domestic and production groups. These larger units may both span more than one generation and incorporate households which are not necessarily co-residential. For example, in generation A, a young man goes as a migrant laborer to South Africa. He remits monies to his parents and sister at home, where they grow food crops and maintain a small herd of cattle. After the parents die, the sister, who remains unmarried but has children, maintains the fields, and her growing sons herd the cattle. In generation B, the now elderly, former migrant laborer keeps the cattle belonging to his dead sister's sons, who now work as migrant laborers. The labor of the sister on the fields and her sons in herding have helped build the herd which, on the death of the now-old man, will be divided among his children and his sister's children.

In other less fortunate cases, the absence of household members may lead to a situation where cattle receive insufficient care, the dwindling herd is a drain rather than a help and cash remittances must be spent to purchase food because of insufficient crop food production. The dependents of migrant laborers may constitute a small unit without involvement in extensive networks of production, or they may be drawn into more successful households' networks, as a client or object of charity; or, without the cohesion and continuity of the larger, more successful groups, they may fragment.

The spatial mobility of Tswana families must also be taken into account in determining appropriate units of analysis. The ideal-typical spatial arrangements of Tswana political and economic systems comprise a central settlement of houses together with the major political and jural institutions; arable fields or "lands" surrounding the central core, and, beyond that, the cattle herding areas or "cattle-posts," which, in turn, merge with hunting areas and no man's land. (These neat divisions among village, lands and cattle posts have been somewhat blurred, however, by the colonial demarcation of Tribal, later District, boundaries; the permanent settlement of inhabitants within these boundaries, and population increases throughout the post-independence period.)

Historically, the Tswana were relatively mobile. Researchers and policy analysts have given considerable attention in the past decade to the question of mobility and whether, in fact, people manage three "homes" in the three traditionally distinct areas. The debate on the movements of people into permanent settlements in the lands (Field 1980) or out of the lands into village settlements (Hesselberg 1982) continues. It is clear that the poorest categories live disproportionately in land areas and that the richest follow the ideal pattern of three residences. For the middle majority, however, there remains variation both by district and sub-district and by level of wealth and type of productive strategy. The ways in which people seek to establish or maintain bases in different parts of a district are influenced by policies and programs, including programs of water development for domestic and agricultural use, of establishing service centers (or "population catchment areas") and of agricultural development and land tenure. Socio-economic processes such as the changing value of land and increasing pressure on resources also influence residence. Whatever overall patterns of multiple residence are in place and developing, there is quite extraordinary mobility of whole domestic units and of individual members and clusters belonging to such units. (See, among others, Roe and Fortmann 1982.)

Implications for the Household as a Unit of Analysis

Gradually accumulating knowledge about diversified Tswana production systems leads us to question the validity of the household as a unit of analysis. It has become clear that many of the processes generating phenomena under investigation—whether rural income, patterns of rural-urban and intra-rural migration, determinants of variable crop outputs and yields, or relative vulnerability to drought conditions—cannot be understood if the household is assumed to be the primary unit of analysis. (See Alverson, Cooper, Kerven, Mahoney, Peters, Roe and Fortmann for direct statements and many of the other cited works for corroborating evidence.) In a recent article specifically addressing the significance of the Botswana case for current FSR models and methods, Behnke and Kerven (1983) express the view of most social researchers when they state that "individual households are not discrete entities . . . [but] are encompassed within larger units which both sustain them and restrict their freedom of action" (p. 12). They also provide illustrative case material demonstrating the ways in which transfers between separate domestic units effectively coalesce them into larger units for different purposes and conclude: "To create an artificially tight definition of the household in such societies is not, therefore, merely to 'tidy up' the data; it is to systematically misconstrue the long-term economic environment in which individuals operate. . . ." (ibid.)

These various critiques all demonstrate that the practices of individual "farming households" occur, and must be investigated, within larger or supra-household networks or units. The issue then becomes how to devise analytical frameworks and field methodologies for carrying out such investigation.

It should be noted, however, that questioning the validity of using households as the sole units of analysis is not a recommendation to abandon the concept of household. In fact, despite shifting boundaries, the household is a concept of particular validity in Southern African rural areas. As Alverson carefully pointed out in 1979, ". . . the household by and large stands as a node in complex structures of exchanges and reciprocities, which currently are vital to the success of the household in its farming enterprise" (p. 45). Both the "node" and the structures within which it operates should be investigated.

Intra-Household Relations and the Place of Gender in Farming Systems Research

We have learned from research that to understand and influence patterns of production, consumption and investment we must move beyond the single dwelling unit or household. We must also look inside the "node." Far less progress has been made in describing or analyzing intra-household processes than inter-household exchanges, yet field studies suggest that the internal composition and organization of the household and the role of women within the household—or, more precisely, gender-related work patterns—are critical to the systems of production that have been documented for Botswana. Attention to sex-related differences in farming has focused almost entirely on "female-headed households." Although this research has produced significant findings and useful hypotheses, it has not only obscured important variations among households headed by women but also diverted attention from the role of Tswana women as farming wives, sisters and daughters.

Ideal-typical statements about the division of labor by sex abound for Africa, including Botswana. Such categorization is useful but it often fails to distinguish the cultural ideal from conventional practice; it also fails to capture variation or the dynamics that generate the observed or stated "norm." A standard description of the sexual division of labor in most southern African agro-pastoral systems is that men look after cattle, clear and plow the land while women carry out all other arable tasks; both look after small stock; women also raise chickens and pigs. While this continues to be an acceptable general statement, studies of the allocation of labor carried out over the past 10 years document far more "crossing" of these gender-related distinctions than the ideal types suggest. One must be wary of accepting the ideal type uncritically. (It is also dangerous to assume that perceived "discrepancies" between observed practices and stated cultural practices reflect radical change or an "erosion" of the division of labor. Current historical studies will help to provide sound evidence but, for the moment, one must be careful in positing broad shifts in the gender-related performance of tasks.)

The adoption of plows at the turn of the century among Tswana groups entailed men's taking over the tilling of the soil, previously done with hoes and digging sticks by women. But field researchers have pointed out that women do plow (Fortmann 1981; Gulbrandsen 1980; Kerven 1979; Solway 1979) and that women play a more direct role in cattle-keeping than conventional statements allow for (Solway). Carol Bond's influential report on *Women's Involvement in Agriculture in Botswana* (1974) documents the greater involvement of women in crop production and the even larger dominance by men in stock-raising. But the figures also led her to stress the degree to which tasks defined as "male" and "female" were carried out, and recognized to be so, by both sexes.

The data from Bond and from the Rural Income Distribution Survey show the relative proportion expended by each sex of the total time spent on a category of task (plowing, weeding, etc.). There are also figures on the allocation of time per 12-hour day expended on different activities by sex (Kossoudji and Mueller 1981). The usefulness of these figures is clear. However, these data have two shortcomings for improving our knowledge about farming systems and our ability to reduce constraints on farming success. First, the figures give us only the broad parameters of a gender-based divison of labor; they cannot tell us about the prevailing farming pattterns followed by different households or clusters of households. Second, they are based on post hoc reporting rather than on, or in addition to, systematic observation. Authors are usually aware of such problems as not sufficiently distinguishing between actual practice and the stated norm (see above) and/or over- or under-reporting for various reasons. But once figures are available they tend to acquire a validity of their own and one stops asking, "What do they really mean?"

While the overall patterns seem acceptable, there are questions that need raising. For example, all available figures on the sexual division of labor suggest that women's involvement in livestock husbandry appears minimal. Yet, in my own interviews with cattle owners, I found over and over again that women were as knowledgeable as their husbands or adult sons regarding the state of the herd. Often, husbands turned to their wives in trying to remember when the last vaccinations or dips had taken place or how many calves had been born or died. Solway (1979) has made similar observations, and a recent report by Van der Wees (1982) states that women take part in decisions about cattle sales.

Survey results and field studies indicate that there is great interdependence in farming between men and women. Van der Wees has explicitly concluded: "Husband and wife [in all households with a husband present, namely 56%] make decisions together [and] also carry out agricultural activities together" (1982, 66). But we have little information on the precise strategies followed by households (and clusters of households) that depend on a division of labor by sex. Until we have more systematic information on these interdependent activities and decisions, our ability to understand and improve current farming systems will remain limited.

My own study[3] of cattle owners who were members of borehole syndicates, i.e., groups which own and jointly use deep bore-wells powered by diesel engines, revealed not only interdependence among households but also critically important interdependence of male and female labor within households. Indeed, the woman appears to be the central lynch-pin in the diversified activities of Tswana household members and is particularly "attached" to the locus of crop production. Wives played a primary role in crop production after plow planting in all but 13 percent of the borehole syndicate members' households (eight out of 62 households). In these few households, which were among the wealthier households, wives either held a professional or semi-professional job, mainly as teachers or nurses, or they looked after a family store. Even in these households, many wives maintained an important managerial role in acquiring sufficient labor for the crop cycle.

In all other households, apart from the few where the wife was ill or had died, the wife played an essential part in the crop cycle. When a man responded that only "his family" worked on the fields after plowing, he was in fact, referring in all cases to his wife, who was helped by children and in some cases by the man himself. A quarter of the households depended not only on the married couple and their children. In just over a quarter the husband and wife said that, when conditions warranted, they called in neighbors for work parties (*molaletsa*), where compensation—formerly, but now rarely, given in beer and meat—was either sugar and tea or cash. In good crop years, 36 percent of the households hired small groups to perform specific tasks for cash or engaged an individual (rarely more than one) to work for the whole or part of the crop season in exchange for a negotiated portion of the final harvest. In all these instances, the wife was the key manager and worker.

"Negative cases" clearly illustrated the importance of adult female labor within the household to successful crop production and, by extension, the "package" of diversified activities on which the household depends. Where a wife's death or illness had removed her from the typical worker-manager role, the men and their households either did not plow or they experienced a series of poor harvests which caused some to withdraw from planting. Only very old widowed men remained long without acquiring another wife. One man whose wife had become frail complained that he would have to sell a beast for cash to hire workers to replace her labor.

Female adult labor is essential not only to the work of the household but also to the links with other households that are the sine qua non of successful production. As indicated, many households require temporary workers for post-plow-planting operations such as weeding and harvesting. Work parties or *molaletsa* are a primary form of short-term contracting. Even when compensation is given and received in the form of sugar and tea or cash (see above), these involve reciprocal exchanges of labor. Today's hirer is tomorrow's hired. Because virtually all of the labor involved in such exchanges—except for bush clearing—is female, the absence of adult female labor from a household's resources is extremely dangerous. (Although some households hire in more labor than they hire out, this imbalance is more accepted by their neighbors if the woman of the household works even occasionally in *molaletsa* on the neighbors' fields.)

The greatest difficulties in acquiring labor were expressed by men who were tractor owners and plowed large areas of land but whose wives did not work on their fields.[4] As one man put it, "The people say why should we work for you when you plow such big fields but do not work on them yourself." He was a retired schoolteacher, active in local politics; his wife, who did not work on his fields, was also a teacher. The social differentiation and social "distancing," symbolized by the wife's removal from the fields, that are taking place in rural areas have repercussions for the management of crop production, at least on a certain scale.

Critical Constraints on Farming:
Gender, Household Type and Inter-Household Exchange

The critical constraints on Tswana families' successful crop production that have received greatest attention are draft power and male labor. "Female-headed households" have been singled out as the category of households that is most lacking in both these crucial factors, with the consequent characteristics of lower crop outputs, higher costs and generally lower levels of welfare. It is significant that, while the label "female-headed" is used to indicate an absence of (adequate) male labor, the parallel label "male-headed" appears to signal no reference to the availability—or not—of female labor. In this case, the gender of household labor becomes noteworthy only where it is male and absent. Yet the success of "male-headed households" in fact depends not only on the presence of male labor or draft power but also on the presence of female labor and female management within the household.[5]

Again and again, reports on Tswana farming households link the range in output and yields discerned in aggregate patterns of production across rural households with particular types of household. Research and analyses published in the last few years suggest that several of the prevailing typologies require rethinking.

During the 1970's, a number of intensive field studies of rural populations, large national surveys such as the Rural Income Distribution Survey (1974) and the National Migration Survey (1979), and numerous other technical and policy papers provided mounting evidence that the critical constraint on successful crop production was draft power. "Female-headed households" were also found to face particularly severe constraints in access to draft, with consequently low crop output. This insecure access was linked to the absence of adult men—either temporary, in the case of women with a migrant husband or son, or permanent, in the case of widowed, divorced or single women. The two factors associated with this male absence were (1) the lack of cattle, or the lack of a man to gain access to cattle, and (2) the lack of male plowing labor (Kerven 1979). Primary emphasis, however, has been placed on draft power, with the result that a key recommendation for policy action, for example, has been for female-headed households to be assured of more timely access to draft animals (Kerven ibid; Gulbrandsen 1980).

The published discussions of this issue indicate a growing appreciation of the variation within the category of "female-headed households." Not all are without access to draft or male labor; not all are uniformly "disadvantaged." One response to capture this variation has been to devise more complex typologies of "female-headed households" (Kerven ibid; Izzard 1979); these have often been so complex that they present problems intellectually and with respect to policy formulation (see Peters 1983b). Another response is to try to differentiate more carefully among members of the research population. A recent article discusses research in two different areas of Botswana that investigated the impact of absenteeism caused by labor migrancy on crop production (Hesselberg and Wikan 1982). Reseachers found, first, that there were no significant differences in size and wealth between households with absent workers and those without, once the "female households" (i.e., those with no able-bodied man as a member) were excluded. (These households, composed of women and children, were "small and poorer than other households on average.") When "female households" were excluded from the rest of the analysis, it was found that there were no significant differences in crop production between "male households" (i.e., house-holds with one or more able-bodied men but no absent migrants) and households with at least one able-bodied man and some absent migrants. Households with all their available men absent either demonstrated a reduced level of crop production or withdrew completely from crop production. A second, related conclusion was that "in spite of the importance of [draft-power], the main reason for non-plowing [is] a shortage of men" (p. 71). Here, then, the emphasis has been shifted from draft to male labor.

In a recent paper, Louise Fortmann (1983), using data extracted from the Waterpoints Survey of 1979-80, found that—predictably, given the present data base—"female-headed households were significantly less likely to plow than male-headed households . . . from 1976 to 1979" (p. 13). When she controlled for cattle ownership, however, this difference disappeared. Her finding was that "economic stratification," specifically the ownership of cattle, was more important than the sex of the household head in determining whether or not the household plowed. This finding would seem to support the emphasis on draft power as being the critical constraint. However, when Fortmann compared the different households, divided by sex of head and cattle holding, with respect to the timeliness of plowing, she was surprised to find that, while male-headed cattle holding households plowed before those with no cattle and while there was no significant difference in the proportions of male- and female-headed cattleless households' plowing dates, "significantly fewer female cattle owners had started by this date than had male cattle-holders" (p. 18). In fact, the female cattle owners plowed even later than the cattleless households. Ruling out the effect of certain hypothesized possible factors, she inferred that female-headed cattle owning households may "depend on the assistance of male relatives," whose first priority is to plow their own fields. Thus, the otherwise disadvantaged female-headed households who are cattleless and who hire both draft and labor "may be relatively advantaged in having greater control over the time of plowing" (p. 24). Fortmann's conclusion stresses the availability of male labor as being as critical a constraint as draft power (but cf. Kerven 1979).

If further differentiation among the "female-headed households" were possible—to distinguish the availability or not of male labor and the particular type, timing and form of this labor in relation to cattle holding and other significant characteristics, such as the age of the female and of any male members, to aid in the separation of life-cycle from other intergenerational or class effects (see Peters 1983b)—more precise associations would be possible.[6]

A more precise understanding of the relative and interactive effects of the shortage of draft and male labor on different types of households is also dependent on greater specification of the inter-household level. The finding that households whose male members are absent migrant workers have lower crop output, and/or higher incidences of the resident female members' working on other peoples' fields, cannot be fully interpreted until we know the placement of these households in larger networks and the relation between different types of households. For example, it may be that much "hiring-out" indicates the development of an agricultural proletariat (Cooper 1981, 1979; Hesselberg 1982). But if these hiring-out households are at a certain stage of development and/or if their "hiring out" is to related households (e.g., parents or others at a more mature stage), the conclusion is different. Both processes are probably in effect[7] but to decipher where, and with what significance for farming and its relation to other sectors, would require both more rigorous examination of household categories and more careful analysis of inter-household relations.

The Importance of Gender

Systematic investigation of the gender-based division of labor and access to resources should be an important dimension of future studies. This needs to be done across categories of households and within households of particular types. Posing the inquiry in these terms enables one to ask even broader questions, e.g., question about the present nature of rural labor markets or about probable future shifts in the diversified income strategies and patterns of investment among rural families.

The relative significance of female labor has remained unexamined despite enormous interest in the significance of male labor for crop production and despite many references to women as being "the primary crop producers." The availability of women's labor is a critical, but unexamined, component of the relative success of male-headed households and even, according to Hesselberg and Wikan, of households that are de facto female-headed but retain one or more male members. Numerous analyses of the production "mix" of Tswana households have pointed out that, with the present relation between migrant wage rates and average earnings from crops, the opportunity cost of men's labor in crop production is very high (Alverson; Gulbrandsen; Lightfoot; Lucas; among others). What this assessment does not include, however, is that the ability of men to take up the option of wage labor often depends on the availability of female labor to maintain other household production activities (not to mention maintenance or "domestic" work). Women are the means for men to reduce their "opportunity cost."

Many still unresolved questions could be answered by more systematic examination of the significance of gender in differently constituted and differently endowed households. For example, in a recent article, Lightfoot (1982) argues that technology per se does not affect yields but that "good management," as demonstrated by timeliness, is the necessary condition for assuring higher yields. He does not present data on the determinants of "poor" or "good" management, but if different levels of management vary within and across categories of resource endowment, as is implied, a key characteristic may be the availability and type of female labor. This is an important next focus for inquiry.

The nature of, and interrelations among, the various factors of production should also be explored. One might ask why female cattle owners who suffer from their dependence on the labor of male relatives for plowing, as Louise Fortmann found, do not use their resources to hire labor elsewhere. Existing information suggests, first, that modes of access to draft power are linked with those of labor allocation, i.e., labor and draft are not discrete factors in rural Botswana. Second, male and female labor is non-equivalent, not only because each sex predominates in certain tasks but also because they do not have the same exchange value. For example, men can gain access to draft animals by offering their labor for plowing and other activities. Women's labor, on the other hand, is exchanged for cash, cash-substitutes such as tea or sugar, and shares of the harvest; it is normally exchanged for draft only within categories of near kin. We must conclude that the types of labor relations and forms of exchange are critical aspects of farming systems, that these social mechanisms of access to labor and resources are far more "personalized" than conventional Western models assume, and that gender is a key dimension.

Implications for Farming Systems Research

Because the diversified production strategies of Tswana families depend on their being part of supra-household networks and on a division of labor by sex within the household, researchers and practitioners seeking to improve crop practices and, hence, income and welfare must investigate and understand both inter- and intra-household relations.

Households are not units with fixed resource endowments. Endowments are altered by inter-household transfers in such a way that hard and fast lines between endogenous and exogenous factors cannot be drawn at the household boundary.

Many inter-household linkages are gender-based, with male and female labor having different exchange values. Because modes of access to draft power and male labor are linked, households possessing cattle adequate both for draft and for drawing in male labor can be "on the up" whereas households lacking both cattle and male labor may typify a downward swing. Female labor also plays a critical role in inter-household exchanges. To ensure adequate labor for weeding and harvesting, households appear to require the presence of adult, able-bodied women. The multiple exchanges needed to "service" the social networks that provide support in the daily routine and in crisis also depend on women. Both male and female labor are also necessary to assure the household's own crop production.

Current research and recent publications are refining our understanding of the links between access to draft power and male labor but we need to pay equal attention to the availability of female labor. It certainly seems worth examining the role of female labor and management when attempting to answer Lightfoot's question about differences among farmers in respect to practices of "good management."

Questions to Be Explored

What do these conclusions imply for new approaches to farming systems research? First is the issue of the appropriate unit of analysis. There are many caveats to be expressed concerning the use of the household as the primary unit of analysis. In practice, current usage in Botswana defines "household" as a residential unit or compound (Tswana *lapa*). But the circumstances of diversified production—the multiple sources of income; transfers of income, resources and personnel; spatial dispersal, and seasonal mobility—entail significant units above the individual household. Research must take this into account in its analytical and methodological frames.

Second, the sets of income strategies and farming practices being documented in Botswana depend on the particular composition of households. The role of household composition should also be included in the research agenda.

To suggest that one must look inside the household—the "node" of the key production units in Botswana's rural sector—is not to fall back into the old trap of regarding individual farmers as the sole units of analysis. It is instead a recognition that households are organizations, dependent on the availability of certain critical combinations of factors.

Age and gender are the critical dimensions of household composition. Gulbrandsen, for example, has shown that there are significant differences in production at different stages of households' developmental cycles.[8] His data demonstrated, in particular, the differences between "senior" and "junior" households—the labels referring to the relative age and, hence, resource endowments of the male heads of the households. He also described the "optimal" household for diversified crop and livestock production as consisting of a middle-aged male head of household with adult sons (cf. Hesselberg and Wikan).

In this paper I have tried to show that female labor is a critical but hitherto underemphasized factor in households' "optimal" production packages. Gender is a key characteristic of labor in rural Botswana, and female labor is as critically important as male labor. Any assumption that one has paid adequate attention to gender by considering "female-headed households" is as distorting as a failure to recognize that the success of male-headed households depends in large part on the availability within the household of female labor.

Third, a thorough understanding of the important inter- and intra-household linkages is necessary for projecting both the short- and long-term effects of any intervention. In Sierra Leone, failure to recognize the age- and gender-specific characteristics of seasonal labor profiles have had negative effects on a rice project (Richards 1983). Over the longer term, the interactive effects of developmental or seasonal cycles and vulnerability of particular types of households—which often result in a cumulative "ratchet effect" on the poor (Chambers 1969)—demand close attention to the processes of inter- and intra-household exchange. An understanding of inter- and intra-household processes is needed in order to project and monitor the ripples through rural systems of any intervention.

How, then, does one select appropriate "recommendation domains"? One established analytical method for research in Botswana has been to divide the research population into categories of farmers or households according to relative income or wealth. The most common indicator is cattle ownership. But, knowing that key production units, or at least networks, crosscut such resource-owning categories, one must question whether these are appropriate target groups. Should one, instead, adopt as recommendation domains the networks or clusters of households that use, if not own, resources together? For example, households with no plow animals and households with 20 or more cattle may be seen as constituting two separate recommendation domains, yet the links between them—the exchange of labor against plow services or a share of the harvest—are critical to understanding how individual households operate within each recommendation domain (Peters 1983c; Behnke and Kerven 1983). The organization of these clusters must be investigated in order to understand the critical parameters of individual households' production performance.

If one wishes to consider the linked clusters as a target group, it is important first to recognize that many networks (e.g., ones focused on a team of oxen) are not corporations. Any one network, or social configuration, may be the product of many different connections which vary from year to year. Some networks last for many years, even across generations, but others represent seasonal contracts. One must decide whether the network observed at a particular point in time has sufficient standing to warrant its being treated as a recipient unit.

One must also recognize that introducing new inputs (resources, information, etc.) into a network will presumably change the significance of its constituent ties and even the shape of the unit itself. The importance of inter-household exchanges suggests that a project's impact on the "community" should be investigated rather than its impact on particular categories of farmers (distinguished by level of assets) (Behnke and Kerven 1983, 13). (But this does not mean that the shape of the "community" is less difficult to determine than a household or household cluster or that the "community" will not be changed as a result of the project.) The ways in which interventions will change the relative weight of available production factors, and modes of access to those factors, require careful tracing, including both prior tracing of likely effects, based on available knowledge of linkages, and post hoc tracing, as part of the monitoring, evaluative and directed feed-back processes of research.

An effective research and action agenda would seem to require a dual approach. The dual strategy would be to identify (1) the significant social units or networks in any particular area and (2) the significant categories of households facing similar constraints or with similar assets. The first approach would require researchers to trace the links out from various "nodes." But the social and economic significance of these particular networks in the larger society would also require the second type of analysis, namely an analysis of how significant categories or types of households are distributed. Categories could include households holding herds of varying sizes; households following different combinations of crops, livestock and off-farm employment, or categories based on multiple characteristics, such as households that are "male-headed with x cattle, y adult females, alpha production mix" and so forth. The choice of significant characteristics could be based on the kinds of research discussed above.

We need to understand the critical inter- and intra-household linkages that make possible current production and income strategies in Botswana. To achieve this, a systematic, rigorous analysis of the key socio-economic relations that constitute Tswana production, consumption and investment units is essential.

Notes

1. Litschauer and Kelly give a figure of 200 kg. per hectare for 1980 data.

2. The distinction between "demand-rights" and "privileges," or "request rights," refers to the fact that in the former case a person owns cattle or holds them on a long loan and thereby has first call on their use. In the latter case, a person must depend on another person in order to gain access to cattle.

3. Research was carried out in 1979–1980 in the Kgatleng District of Botswana. This research was made possible by doctoral research funds from the Social Science Research Council/American Council of Learned Societies and the National Science Foundation.

4. Some men in this category were able to rely on semi-tied dependents for field labor. These included large cattle-owners with cattle posts in remote areas of the district, where they had access to the families of San and/or Kgalagadi herders, or men from families of high rank who still retained descendents of the servant families of their fathers.

5. The "invisibility" of females in the category of "male-headed households" and the non-equivalence of the opposition between "male-headed" and "female-headed" as labels will not be surprising to many who have concerned themselves with examining the organization and ideology of domestic units. The underlying dichotomy of the two labels is, of course, the complete vs. the incomplete household.

6. It is noticeable that each separate study makes certain distinctions that are useful but never all of those that seem significant. Thus, Hesselberg and Wikan's finding is important, but the exclusion of households with no males present leaves a significant gap. Fortmann's paper, on the other hand, does not differentiate within the "female-headed" category according to the actual presence of males.

7. This seems to be a conclusion one draws by comparing findings from the articles cited. Although each individually emphasizes one aspect/issue/household type/argument, together they provide a useful foundation for further refinement of research questions and methods.

8. The differences relating to developmental cycles he describes are not those of an individual household's cycle, as in the classic Chayanovian shifts in C/W ratios; because of inter-household linkages, Tswana developmental cycles are more complex.

9

Agricultural Production, Social Status, and Intra-Compound Relationships

Helga Vierich

To understand the causes of variation in productivity from farm to farm, it is necessary to look at the cultural context within which the farming system operates. The structure and institutions of society affect the farming system in three ways: first, they create pressures that require particular individuals to produce more than they need for subsistence; second, through marriage customs and group insurance systems, they cause the disposal and investment of accumulated wealth in ways that may, or may not, benefit agriculture; and third, they create differential access to important resources, including land and labor.

This paper examines several hypotheses concerning the cultural and organizational causes of variation in productivity among different farming units. These hypotheses relate to the roles played by family composition, social status and ethnicity—all of which affect access by the production unit to resources, land and labor.

The case study analyzed here illustrates relationships between the nature of the production groups and the levels of agricultural production that must be taken into account in proposals for technological change. Different technological packages may be appropriate for different kinds of production units, depending on the units' structure and composition. Moreover, not all farms are affected equally by such factors as population growth and declining soil fertility. Differences in response to such factors must be taken into account in long-term planning and technology development.

The Village Case

The case study presented here is drawn from Koho, one of six villages participating in long-term socio-economic studies carried out by the

155

International Crops Research Institute for Semi-Arid Tropics (ICRISAT) in Ouagadougou, Burkina Faso (formerly Upper Volta).

The village of Koho is located about 200 kilometers west of Ouagadougou in a zone of semi-arid tropical tree savanna. Average long-term rainfall for the region is about 1,000 mm. Since the study was begun in 1981, rainfall in the village has been below average—by 13 percent in 1982 and 21 percent in 1983. In 1982, Koho was a village of approximately 1,200 people from three major ethnic groups: the Dagara-djula (62 percent of the population), the Bwaba or Bwa (34 percent) and the Fulani (4 percent).[1]

Ethnographic Background

Each of the ethnic groups is composed of a number of lineages which are the major political and land-holding groups of the society. The compound is the smallest fragment of lineage.

In 1982, each compound was a family cluster frequently consisting of the households of a father and his married sons. Leadership and responsibility for the well-being of the entire compound group, which might include several production groups, was vested in the most senior man living in the compound. Thus, in every compound there was one household head who wore two hats: household head and compound leader.

Agricultural production units were organized within the compounds, and each compound leader allocated land to the various production units within his compound, including his own farm. Each agricultural production unit was usually composed of more than one conjugal household and was headed by the most senior household head among the cooperating households; this was the father, in the case of a production unit composed of a household headed by a father and a household headed by his son, or the eldest brother, in the case of a production unit composed of the households of brothers.[2]

The amount of land each production unit worked depended on two major factors: the number of workers available, and the type of technology used. These factors were difficult to analyse separately, because most farms with animal traction appeared to have been among the larger, more productive enterprises before they began to use plows. Their adoption of animal traction indicated a pre-existing tendency to invest in agriculture. Animal traction equipment, which consisted mainly of ox-drawn plows and donkey carts, had been adopted by 22 percent of the village farms since it was first introduced into the village in 1965. Adoption proceeded very slowly until the late 70s, and about half of the plows were purchased after 1978.

The major crops produced in Koho are white sorghum (32 percent of surface area cultivated), cotton (28 percent), millet (27 percent), red sorghum (7 percent) and maize (6 percent). Rice, groundnuts, cowpeas, tobacco, calabashes and various vegetables and condiments—some 40 varieties in all—complete the agricultural roster. For most cereals, yields per hectare are low, averaging 300–500 kg.

Variation in Production Among Farms

Preliminary analysis of the production data from the Koho sample farms indicated a great deal of variation in the amount of cereal produced per agricultural worker. On some farms each working member of the farm unit produced less than a hundred kilograms of cereal, while on other farms, each worker produced over 300 kilograms. The range was 30 to 902 kilograms per worker. One of the first hypotheses explored to explain this variation was that it might be related to family composition.

Tests of "Chayanov's Rule"

It has been proposed that there is a positive relationship between the ratio of dependents per worker and production per worker, i.e., that productivity per worker will rise as the ratio of consumers to workers increases. (Chayanov 1966). Sometimes called "Chayanov's Rule," this relationship between family composition (ratio of dependent consumers to active consumers) and agricultural productivity is conventionally measured in terms of hectares cultivated per worker and cereal production per worker. As the dependency ratio rises, so should these two parameters.

Chayanov's work pertained to peasants in Czarist Russia. While there are numerous differences between the peasant economy of Czarist Russia and the economy of the lineage or clan-based societies of Africa, studies in Africa have confirmed that Chayanov's relationship between family composition and agricultural production does hold in a general way (Norman et al. 1981; Sahlins 1972).

Chayanov's Rule was tested in Koho, and confirmed, as it was in the other villages in the ICRISAT study where it was tested. Measured in terms of hectares cultivated per worker and cereal production per worker, there appeared to be a tendency for both parameters to rise with the dependency ratio of the producing unit. Correlation analysis showed the dependency ratio and area cultivated per worker to be significantly correlated at the 5 percent level.

As was the case with Chayanov's data, there was a tendency for the variation to increase at both the high and low ends of the continuum of dependency ratios and for hectares cultivated and production per worker to drop off again at the highest dependency ratio. Possibly the ease of subsistence at low dependency ratios and the overburdening of the few workers at high ratios may have led to investment in other economic pursuits at either end of the spectrum of family composition. (See Table 9.1.)

Technology and Ethnicity

Chayanov's Rule expresses a tendency, nothing more. It cannot explain the great variations in productivity among farmers in the same range of dependency ratios. For instance, three production units in our sample with nearly identical dependency ratios (1.60, 1.60 and 1.57) cultivated very different areas per worker (.33 ha, .87 ha and 1.24 ha respectively).

One possible reason for variation among farms with similar family composition is that some farmers cultivated with hoes while others used ox-drawn plows and weeders. When the farms were divided into two types—those using the traditional hand-tool cultivation methods and those which possessed ox-drawn plows and weeders—there were clear-cut differences between the two groups of farmers. However, it was on farms with a dependency ratio of 1.55–1.79 that animal traction equipment was most frequently found (Table 9.1). In fact, the frequency of investment in plows, carts and weeders tended to follow the same pattern in relation to dependency ratios as did hectares cultivated per worker, peaking at dependency ratios of 1.50–1.74 and dropping to nothing at the lowest and highest dependency ratios.

It is probable that when the dependency ratio rose beyond 1.25 in a production unit, the leader started to look for ways of increasing production potential and decreasing the drudgery of necessary farmwork. If he could assemble the capital and extra labor, he was likely to invest in plows and carts. If not, he might turn to other sources of income, such as petty trade, craftwork, hired cropwork and wage work in towns.

Variation in access to land of different types also led to important differences among farms. Farmers with poor land were apparently obliged to cultivate a larger area in order to achieve the same production level. This point can be illustrated by comparing the two major agricultural ethnic groups in the village.

The Bwa settlers had recently arrived in the village and were politically subordinate to the Dagara-djula. As a group, the Bwa were found to have very little land in the higher-potential river valley and lower slopes and to cultivate proportionally more upland soils than the Dagara farmers. Even the gardens around the houses of the Bwa, fertilized by compound sweepings, were cultivated by the Dagara-djula (Table 9.2).

Ethnicity, and by implication access to favorable land, clearly modified the effects of technology on cereal production. In 1982, the Dagara-

TABLE 9.1
Tests of Chayanov's Rule in the ICRISAT Study Villages, 1982

Dependency Ratios (ranges)	1:00-1:24	1:25-1:49	1:50-1:74	1:75-1:99	2:00+
Sahel Zone: Oure					
No. of farms	3.00	7.00	4.00	5.00	2.00
No. of farms with animal traction	0.00	2.00	2.00	1.00	0.00
Hectares/worker	1.03	1.49	1.12	2.62	2.02
Cereal production/worker (kg)	114.70	255.10	258.60	551.30	362.20
Sudanian Zone: Kolbila					
No. of farms	3.00	8.00	5.00	4.00	2.00
No. of farms with animal traction	0.00	3.00	2.00	2.00	0.00
Hectares/worker	0.62	0.74	1.16	1.02	0.62
Cereal production/worker (kg)	162.90	219.60	304.90	302.20	221.90
Northern Guinean Zone: Koho					
No. of farms	5.00	4.00	9.00	4.00	2.00
No. of farms with animal traction	0.00	1.00	9.00	4.00	0.00
Hectares/worker	0.67	0.75	0.81	1.06	1.26
Cereal production/worker (kg)	191.60	117.30	214.10	301.50	161.00
Total (3 villages)					
No. of farms	9.00	19.00	19.00	13.00	6.00
No. of farms with animal traction	0.00	6.00	14.00	7.00	0.00
Hectares per worker	0.77	0.99	1.03	1.56	1.30
Cereal per worker	156.40	197.30	259.20	384.90	248.40

TABLE 9.2
Ethnic Differences in Access to Arable Land, Koho, 1982

| | Ethnic Group | | | |
| | Bwa | | Dagara-djula | |
Land Types	Hectares cultivated	% of total land of each land type	Hectares cultivated	% of total land of each type
River valley bottom	0.14	3	5.75	97
Lower slopes	1.80	17	8.75	83
Middle slopes	15.14	42	21.19	58
Uplands	43.06	49	47.67	51
Totals	60.14	42	83.06	58
Area cultivated per capita (hectares)	0.409		0.336	

djula with traction equipment cultivated only slightly more land than the Bwa using hand tools (.87 ha per worker vs. .83 ha per worker). Depending on their access to better soils, farmers appeared to choose a different balance between cereal crops and cotton. One reason for this may be that the cotton extension service provided fertilizer at subsidized rates which made it possible to cultivate the upland soils continuously and to produce cereal crops on the residual fertilizer in a rotation following cotton.

The Bwa farmers had 35.5 percent of their land planted in cotton in 1982, while the Dagara had only about 15 percent of their land under cotton. This difference was significant at a 2.5 percent level. Thus cotton production appeared to be far more important among the Bwa than among the Dagara-djula. In fact, among Bwa farmers working with hand tools, cotton rather than cereal was the main crop. These Bwa families did not produce enough cereal for subsistence and were found to be purchasing up to 60 percent of their cereals. By contrast, the Bwa farmers using traction equipment were found to purchase only about 19 percent of their cereals.

Among the Dagara-djula, both the farmers using traction and those using hand tools devoted about 15 percent of their farm land to cotton and purchased about 45 percent of their cereals. The Dagara farmers with traction equipment did not seem to follow a different farming or production strategy from the Dagara using hand tools. Yet average cereal production per worker was higher in units with traction equipment.

This might be explained by the greater use of organic and chemical fertilizers among traction households (Jaeger 1983).

Social Status and Agricultural Production

The social status of the head of the production unit was also found to be a major factor in agricultural production. Compound leaders headed all of the traction-owning production units among the Dagara-djula, whereas only 11 percent of the units led by ordinary household heads possessed traction equipment. Differences in agricultural production were thus also highly correlated with the social status of the head of the production unit.

To determine the possible role of social status in agricultural production, the Dagara-djula sample[3] in Koho was divided into two groups: those who were heads of compounds as well as being heads of their own households and of a production unit and those who were simply heads of households and production units, living within a compound led by someone older.

Among the Dagara-djula, the following differences related to the status of compound head: (1) production units headed by compound leaders were, on the average, twice as large as those headed by ordinary household heads; (2) cereal production per worker was nearly double that of production units headed by ordinary household heads, and (3) the amount of cash involved in livestock transactions (sales and purchases) was far greater in production units headed by compound leaders than the amount involved in units headed by ordinary household heads. There was also a significant age difference between the leaders of the two types of production units, with compound leaders tending to be about 10 years older (Table 9.3).

The dependency ratios of the two types of production units averaged about the same (around 1.57), and the percentages of cereal purchased and farmland under cotton were nearly identical. The area cultivated per worker was slightly greater in production units headed by compound leaders (about 0.1 hectares), but this could scarcely account for the differences in production per worker.

Factors Leading to Greater Production by Units Led by Compound Heads

The difference in productivity between farming units led by compound heads and those led by ordinary household heads probably resulted from two factors: (1) compound heads were under far more pressure to produce surplus than the ordinary heads of households and (2)

TABLE 9.3

Comparison of Characteristics of Production Units of Compound Heads and Simple Household Heads among the Dagara-djula of Koho, 1982.

	Heads of Compounds	Heads of Households
Number of Production Units	6	9
Size of production units	23°	10°
Age of head	60*	51*
Dependency ratio	1.55	1.56
% Possess animal traction	100°	11°
Cereal production/worker	256*	173*
Cotton production/worker	146	103
Cereal production/consumer	179.5	121
Cereal purchased/consumer	144	98
% purchased cereal	47	45
% area planted to cotton	15	15
Sale of animals (CFA)	836,034*	18,294*
Purchase of animals (CFA)	140,313*	25,197*

*Significant at 10% level
°No test of significance was done
Note: Tests of significance used were one tailed T-tests.

compound heads had better access to land, labor and capital resources than ordinary household heads. Both of these differences stem from the rights and responsibilities that went with the social status and political role of the compound leader.

The compound leader represented the interests of the whole group in the larger field of lineage and village politics. Furthermore, he had the authority and responsibility to request land from the lineage head and to arrange and, often, to finance the marriages, baptisms, funerals and group labor invitations that took place within the compound group, even when these were for the benefit of an ordinary household within the group.

The compound head was under greater pressure than ordinary household heads to have abundant grain on hand to meet his extra social and political obligations. These included obligations to share, to provide hospitality, to provide for the less fortunate, and to provide food and drink in exchange for group labor at weeding, harvest, threshing and household-building parties. It was the compound head who usually took responsibility for handicapped, infirm and aged family members.

Finally, household units too inexperienced or small to be viable on their own were often included in the production unit of the compound leader.

The compound leader also had certain privileges. He often had access to the accumulated savings and investments of the extended family. Investments in cattle clearly accounted for the enormous differences between compound and ordinary household heads in terms of livestock sales and purchases. The compound leader also had access to the best land within the family allocation for his own production unit, and was entitled to contributions of labor from other production units within his compound. Furthermore the compound leader, because of his higher political status, was in a good position to secure labor from other compounds within his lineage.[4]

The compound leader could not easily abuse these privileges or he would lose the support of his juniors and, with it, his access to extra labor, land and capital. For every improvement in his own conditions, the compound head was also obliged to improve the security of his junior production units. Junior production units which did not produce enough for the year were assisted by their compound heads. Compound leaders may even have raised their annual cereal requirements in anticipation of a certain frequency of failure, because of illness or other misfortune, within the smaller production units sharing their compound. Moreover, given their understanding that the senior unit would provide for their families in case of a deficit, junior men could afford to pursue other sources of income such as trade, wage labor and craft production, which might otherwise have been prohibited by the requirements of crop work.

Organization of the society into compounds provided more vulnerable units with a form of buffer against misfortune. It would seem, therefore, that the higher production per worker noted in farm units headed by compound leaders compensated to some extent for the occasional insufficiencies of the ordinary farm unit's subsistence efforts. This may explain why compound heads bought large quantities of cereal[5] despite the fact that their cereal production was often manifestly in excess of the requirements of their production group. In 1982, Dagara-djula compound heads purchased an average of 144 kilograms of cereal per consumer (Table 9.3). This, in addition to the cereal production of 179.5 kg per consumer, gave a total of 323.5 kg, which was much more than the 190–200 kg per consumer normally estimated by the FAO.

If one considers the special rights and obligations of the compound head, one can better understand the economic performance of the production units that they lead. The compound leaders covered in the study were at one time simple household heads within the compounds of their elder kinsmen. It is probable that their production profile at that time resembled those of production units led by the ordinary household heads in the present study. With their ascent to compound leadership, the pressures and privileges of their position pushed—and permitted—them to invest more in agriculture and to produce at surplus intensities.

Conclusions

In Koho there were clearly close links between the village institutions that organized economic activities and agricultural performance. The rate and impact of the adoption of new technology was found to vary by ethnic group in timing and in impact on the farming system. Access to land of different types had an important effect on the degree of cash cropping and modified the uses to which new technology was put. Furthermore, it appeared that investment in new technology was proceeding without serious disturbance to existing patterns of investment and social organization, as indicated by the high correlation between the possession of traction equipment and social status.

New technology was adopted both where pressures for increased productivity were greatest, according to the existing social organization of production, and where privileges accorded to social status brought access to labor resources and accumulated capital within the compound unit. By the same token, the greater pressure on land among the Bwa farmers and the poorer quality of their land, determined by ethnic relations and historical events, resulted in cropping patterns and uses of new technologies quite different from those employed by the Dagaradjula within the same village setting.

Notes

1. Because the Fulani are a herder group that practices very limited agriculture, it has been omitted from this analysis.

2. In this paper, the farm "production unit" has been used interchangeably with "farm" or "farm family."

3. The Bwa sample members were not included in this analysis because of the differences in production and cereal purchases between the two ethnic groups, noted above, and because virtually all of the Bwa sample were compound heads. Therefore a correlation of status and production in the Bwa group was not possible.

4. The compound head's access to outside labor called into question, of course, the original calculation of dependency ratios which was based on the breakdown of dependent consumers to active workers usually found in a normal production unit. It appears that the supply of outside labor available to compound heads was in some cases sufficiently regular to make the number of workers

counted within the production unit an inaccurate measure of the unit's labor resources.

5. The cereal purchases referred to here were those made for home consumption, not for speculation. These two categories of purchases were distinguished during the data collection.

10

Sheep and Goats, Men and Women: Household Relations and Small Ruminant Production in Southwest Nigeria

C. Okali and J. E. Sumberg

Small ruminants are a unique development resource in humid West Africa. With low capital and management inputs, small ruminant production offers excellent but highly variable returns. It also makes an important contribution to animal protein supplies in the rural areas. Yet small ruminant production, as a minor farm enterprise, is not well integrated with efforts to improve crop production.

The International Livestock Centre for Africa (ILCA) is currently evaluating the possibility of improving small-scale sheep and goat production systems. Two models of improved small ruminant feed production are under consideration: the first is an "alley farming" model which links crop and livestock production through leguminous browse trees; the second is an "intensive feed garden" model which is used where animals are confined and land is scarce. The background and rationale underlying the development of these models are outlined below, and each model is reviewed in light of the resources available to farmers and of household decision-making processes.

Sheep and Goats

Because the disease, trypanosomiasis, has generally limited livestock production in the humid zone of West Africa, most indigenous animals are the trypanosomiasis-tolerant dwarf breeds. Dwarf sheep and goats are the most common ruminant species found; there were an estimated 14 million dwarf sheep and goats within the humid zone in 1979 (Jahnke 1982).

Small ruminants are a major under-exploited food and capital resource in the zone. There has been no systematic attempt by farmers or development agencies to increase small ruminant production, and small ruminants are only rarely mentioned in descriptions of area farming systems. Yet these animals constitute an important source of meat, provide farming households with a flexible financial reserve and play important social and cultural roles.

Rural owners are generally male farmers involved in food or tree crop production and women involved in food processing or marketing. Both groups of owners have relatively limited skills in animal husbandry. Individual owners typically keep two to four breeding animals, with goats being more common than sheep. Although small ruminant management systems vary within the zone, the vast majority of animals are free-roaming and require only limited capital or management inputs. In general, the owners of these free-roaming animals provide no special feed, housing or veterinary care: the major investment is in acquiring new stock.

Although capital and management input requirements are limited, small ruminant production entails a considerable degree of uncertainty, mainly because mortalities from disease are high, particularly among goats. *Peste de petits ruminants* (PPR) is probably the most important killer and can quickly decimate whole flocks. Nevertheless, despite high mortality rates, the potential returns from sheep- and goat-keeping under the traditional management system are high (Upton 1984).

Small Ruminant Production as a Factor in the Rural Economy

Small ruminant production is one of a number of minor farm enterprises that lend a measure of diversity to the larger farm economy. In the humid zone it is not generally integrated with crop production. Forage crops are not grown to support small ruminants, and the animals' manure is not returned for cultivation of food crop plots.

Although small ruminants are mainly owned by individuals for consumption at public ceremonies, once these requirements are met the surplus is sold. Because animals produced in the south are generally insufficient for households' consumption, few animals are currently available for the market. This suggests that there is great market potential for small ruminants in the south, even in the rural areas which currently import animals from the major urban markets in the north to meet internal demand.

Sheep are consumed primarily during Muslim religious holidays, whereas goats are consumed at all ceremonies throughout the year, including births, deaths and marriages; they are also eaten at festivals. As a result, the demand for sheep is seasonal but the demand for goats

FIGURE 10.1

Mean Daily Supplies of Dwarf Sheep and Goats in Four Rural Markets in Southwest Nigeria, 1983

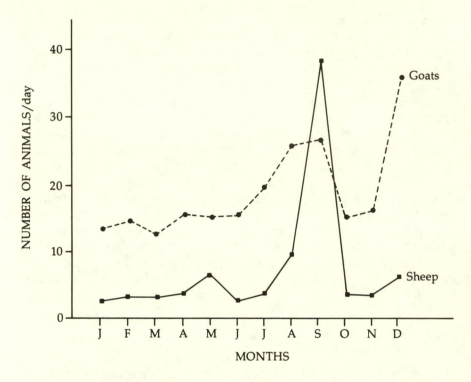

Source: ILCA Annual Report 1984. Humid Zone Programme, Ibadan, Nigeria.

is consistently high. Figure 10.1 shows the mean daily supplies over a year of dwarf sheep and goats in four rural markets in southwest Nigeria.

There is a clear price premium for male sheep during the festival period. Largely because of this price premium, sheep appear to yield a higher output and rate of return than goats. Although goats are more prolific, sheep are bigger and heavier and experience fewer mortalities (Upton 1984).

Current Production Systems

Because of their tendency to wander and damage crops, sheep require more attention than goats and are often tied or tethered during the cropping season. As a result, small-scale sheep production is a somewhat more specialized enterprise than goat-rearing, demanding greater management input. This specialization often involves older men with available time. A direct response to market forces, it illustrates one potential development option for small ruminants in the humid zone.

Many women in the rural areas combine goat production with their food processing activities. Cassava peels or other crop by-products of small-scale food production, combined with household wastes, are important feed resources, available without the need for goats' having direct access to land or fodder crops. For these women, owning a small number of animals is an attractive, efficient subsidiary enterprise.

External forces powerfully affect the characteristics of small ruminant production systems. In southeast Nigeria, for example, traditional animal husbandry systems are being modified by high human population density and increasing pressure on agricultural land. As land use becomes more intensive, free-roaming animals pose an increasingly important threat to growing crops. Indeed, in many parts of this area, free-roaming animals have been banned, and sheep and goats must be kept in pens or tethered. A recent survey of 26 Local Government Areas (LGAs) in four southeastern states indicates that restriction of animal movement exists where open, derived-savanna vegetation predominates but is less common in more heavily forested areas. In 15 LGAs in Anambra and Imo states, for example, 86 percent of the households restricted movement of their animals either during the whole year or during at least the cropping season. In contrast, only 16 percent of the households in the more heavily forested Rivers and Bendel states restricted animal movement at any time during the year. It would appear from these data that restriction of animal movement is a forced response directly related to the intensity of agricultural land use.

Once animal movement is restricted, housing, feed and water become critical. Restricted animals require a higher level of input and management than free-roaming animals; this is most clear in the need for daily feed. Given these conditions, small ruminant production could evolve from a low-input minor farm enterprise into a more intensive, specialized enterprise, particularly as specialized feed production systems are introduced to fulfill the daily demand for high quality feed.

Further development of sheep and goat production to benefit rural households in the humid zone will need not only to exploit the biological potential of the animals but also to take advantage of traditional production relations within the family. The most important intra-household relations are the relations between men and women governing the control and use of resources.

Men and Women

Beginning with Boserup in 1970, many observers have expressed concern about the ways in which African men and women appear to be unequally involved in the development process. In agriculture, this situation can be partly explained by the fact that in many countries land resources are traditionally held by men on behalf of group members. But small ruminants appear to be held by individual men and women, rather than by domestic units or kin groups, and in this respect may represent a unique resource.

All the available evidence indicates that a large proportion of the rural population in the humid zone own small ruminants. ILCA's village surveys in southwest Nigeria indicate that up to 75 percent of the population in some villages may own animals. This is illustrated in Table 10.1.

As suggested, goat ownership is far more widespread than sheep ownership. Sheep are banned in many households, communities and ethnic groups, including the dominant Yoruba, because of their destructive grazing habits and/or for ritual reasons.

Although both sheep and goats are grouped as small ruminants, the ways in which they are owned and managed differ. Because a large part of the woman's day is spent around the compound, women often argue that they cannot keep sheep because of their grazing habits. Goats, which are notorious for staying near the house and even for sleeping in outdoor fireplaces, appear to be more appropriate livestock for women. In fact, women restrict themselves almost entirely to goat production. Sheep, which are often in the fields or near the roadside, are generally kept by men and older people with available time. (See Table 10.2).

Women have a distinct advantage over men when it comes to providing feed supplements in the form of crop by-products, including not only kitchen wastes, which are available daily if food is cooked in the house, but also by-products of food processing. Both food preparation and food processing are exclusively female concerns, and Yoruba women in particular spend less time on farming than on food processing (and trading). The occupational distribution of small ruminant owners by age and sex in two villages in southwest Nigeria is illustrated in Table 10.3.

Because livestock usually require more continuous management than crops, households in parts of southwest Nigeria, where people often maintain two residences, face special problems. These families generally celebrate most festivals and ceremonies in their urban home, leaving animals unattended near their village or farm camp for long periods of time. Married Yoruba women are the more regular rural residents; even when men are resident, they work away from the house and women

TABLE 10.1
Small Ruminant Flock Characteristics in Two Villages in Southwest Nigeria.*

| Flock type | Prevalence | | Mean flock size | |
	Eruwa	Badeku	Eruwa	Badeku
	%	%	Animals/Owner	
Goats only	80.3	50.0	3.7	2.9
Sheep only	1.5	22.9	3.0	2.2
Goats & sheep	18.2	27.1	5.4	5.1
All flocks	—	—	4.0	3.2

*59.4 and 74.2% of adult population owning some small ruminants in Eruwa and Badeku, respectively.

TABLE 10.2
Ownership of Small Ruminants by Age and Sex in Two Villages in Southwest Nigeria.

| Age of Owner | Goats | | Sheep | |
	Men	Women	Men	Women
years	% of goats		% of sheep	
29	6.0	3.5	1.7	—
30 − 39	12.0	4.6	15.7	—
40 − 49	25.3	14.7	20.0	4.2
50 − 59	8.2	7.4	19.2	10.0
60+	10.9	7.4	24.2	5.0
Number of animals	229	138	97	23

more commonly care for the animals. A woman's responsibility may even extend to caring for animals owned by co-wives or other relatives who normally live in an urban area. Women and other rural residents providing caretaking services usually acquire the kids or lambs of breeding animals. Caretaking is common in southwest Nigeria; borrowing for breeding is also practiced throughout the south, probably because there is an overall shortage of breeding stock and because disease-prone markets are an unsuitable source for the purchase of breeding stock.

As suggested above, small ruminants may be an important source of income for individual owners, including women. To fulfill their obligation

TABLE 10.3
Occupational Distribution of Small Ruminant Owners by Age and Sex in Two
Villages in Southwest Nigeria.

Occupation	Eruwa Men	Eruwa Women	Badeku Men	Badeku Women	Total Men	Total Women
		%		%		%
Farming only	59	10	53	5	56	8
Trading only	3	50	—	9	1	34
Food Processing only	—	—	—	38	—	15
Farming and trading	12	31	16	5	14	21
Farming and other occupy	20	—	31	5	26	2
Other occupations	3	3	—	38	1	17
No occupation	3	6	—	—	1	3
Number in Sample	34	32	49	21	83	53

to provide daily food, women require small amounts of cash on a daily
basis. They can earn this by selling food, palm kernels and firewood.
Income from small ruminant production, however, could be large enough
to provide for capital investment. As a result, goats and sheep may be
a highly suitable development resource that can help to equalize development within rural areas and provide women, as well as men, with
capital for other activities.

A Development Strategy

It is clear that small ruminants are a widely available resource with a
clear potential for more efficient exploitation, but a fundamental choice
must be made about what development strategy to pursue. This choice
is whether to strengthen the role of small-stock production as a minor
farm enterprise easily accessible to most households or whether to
develop specialized production systems in which small ruminant production becomes the primary economic activity of a limited number of
individuals.

Although the development of specialized small ruminant production
systems has been advocated as a means of increasing aggregate meat

supplies, even relatively small increases in productivity over a wide area would have a major impact on overall meat supplies. Moreover, the enhancement of small-holder production systems could make an important contribution to rural welfare.

Enhancing the Existing Farm Enterprise

The rationale for a development strategy that seeks to enhance the existing subsidiary farm enterprise is founded on the principle of complementarity among activities within the farming system. Complementary activities generally permit more efficient use of resources such as land, labor and capital and, in so doing, increase the overall returns to the system. Complementarity plays an important role in complex traditional farming systems, implying that there is some mutual benefit to two or more activities; a primary example in some systems is complementary crop and livestock activities. Recognizing the value of complementary relationships, particularly those involving minor farm enterprises, de-emphasizes the importance of "single-enterprise maximization" as an agricultural development strategy. Risk reduction, which is assumed to result from complementarity among farm enterprises, remains a major goal of small-scale producers and should not be discounted in development.

As indicated above, small ruminant production in the humid zone of West Africa has been relatively independent of other farm enterprises— the notable exception being the strong complementarity between goat rearing and small-scale food processing by village women. The natural links between cropping and livestock husbandry have never developed within much of the zone because readily available vegetation has been generally sufficient to fulfill the food requirements of the low-density small ruminant population. As a result, systematic fodder production has not been practiced, and the manure of free-roaming animals is essentially lost to the system.

This present state of low-level equilibrium has presumably been maintained by the disease PPR, which has severely restricted the expansion of sheep and goat populations. Widespread control of PPR could have major effects on the production system, not the least of which could be the eventual development of feed deficits. Preliminary results from ILCA's Small Ruminant Programme in Ibadan and from other field studies in West Africa now indicate that PPR can be effectively controlled under village conditions with an annual vaccination of tissue culture rinderpest vaccine (TCRV). Although widespread vaccination of small ruminants with TCRV will depend on large-scale government programs similar to those for rinderpest control in cattle, the cost-benefit relationship of such an activity appears very attractive (ILCA, unpublished data).

The goal of ILCA's Small Ruminant Programme is to develop improved sheep and goat production systems which make a significant contribution to farm enterprise. A major component of ILCA's approach is improved feed, the need for which should become increasingly evident as PPR control causes growth in animal population. Where possible, the program also seeks to link small ruminant production with crop production, the major farm enterprise, thus developing a new measure of complementarity within the farming system. The primary elements of this new relationship are a chronic soil fertility problem manifested through low crop yields, a projected livestock fodder shortage and fast-growing leguminous browse trees.

The Models

Two specific models of improved small ruminant feed production are being developed and tested. (Both are predicated on the control of PPR.) In areas such as southwest Nigeria, where animals are free-roaming, integrated alley farming systems, linking crop and livestock production, are emphasized. In areas such as southeast Nigeria, where animal movement is restricted, a more specialized feed production system, called an "intensive feed garden," is being developed.

The fast-growing leguminous trees *Leucaena leucocephala* and *Cliricidia sepium*, which can provide both high quality fodder and nitrogen-rich mulch for crop production, are central elements in both models. Properly managed, the trees will provide fodder throughout the year. (Unlike grasses and some herbaceous legumes, browse shows relatively little decline in nutritional quality during the dry season.) Trees have traditionally played an important role in the farming systems of the humid zone of West Africa, and the browse trees forming the basis of the two models can be seen as an extension of this tradition.

Integrated Alley Farming Approach

The integrated alley farming approach is based on the initial work of the Farming Systems Program of the International Institute of Tropical Agriculture (IITA) (Kang, Wilson, and Sipkens 1981). Crops are grown in four-meter-wide alleys between rows of densely planted trees, which are pruned three to five times during each growing season. Trees managed in this way can produce four to eight tonnes of mulch dry matter/hectare/year, yielding over 100kg of nitrogen for crop production.

The trees in an alley farming system are effective nutrient pumps, bringing minerals from the lower soil profile to the surface, where they can be used by the growing crop. If leguminous trees are used, significant quantities of nitrogen are added to the soil indirectly from the foliage (as mulch) and directly from decaying roots and nodules. This large input of minerals and organic matter can apparently support continuous cropping at intermediate yield levels with little or no fertilizer. In addition, alley farming addresses two issues related to the decreasing efficacy of the bush fallow strategy for maintaining soil fertility in the humid zone: a rural labor shortage for bush clearing and an inability to maintain soil fertility with ever shorter fallow periods.

Small ruminant production can be integrated with alley cropping through cut-and-carry feeding of some portion of the tree foliage. The cut-and-carry system is highly flexible and can be used with either free-roaming or confined animals. Depending on the availability and quality of other feed, a range of browse feeding strategies can be developed. Browse may be fed, for example, as a protein supplement or as a sole feed and may be used on a year-round basis or only during the dry season. Feeding browse to only particular classes of animals, such as growing weaners or lactating dams, may be desirable in some circumstances. In order to give sufficient benefit to the crop and avoid the possibility of soil mining, approximately 75 percent of the available tree foliage should be applied to the soil as mulch. An annual tree foliage yield of 4 tonnes of dry matter per hectare would then give 1 tonne for feed. This amount would be sufficient to support 14 adult animals per hectare as a supplement (25 percent of feed intake) or four animals per hectare as a sole feed.

At a somewhat higher management level, short-term alley fallows, including browse trees, can be grazed. While the cut-and-carry system is applicable to both sheep and goats, the goats' propensity to de-bark the trees excludes them from the grazing system. A preliminary evaluation of the grazed fallow system indicates that with continuous grazing, 12 to 16 breeding ewes may be supported per hectare. At this stocking rate, potential returns from alley grazing are similar to those expected from maize/cassava intercropping. ILCA has also developed an inexpensive living fence woven from *Leucaena* (Sumberg 1983); this eliminates the need for purchased fencing, which usually limits the potential of grazing systems for small-scale farmers.

The use of natural fallow vegetation has been stressed to avoid the problems inherent in the establishment, management and eventual eradication of introduced pasture species. In any case, it would probably not be realistic to establish pasture species for the small flocks and relatively short-term fallows envisioned in this system. The grazed fallow system as it is now being evaluated consists of a rotation of blocks of alleys with three to five years of alley cropping followed by two to three years of grazing.

Intensive Feed Garden Approach

The intensive feed garden, in an earlier stage of development and evaluation, currently consists of a small plot containing browse trees and productive fodder grasses. The objective of the garden is to produce the maximum amount of seasonally useful fodder from a limited land area. The garden is predicated on intensive nutrient cycling promoted by the periodic application of manure, bedding and refused feed from confined animals. The intensive feed garden is a specialized feed production strategy designed to address the problem of feed shortage with confined animals. (It does not have any direct relationship to food crop production.)

While the alley farming and the intensive feed garden models are intended for use under different circumstances, their eventual adaptation may result in considerable overlapping. The reasons for this can be illustrated by a discussion of the requirements of each of the respective models.

Requirements for the Two Models

Alley farming is primarily a crop production strategy; as such, it requires both long-term access to land and a continuing interest in food crop farming. The alley farming model currently used in ILCA's on-farm research and in a government-sponsored pilot development program is based on an initial plot of 0.33 hectare. Since the average farm in southwest Nigeria ranges from one to five hectares, the initial alley farming plot constitutes a relatively small part of the total farm. The trees are established from seed within a food crop; during the establishment year, the trees are weeded when the crops are weeded. As a result, tree establishment requires little additional labor. Although the labor needed for tree pruning during subsequent years is not unsubstantial, alley farming provides for continuous cropping, thus greatly reducing overall labor for clearing of fallow lands.

The intensive feed garden is a small plot (200–500m^2) used solely for fodder production. Although the labor required for land preparation, planting and establishment is additional to other farm labor demands, the small size of the garden insures that the additional inputs will be limited. Since the feed garden should eventually contribute significantly to the feed requirements of two to five animals, the labor required for locating and transporting cut-and-carry feed may actually be reduced over the long term.

A feed garden could be located on a plot of land unsuited to crop production, which might diminish problems of land availability—particularly for women not actively engaged in farming. Although the feed garden was originally conceived to meet the requirements of confined animals, it could be used equally well to supply supplementary feed to free-roaming animals. This option might be particularly attractive to women who have limited access to land or who do not have sufficient labor resources to initiate alley farming. (Conversely, there is no reason why alley farming cannot be used to supply feed for confined animals, but alley farming was not considered a viable first option in southeast Nigeria because the land-preparation techniques required for yam cultivation produce large mounds, with relatively little topsoil between them for tree cultivation.)

Both of these models are based on the premise that any development of small ruminant production must take place within the context of existing farming systems and their economies. Intra-household processes also have important implications for applications of the models.

The Models and Intra-Household Processes

Rural women have been disadvantaged when improved systems have been introduced that require independent access to land and considerable labor inputs. Access to resources, commonly gender-related, is a factor that must be considered in new development approaches.

In the humid zone, women's access to land varies within and between ethnic groups. In most groups, both women and men living in their home areas have land-use rights as community members. Yoruba women may inherit land from their fathers just as Yoruba men do (Marshall 1964). Away from their home areas, as strangers, women may acquire rights through others, usually their spouses, or they may rent land (Green 1964). In Yorubaland, the dual practices of exogamy and patrilocal residence place most married women in the position of strangers, and independent farming is never emphasized as an activity for them. Among the Ibo of the southeast, a married woman's farming rights are in her husband's village, and the amount of farm land she may use depends on his standing in the community.

It has been indicated above that the free-roaming systems of small ruminant production, particularly goat production, do not make heavy demands on time, cash or management resources. It should also be noted that, because the land used in these activities is the common land of the village, even the landless may engage in small ruminant production (Matthewman 1980). This has important implications for rural women without land use rights.

If land is plentiful, as it is in many parts of the zone, the ability to mobilize labor is even more important than land-use rights. Alternative employment opportunities have led to a reduction in the population of working men in rural areas, and widespread education has reduced the available child labor on which women, in particular, traditionally relied for assistance. Although some labor is available for hire, only the wealthiest farmers can (and do) pay promptly.

Within the household, female members traditionally share roles, but rural households are no longer large, and labor, even for domestic work, is limited. Current household statistics from a large village in Oyo State, Owu-Ile, where the population is permanently resident, demonstrate this clearly. With 40 percent of the population being adults, just over 33 percent of the occupied houses have only one female adult while a further 25 percent have two female occupants. This contrasts strongly with the commonly held view of the large rural household. This situation also applies in households where women are in polygamous unions since co-wives rarely live in the same house. In each of ILCA's 16 alley farming households in Oyo State, there is only one resident wife regardless of whether she has one, two or three co-wives. Because they must provide food, married women generally have less time to spend on their own economic activities. For women with young children, their own time is a particularly valuable resource.

Income Strategies

While the difference in individuals' access to resources are reasonably well documented, their strategies for exploiting these resources are poorly understood. Among the Yoruba, husbands and wives each contribute separately to the upkeep of the domestic unit, although responsibilities are not always clear-cut. In general, women provide food and a large proportion of clothing for themselves and their children. Yoruba women also have independent responsibilities as daughters, sisters, wives and mothers. Marshall (1964) demonstrated how reciprocal obligations among kinsmen help women to achieve their goals. Households in southwest Nigeria and elsewhere use various means for assisting individuals to fulfill their obligations despite differences among them in terms of access to land and labor resources.

In the case of land, more than one household member may plant the same piece of land with different crops. Women often plant vegetables and other crops to meet daily subsistence requirements, while the men may plant the basic staple, a root or cereal crop. Where more than one woman is involved, a farm may be shared between them, a system practiced by Akan cocoa farmers in Ghana. Where women do not farm and have no alternative roles, they may concentrate on processing crops produced by men. Cassava and palm nuts, for instance, have essentially little or no value before processing, and the market for these raw materials is limited outside the rural areas. In these cases, there are frequently monetary exchanges between the parties involved, even if the exchange is between spouse and kinsman.

The diversity of rural households' agricultural income sources is illustrated by Ay (1978) for an old cocoa area of southwest Nigeria. About 50 income sources are listed, excluding varieties of the same crop. Among these are about 20 trees and 30 arable crops. Fuel wood is also noted as an income source, particularly for women. For many men in the Badeku area, cocoa is the major source of farm income. Most of the rural area is marginal for food crop production, although, Ay notes, there are some wealthy food farmers.

In such an area, it is relevant to consider the alternatives to further investment in livestock production. For women, these alternatives may be food processing and marketing, to which small ruminant production is already closely linked. Households, however, need to invest in a variety of items to enable all members to earn incomes with the minimum investment of scarce resources. This is true of all ages and sex groups. In rural surveys, adults are rarely recorded as unemployed, or even retired. Farming systems research must consider this, since technical innovations may result in individual income losses and thus reduce total welfare. For example, in southeast Nigeria, the introduction of power-operated oil extraction mills caused women to lose the palm kernels and a portion of the oil. In addition, men lost income because poor quality fruit was not acceptable to the mill (Lagemann 1977).

Users of ILCA's Improved Systems

ILCA's improved systems focus on small ruminant producers who have access to farm land. The alley farming model requires that individuals who grow the trees have an active interest in arable crop farming, which permits them to establish trees at little or no extra cost. The double use of browse as feed and mulch, however, allows it to be used by individuals with different economic roles. The present proposed strategy of allowing 75 percent of the browse to be used as mulch allows the major benefit to accrue to the individual with direct land-use rights and the major responsibility for producing arable crops.

Although the strategy of alley grazing potentially places some re-strictions on the multiple uses of land, it is proposed for fallow periods and would not cover all the available land at any one time. Moreover, alley grazing is a system for sheep producers, who tend to be older men in smaller households where the problem of meeting a variety of needs is less important.

In Yorubaland it is largely the men who hold direct land-use rights and are responsible for producing crops; as a result, men will accrue the principal benefits from the proposed alley farming model. The major issue in intra-household decision-making is whether the women will be allowed to use the browse to feed their own animals.

Although the comparative independence of the West African woman is now well documented, she tends to be more independent in her use of money than in other aspects of decision-making. Married women are even reluctant to discuss the decision making process. All of the wives of ILCA's 16 alley farmers claimed that their spouses took most decisions—even those connected with the sale of their own animals. They also reported that they rarely disagreed with their spouses on any subject and that disagreements were in any case rarely voiced. It is clear that these women perceive male-female relationships in terms of dominant male models, as is reported by Karanja (1983) for educated Yoruba women in Lagos. Given this perception, the only way to determine if the trees will be shared is to monitor actual browse use from alley farms.

To date, ILCA has established 16 alley farms on farmers' fields and used these farms to work out appropriate establishment strategies and alternative ways of using the browse. Only in the two oldest farms have the trees grown sufficiently to allow feed to be used. An initial reaction of the oldest farm's owner was to confine the animals all the time and to attempt to use the browse as a sole feed during the dry season, when the feed first became available. He had little interest in using the browse as feed during the wet season. This experience suggests even greater flexibility in the alley farming system than had been foreseen.

As yet, no alley farms have been established by women, and the women in the households with the oldest farms claim they have no knowledge of them. In 1984, 30 women are participating in a pilot development project, organized by the Livestock Project Unit of the Federal Livestock Department, that includes alley farming. Each of these women either has a separate piece of land to farm or farms her husband's land. The first part of the monitoring work involves watching and recording men's and women's levels of participation in the establishment of the trees. Browse for use as feed will not be available until the beginning of the second year.

The intensive feed garden, although adapted to areas where land preparation techniques make the establishment of alley farms difficult, also presents itself as a suitable alternative in other areas for men and women with little or no interest in farming. Grass cutting and the routine pruning of browse trees are the only extra labor required. Each adult animal needs only 1 kg of browse for 25 percent of its diet. Since a woman must harvest food for the house daily, from her own or her husband's farm, this amount of browse can be collected at the same time with little additional labor.

Conclusion

The overall objective of the development approach and feed production models discussed in this paper is to increase the viability of small-scale sheep and goat production. The program confronts two kinds of issues: highly focused issues requiring specific technical solutions, such as PPR control, and more diffuse issues relating to the links between small ruminants and other components of the farming system. These diffuse issues will take on increased importance as disease control releases the development potential of small ruminants. The research challenge is to formalize the processes by which farmers have successfully incorporated other new resources, for example cocoa and cassava, into their farming systems.

Notes

A different version of this paper appeared in *Agricultural Systems*, vol. 18, no. 1 (1985), pp. 39–59. Permission to use this material was granted by the publisher.

11

Training Staff for Farming Systems Research in Africa

Mandivamba Rukuni

This paper identifies issues that must be resolved in planning and carrying out programs to train field staff for farming systems research in Africa. It also describes training activities being carried out in East and southern Africa by the International Maize and Wheat Improvement Center (CIMMYT) and by the University of Zimbabwe, with strong support from CIMMYT.

Issues in Farming Systems Research Training

In addressing the issues of training for farming systems research, it is useful to start by examining the extent to which FSR is institutionalized in national programs. This, of course, varies from place to place and is usually determined by a policy decision at the ministerial level.

Policymakers must decide first, whether an FSR team is needed and, if so, where it should be located. The team can be located within an existing national institution—a research department or ministry, where positions are funded by the government, transport is provided, etc.—or in an international organization. The question of the team's location is related to the question of its longevity; a "permanent" team would be one that is housed within a government institution, but a "temporary" team may be funded by AID or another foreign donor, with no commitment from the host government to take it over. The composition of the team is also a factor in institutionalization, e.g., whether the team will be composed of persons selected from various government departments.

If FSR is (rightly) viewed as supporting on-station research, and not competing with it, then a policy decision must be made about funding and, in particular, the proportion of the available agricultural research budget that will be allocated to farming systems research. Relevant questions include the extent of funds available to support the recurrent expenditures that are involved in carrying out long-term work and whether transportation will be provided for field visits.

Questions relating to the institutionalization of farming systems research are basic—the "to be or not to be" questions. If these kinds of questions cannot be answered, it becomes difficult to know where training activities should be located, what kinds of training to provide and how much to allocate to training. Although many external aid agencies are looking at how FSR is institutionalized, this question may warrant even more careful study since the nature of the institutionalization directly affects work-sharing between national programs and international agencies.

A second major issue to be addressed relates to the nature of FSR training. How FSR practitioners acquire skills is a gray area that requires thought. A number of key questions and possibilities must be considered.

For example, should we give priority to on-the-job training or to more formal, academic training? At the moment, it may be wise to focus on in-service training. It has clearly been effective in turning normal, "run-of-the-mill" researchers into FSR practitioners. Moreover, if FSR is viewed as a process, and not as a discipline, then the need for formal FSR training, in colleges and universities, is obviated. At the same time, it might be a good idea to incorporate training and materials in university-level social science education programs so that graduates will be better equipped to take up farming systems research. Such efforts could include training in techniques of the kind that is now offered at the special University of Zimbabwe workshops described below.

Another question relating to the nature of training is whether training should be "project-based" or "problem-oriented." Should we undertake training only when foreign aid is available to support FSR activities, or should persons be trained because the need is there, in anticipation of possible future national or international funding?

A related question is whether efforts should be made to train "generalists" or "specialists." CIMMYT has always said that the FSR team should be composed of "generalists" from different disciplines, i.e., a generalist social scientist and a generalist technical scientist. But in East and southern Africa there is no massive pool of scientists on which to draw. If someone releases a single scientist for FSR, e.g., an agronomist, this person must be a jack-of-all-trades. If he does not himself know all the answers, he must know when to call in a specialist. It is also true that, because the supply of commodity researchers is very small, the assignment of a specialist to FSR may impair the basic research program to which FSR relates. Some compromises must be made. It is a give-and-take situation—although this may be more true of national and local institutions than of international organizations which can themselves provide personnel, as well as the funds needed to cover recurrent expenses and such essentials as transport.

Planners must also consider whether training should be based locally or abroad. In my own view, both may be involved. Local training is appropriate for the kinds of programs offered by CIMMYT and the University of Zimbabwe, but some supplementary foreign training might be desirable to expose researchers to work being done on gender-related issues, intra-household studies, etc. Graduate students at the University of Zimbabwe working on longer-term projects that are relevant for FSR might benefit from training abroad. Other kinds of training abroad which might be valuable include training in data-gathering skills and/ or development concepts. In this connection, it might be desirable to establish an African studies center or institute that could collate, and make available to FSR researchers, relevant social science studies on Africa; alternatively, an information network or networks on relevant issues, e.g., intra-household studies, could be valuable. FSR researchers in Africa would benefit from such basic studies and background information.

Another kind of issue to be addressed is whether to cover concepts in training or to offer practical training. There are obviously a number of conceptual or philosophical issues in which practitioners should have some grounding before focusing on specifics.

The length of training is also an issue, especially when it relates to training people employed by national programs. These people are civil servants, employed on a full-time basis, and often cannot be released for long periods of time. As indicated below, the length of training programs at the University of Zimbabwe has been reduced to two or three weeks in order to accommodate civil servants who could not be released by their ministries or employers for longer periods.

A final question is whether training should be disciplinary, i.e., designed to improve the skills of practitioners in particular fields, or interdisciplinary, i.e., aimed at getting FSR teams of social and technical scientists to adopt a common approach when they talk with farmers. I have found that, before they meet with farmers, the social scientists and the technical scientists often have many differences in approach, style and objectives. In this situation, the farmer himself or herself has been a unifying factor. Once the technical and social scientists are face to face with the farmer, they quickly realize that none of them is on the right track; that the farmer has problems; and that these problems must be resolved, by compromise if necessary, rather than according to the dictates of a particular discipline. The fact that training today is more specialized than it was in the past contributes to difficulties in bringing about an interdisciplinary approach; in the old days, an agronomist was often raised as a farmer and exposed to the realities of rural life; today, a graduate in agriculture often comes from an urban area and lacks direct experience of farming—yet we must train him to be a farming systems scientist.

Objectives and Content of FSR Training in Zimbabwe

Many of the issues outlined above have been considered in planning and carrying out training programs in Zimbabwe. When we examine the questions of objectives, content, variety of courses and who should train, the case for short-term on-the-job training is strengthened. Although subjects like FSR concepts and philosophy should be treated in formal academic institutions, practical training for FSR practitioners is probably best provided on an in-service basis.

FSR training should have the following objectives:

1. Expose and interest teachers and researchers in the problems of small farmers.
2. Develop professional expertise for in-depth dialogue with farmers in order to diagnose the constraints that affect them and to explore opportunities for development of the farming system.[1]
3. Design and plan new experiments or research programs focusing on specific farmer problems.
4. Develop skills for understanding farmers' logic and rationale in evaluating technology, as a basis for assessing experimental data and making recommendations.
5. Develop skills for working in an interdisciplinary team.

The content of training courses should be largely determined by the objectives of the FSR program. For example, FSR has been used effectively to generate technology through on-farm experiments, including by CIMMYT in East and southern Africa. CIMMYT has now developed a program that not only helps national programs to launch on-farm research but also supports these efforts with two types of in-service training for nationals of the countries involved. The first type of in-service training concentrates on training a team from a specific country, using a local on-farm research program for field and workshop exercises. The second involves regional training workshops, organized in conjunction with the University of Zimbabwe. These offer a year-long training cycle for nationals from approximately 10 East and southern African countries who are expected to form core FSR teams in their own countries. The

TABLE 11.1
CIMMYT-Supported Training Programs in East and Southern Africa

Content	In-Country Training	Regional Training Workshop
1. Concepts; Background Information	1 week	3 weeks Diagnostic Phase
2. Informal Survey	1 week	
3. Verification Survey	1 week	
4. Prioritize Research Opportunities	1 week	
5. Trial Design and Implementation	1 week	
6. Management of Trials	1 week	2 weeks Experimental Phase
7. Statistical Economic Evaluation	1 week	

two types of training are basically similar in approach and concepts and offer solid grounding for on-farm experiments and technology development.

Because training is given to those already involved in on-farm research, courses cannot be too long or employees will be overly distracted from their primary work. For this reason, the CIMMYT in-country training programs take about seven weeks, one week at a time, spread over about 18 months. The University of Zimbabwe regional training workshops are divided into two parts: a three-week diagnostic phase and a two-week experimental phase. See Table 11.1.

In developing these short training programs, it is difficult to balance the conceptual aspects with the practical aspects. It is essential to put across a minimum content of concepts, yet the practical aspects consume a lot more training time. Although more effective lectures and materials on concepts could be prepared, it is more difficult to reduce the time allotted to practical training. The background and prior training of participating researchers also dictates how much training in FSR concepts they need in order to appreciate the procedures. Researchers already well read in various aspects of African intra-household processes and general social science analysis would more quickly develop an appreciation of FSR concepts. It appears that a good bit of household and social analysis has already been done and is ongoing in Africa, but

African researchers have few effective links for keeping up-to-date with developments elsewhere on the continent. As suggested above, farming systems researchers in Africa would benefit from a network providing access to some of the longer-term in-depth studies that are often missing from or given low priority by on-farm research. These studies could cover a whole range of subjects from farm management to sociological and anthropological studies.

A careful look at the content of training courses shows that trainers must be experienced people, since most of the training is practical. Trainers should have considerable experience with on-farm diagnosis and on-farm experimentation. This is one reason why formal educational institutions may not be the best places for FSR training. To have personnel capable of providing training, formal educational institutions would have to be actively involved in on-farm research. The question of who are the best trainers in FSR also largely depends on the objectives and level of training to be provided. Farming systems research involves generalists as well as specialists, whose skills and experiences find common ground in the farmer and his or her problems; it is not a discipline but, rather, an effective process, open to participation by persons from various disciplines who are interested in a given set of farmers and their farming system.

In conclusion, if one looks at training in terms of the significance attached to farming systems research and on-farm research activities by national agricultural research programs, it is apparent that the quickest and most effective way of training practitioners is through short courses, on the job. This kind of training must be extended to include both biological and social scientists. It should cover enough substance to make scientists aware of the circumstances and problems of small farmers, sharpen their ability to carry on a dialogue with farmers and strengthen their ability to analyze problems and prescribe possible solutions. Scientists must re-orient their traditional ways of thinking and adopt the farmer's rationale when considering on-farm research and its possible results. Academic institutions must support FSR training through developing clearer concepts and disseminating literature and research publications that enrich the field worker's perceptions of the African farmer and African farming households.

Notes

1. Farming systems researchers seem quite different from other agricultural scientists in their ability to go into rural areas and intuitively or intellectually identify the problems that are affecting farmers and propose solutions for those problems. This is an important skill, but it is difficult to see how to design training programs to develop this ability.

12

Household Analysis as an Aid to Farming Systems Research: Methodological Issues

Katharine McKee

It is now clear that improved understanding of such intra-household processes as labor allocation, decision-making, deployment of non-labor resources and incentives can help at each stage of the FSR process. These include the diagnostic stage aimed at identifying key household-level constraints within the farming system, the technology design stage, the evaluation stage and the extension stage. Better understanding of intra-household processes can also help us to identify policy changes needed to improve the distribution of costs and benefits from new technology, enable us to develop new technologies that are more appropriate for particularly disadvantaged households and even enhance our ability to address perplexing issues, including questions about the often tenuous relationships between technological change, on the one hand, and actual improvements in the productivity and welfare of intended beneficiaries, on the other.

It also seems clear that many of the concepts and methodologies employed in household studies require modification if they are to be used effectively by FSR institutions and scientists who are operating under numerous constraints in their efforts to develop, test and extend improved agricultural technologies. Household analysts and FSR practitioners are being challenged to develop manageable means of incorporating useful household studies methodologies, particularly the analytic constructs and techniques developed by anthropologists, into farming systems research. They must also determine what types of investigation are required to strengthen our understanding of how intra- and inter-household processes affect, and are affected by, changes in agricultural technologies and systems.

This paper identifies a limited number of household variables and interactions for possible examination in farming systems research, suggests disciplinary approaches and specific techniques that farming systems researchers might employ in studying these variables, and proposes several types of research that might be carried out to improve our understanding of how household processes relate to technology needs and adoption.

Methodological Challenges

There are two key conceptual and methodological challenges in the use of intra-household analysis to strengthen the FSR process. First, the FSR team must determine the appropriate unit (or units) of analysis for investigation. Second, it must develop a strategy for identifying the unit's primary objectives with respect to agriculture and improved technologies.

Determining the Unit of Analysis

Before the FSR team can begin its diagnostic fieldwork and testing in earnest, it must designate its clients and research subjects and consider how possible technological interventions can be tailored to the needs of various user groups. These questions raise a number of methodological difficulties.

How, for example, do we delineate the boundaries of the "farm household" or "family farm"? Typically, FSR teams consider these to be the locus for agricultural decision-making and behavior, and the target for most FSR interventions. More specifically, who is (are) the farmer(s) within the household to whom research questions, the technology design and testing processes should be directed? Should the "farm household" be defined in terms of its production, consumption, residence, managerial, income or investment functions? Should we try to formulate typologies of household composition as one criterion for selecting the sample to be included in a recommendation domain? Which units of analysis— individual, household, compound, extended family, lineage—should be used for which FSR purposes?

A closely related methodological problem is that of defining the "farming system." How do we determine what is endogenous and what is exogenous to the system? How much do we need to know about the household's overall system of production and consumption in order to specify a production subsystem that can be the focus for farming systems research? How can we determine the hierarchy of constraints or needs?

The papers in this volume suggest that the task of setting justifiable but manageable boundaries on the "farm household" and "farming system" is far more complex than relying, for example, on residence or consumption units, since both intra- and inter-household relationships may affect agricultural behavior and goals. In fact, these relationships and processes may be a more important subject for analysis in farming systems research than the units of analysis themselves. Moreover, the units of analysis may change, depending on the question or technology at hand. It is also worth recalling that the task of FSR is not to model farming households and systems, in all their variations and complexities, but to provide insights into the factors—units or relationships—that drive agricultural behavior at the micro-level. This is not to suggest that FSR researchers should seek to assemble copious quantitative data on variables; their objective, rather, is to apply techniques of the social sciences and other disciplines for the purpose of achieving a better understanding of the goals, characteristics and potential of their clients.

Determining Farmers' Objectives

Once the FSR team has determined the appropriate unit(s) of analysis, it must determine the objectives of the unit. How do we assess its goals with respect to crop and livestock production, complementary enterprises and off-farm activities?

Here again it is important to recognize that the household is both a production and consumption unit. It has different hierarchies of objectives to be maximized; these may include increasing the yield of specific crops, achieving marketable surpluses for sale or barter, assuring an adequate food supply from its agricultural production, or optimizing use of scarce resources. Because households' objectives have been posited as the most important determinant of the technology development process, we must assess them accurately. This requires an in-depth understanding of household composition and intra-household processes.

Assessing Interactions Within and Between Households

In assessing the complex web of intra-familial interactions as a means of determining the household's acceptance of, and benefits from, new agricultural technologies, it is important to examine three key relationships: (1) units and patterns of decision-making and resource control by various household members, (2) allocation of family labor among agricultural tasks and other activities that compete for family members' time and (3) the economic and non-economic incentives for different household members to engage in the new or reorganized enterprises that are required by the agricultural technology at hand.

Recommended Methodologies

In determining what data should be collected, at which points within the FSR process, and for what purposes, two general issues must be addressed. First, the expense and complexity of FSR field studies places the burden upon the FSR team to carefully prioritize a limited number of intra-household variables and interactions for examination, based upon its understanding of local production systems, constraints, and socio-economic conditions. And second, there is a challenge, particularly for social scientists involved in FSR (including economists), to develop and adapt from their respective disciplines more "streamlined" methodologies for intra-household measurement and analysis. Various approaches and methodologies that might be employed in examining household decision-making patterns, allocations of family labor, and family members' incentives are outlined below.

Intra-Household Decision-Making

The most important areas for examination in relation to intra-household decision-making and resource control are (1) responsibility for day-to-day farm management, (2) investment decisions in agricultural activities and (3) choices about household consumption of agricultural commodities. Just as different family members have different paid and unpaid work responsibilities, so have they different rights and responsibilities for decision-making and the allocation of non-labor resources among household enterprises. Sometimes these correspond to the labor allocation patterns or resource endowments, but often they do not. Many decisions involve more than one family member. (A study of 5,000 Senegalese households has shown, for example, that 12,000 distinct decision-makers are involved in rice production.)

The complexities of decision-making processes present many methodological challenges for FSR teams in the field. Moreover, experienced social scientists do not agree about whether and how "decision making" can be quantified and analyzed. Many argue that the result of efforts to determine which individuals are responsible for which farming-related decisions are problematic and that this area of human interaction is best analyzed through its outcomes, i.e. observed behavior.

A few rules of thumb may help to guide practitioners in investigating these concerns and obtaining responses with adequate levels of accuracy.

First, it should be possible, through a review of the secondary literature, informal observations and the exploratory survey or other form of rapid rural appraisal, to determine roughly how tasks and responsibilities are distributed within farm families by gender, age or position within the household. Once this has been accomplished, FSR team members should address their questions to the apparently appropriate decision-maker(s). Depending on the likely type and demands of the technological interventions, the "appropriateness" of the interventions may be assessed according to whose labor will be involved, who manages the activities, who owns the resource or asset to be mobilized, and/or whose cash will be invested.

Second, when an FSR team relies on the household head as essentially the "key informant" for other members of his/her household, it may be necessary to cross-check answers to especially important questions through interviews or informal discussions with other family members who are observed to have significant responsibility in those farming activities and decisions.

A third approach, which has worked in some situations, is to pose "what if" questions to family members whose labor and other resources are likely to be affected by proposed interventions.

Allocation of Family Labor

In its simplest form, this concern could be stated as: "Who will do the additional work required by the new agricultural technology?"

Despite the implications of the "household labor profile" typically employed in agricultural research, household labor is not an undifferentiated commodity which can be aggregated to determine accurately the overall labor available to the household. While a certain amount of substitutability undoubtedly exists within the family labor pool, responsibility for specific crops, operations, off-farm production and unpaid household maintenance tasks is usually allocated among different members according to their sex, age, abilities and experience, and status within the household. This specialization of labor means that different family members have different labor profiles throughout the year.

Even in a basically labor-surplus rural economy or when the household as a whole is judged to have idle labor, certain family members may be overemployed at certain times of the year in essential but unpaid and/or low-productivity tasks (e.g., water and fuel collection, food preparation). Although labor may be required for new tasks resulting from changes in agricultural technology, other family members may be unwilling to perform that work displaced by new demands. The gender-based division of labor, for example, may cause significant sex differentials in labor bottlenecks throughout the agricultural year, with important implications for FSR problems and strategies. When a review of the existing literature and early FSR diagnostic work shows that labor is a more critical constraint to target clients than land, appropriate measurement and valuation of labor by different categories of household members become especially important.

Improved or modified methods are needed for characterizing the sexual division of labor for measuring labor inputs, disaggregated by age and sex. Although there is an enormous worldwide reservoir of data on labor and time-use, much of it has not been analyzed owing to the unwieldiness and sheer volume of the data. In any case, such methodologies may be inappropriate for FSR, since timeliness and clarity are essential measurements of any data's value to the FSR team. Some research questions, of course, require detailed quantitative measures of labor allocation and availability throughout the agricultural year, disaggregated by gender at a minimum, for reasons that have been amply illustrated elsewhere in this volume. But in other cases, far simpler measures of "who does what" and "which family members are overextended when" would be sufficient for the research problem at hand. Both FSR and anthropological methodologies can offer qualitative survey, observation and group interview techniques to obtain this understanding.

Improved methods are also needed for valuating labor and determining appropriate opportunity costs. Several papers in this volume demonstrate the pitfalls of conventional labor valuation assumptions—"wages" or "exchange value," for example, may vary depending on whether a woman is working for her husband, her relative, a neighbor or a stranger, and her "opportunity cost," as measured by economists, may be still another figure. We have traditionally assumed there is a low opportunity cost for female labor, yet we need to analyze, for example, the labor displacement which occurs within a household as a result of technological interventions. What value should we attach to the lost goods and services resulting from these changes, which may not have an obvious market "price" but have a high subsistence value to the household? The tendency for FSR, as currently practiced, to rely implicitly or explicitly on the market mechanism for valuation of women's labor is problematic.

Incentives

The incentive structure within the household bears a crucial relationship to both the ability and the willingness of the household and its members to adopt and modify new technologies. Two questions are central to any analysis: (1) who benefits from the intervention and who will control the output, whether in the form of more cash, more agricultural products, freed land or freed time? (2) What are the implications for agricultural investment and technology adoption of the distribution of an intervention's benefits and costs among members within a household?

Recent evidence has challenged the underlying assumption of microeconomic analysis that the household's interests can be aggregated into a single utility function, with its implicit corollary that the production and consumption objectives of individual family members are complementary, rather than conflicting, and that the benefits and costs of change will be distributed equitably. These assumptions are especially problematic in the many societies where the division of obligations for family maintenance is highly gender-specific; in these societies, men and women allocate the resources under their control to activities that best enable them to fulfill their obligations rather than to activities that are most productive from an aggregate household perspective. A very clear example of this is the case of polygamous households, in which household income generally is not pooled and each wife has clear and distinct responsibilities for herself and her children. In such cases, rather than viewing the household as a single maximizing small firm, we should view it as a composite of small firms, with resources allocated according to separate utility functions. Analyzing incentive structures within the household helps to explain the abundant evidence of women's search for and protection of independent income sources as well as their preferences for allocating their labor to activities where they control the product, e.g., to dairy processing for household consumption and sale rather than to the unpaid weeding of cereal fields that their husbands control.

In seeking to monitor and assess a new technology's impacts and distributional consequences within the household, the FSR team should note, first, that relevant evaluation criteria may vary according to the perspective of different household members. If the new technology requires that individuals allocate additional labor, cash, or other resources, conflicts may arise unless they are compensated with a share of the increased output. The evaluation criteria may encompass such technology characteristics as cooking quality, taste or milk offtake that are not generally considered to be of high priority by the research station or in field trials. As we have seen, gender often plays a central role in differentially allocating the fruits of innovation, especially when the sexual division of labor and economic responsibility is quite distinct.

Because relatively few FSR programs have proceeded to the evaluation stage, there may be opportunity to introduce these considerations about incentives into future research strategies and methodologies. How can we best monitor and assess the second-order consequences of technological interventions, for example, in terms of income, nutrition, workload and status? The preceding discussion suggests that, at a minimum, in contexts where the division of labor, responsibilities and resource-holding within the household are differentiated along gender lines, sex-differentiated data should be collected to assess the consequences of technological interventions. Such data could be obtained through formal surveys or through individual and group interviews (with female as well as male farmers and laborers), observation and/or case studies to collect information of a more qualitative nature.

It should be emphasized that monitoring and evaluating the gender-differentiated effects of agricultural technologies does not necessarily mean that the FSR team has adopted "equity between the sexes" as a priority goal for technology development nor "women farmers" as a key client group. Rather, gender-sensitive monitoring and evaluation relate directly to the FSR objective of gaining insights into the field characteristics and appropriateness of proposed interventions through observation of farmer responses, which in turn can be conveyed to those who are responsible for determining the priorities for technology development and testing. It is important to know how the household and its members have adjusted and reallocated their resources to accommodate the new technology so that this information may be fed back into the FSR process and used to assess the "extendability" of the technology package.

Improving Our Methods of Analysis

Although we are still far from having a full complement of streamlined robust methodologies in our tool kit, there are feasible means for improving our analysis of intra-household data within current FSR frameworks.

Suggested Methodologies in the Different Stages of FSR

At the pre-diagnostic stage, it may be useful to conduct a complete review of the existing anthropological and sociological literature which disaggregates the household's division of labor, decision-making patterns and control of returns from production for the specific recommendation domains or sample areas to be studied. This may suggest the most important intra-household interactions to be examined during the iterative research process which follows. The literature on the African household is rich and growing—why is it so seldom reviewed as an integral part of FSR as practiced in the field?

At the diagnostic stage, we may wish to consider household type and composition as important variables in selecting the recommendation domain and the households to be sampled within that domain. Indeed, it might be useful to formulate typologies of household composition and resource endowment as one criterion in selecting the sample within the recommendation domain. For example, if many households are headed by women, and if we have reason to believe that their resource access and farming strategies are different from those of male-headed households, we may wish to include such households in our sample, as this characteristic may shape household priorities for technology design and responses to new technologies at the testing stage. This relates to a larger question within farming systems analysis—how do we determine what constitutes a "representative farmer" within a specific context?

In assessing the highest priority interventions from a sample household's perspective, we should try to interview the appropriate decision-makers and then make a quick-and-fairly-clean attempt to assess which technologies would be improvements from the viewpoint of different family members. Since the formal field diagnostic survey often includes qualitative questions, it may be used to assess these variables. If critical labor, decision-making and incentive issues are identified, complementary studies may be needed for their analysis.

At the technology design stage, the input of national scientists and field workers, including women, may reduce the incidence of incorrect assumptions about relationships within the household, as well as the perceived "complexity" of the local environment and socio-economic system.

At the testing stage, accuracy of response may be increased by involving the appropriate family members in the field tests, with "appropriateness" being determined according to who contributes the labor, who decides about application of the new technology and who will benefit. This is obviously most important when the testing stage is farmer-managed or jointly farmer/scientist-managed. It may also be useful to monitor how the farm household copes with the reallocation of resources that the new technology requires.

At the extension stage, it is, of course, important to involve women farmers and farm workers, as well as female extension agents, in diffusing technologies for crops and tasks in which women predominate.

Need for a Mixture of Approaches

The utility of employing different methodologies for gathering data and developing insights has been suggested above. Quantitative and qualitative data collection, observation and interpretation should be mixed. Informal participant interviews; unstructured survey methodologies that employ iterative questions, enabling team members to focus quickly on priority issues; and direct observation, including that by biological scientists, should all be employed.

Types of Research Needed

Several researchers writing in this volume have expressed the view that FSR may produce a relatively narrow, static and short-term picture of African realities and that a new research agenda, parallel and broader, may be needed. A consensus is also emerging on the need to distinguish among different types of research, which should be viewed as complementary and benefiting from feedback and iteration with each other.

Three levels of investigation can contribute to strengthening our understanding of how intra- and inter-household processes affect and are affected by new agricultural technologies and changes in farming systems, on the one hand, and of which interventions show greatest promise for addressing Africa's food and poverty problems, on the other.

The different levels of investigation have different objectives, time-frames, methodological problems and financial implications. The need for each, and the appropriate balance among them in an overall research strategy, depend largely on the context in which the research is carried out. Relevant factors include the national policy setting, the severity of constraints in the agricultural system, the available backlog of testable technology, and user group characteristics.

The first type of research is socio-economic analysis undertaken directly within an FSR framework at the diagnostic, experimental, testing and evaluation stages. Given the resource constraints that FSR teams typically confront, this type of analysis must focus on those few intra- and inter-household relationships which the team regards as having highest priority for its technology development activities. Various efforts are being made to strengthen farming systems research by incorporating such concerns, but the unexploited potential of this type of research is undoubtedly great. As suggested above, new training strategies and more manageable methodologies must be developed so as to incorporate these concerns more effectively.

A second category of research relating intra- and inter-household variables to farming systems and agricultural technology is in-depth studies on specific issues raised in the course of diagnostic or on-farm experimentation work. Although such studies may be undertaken outside the narrow framework of the particular FSR program, they should nevertheless relate directly to its problem-solving process. For maximum utility, they should focus on a small number of specific topics, e.g., determinants of crop management practices, labor peaks for different households and household members, labor exchange mechanisms, patterns and strategies for mobilizing draft animals or other farming inputs, and/or specific subcategories of technology users. Moreover, their scale and complexity must be limited so that a relatively short period is needed for analysis and feedback into the FSR priority-setting and experimentation process.

The third, indispensable type of research needed is the more basic, longer-term, comparative and often longitudinal research which illuminates the processes of agricultural change and builds the pool of knowledge for future development strategies. Future research of this kind should be empirically grounded and aimed at generating hypotheses and generalizations that can guide the development of technology and policy. Furthermore, it should examine spontaneous change as well as planned agrarian change through introduction of new technologies, programs, or projects.

The FSR process could be greatly strengthened, for example, by an exploration of the relationships among household composition, resource access and mobilization, and agricultural production patterns. FSR would also benefit from research that would permit better ex ante prediction of the adoption of, and adjustment to, different types of interventions. Improved understanding is also needed of what determines the relative bargaining power of different types of individuals and household units and of their motivation to use current resources, or to mobilize new resources, toward agricultural ends.

These kinds of studies would give us a better understanding of underlying development processes. They would also make it feasible to target technology development efforts to different types of farming households (and individuals), especially those disadvantaged by their asset base, composition or lack of extra-household resources. Analyses of these kinds could also strengthen our capabilities for ex post facto monitoring and evaluation of the distributional consequences of major interventions and of the more general processes of change. An accurate reading of dynamic adjustment mechanisms, could, in turn, feed back to the starting points of FSR—the basic understanding of complex farming systems; the conceptualization and ordering of production problems; and the implementation of experimental, iterative strategies for developing and testing improved technologies.

13

Macro-Policy Implications of Research on Rural Households and Farming Systems

Sara Berry

This paper will address such questions as how do detailed studies of rural households and farming systems help to elucidate the role of agriculture in economic development? How do they clarify the impacts of macro-policies on agricultural performance and rural standards of living? How do they help to explain Africans' increasing inability to feed themselves—either directly, through expanded food production, or indirectly, through increased production of export crops? What do these studies add to our understanding of ways in which the food supply problem can be alleviated without exacerbating foreign indebtedness, domestic stagnation, inequality and underemployment?

Macro-Policies and Agricultural Performance: Issues and Arguments

The inadequacy of basic agronomic research and the lagging development of improved techniques of cultivation appropriate to the African environment and economy are major constraints impeding increased agricultural production and the provision of adequate food supplies. But they are not the only constraints. Recent literature has also criticized the economic development policies adopted by many African governments.

Guided by the prevailing view that accelerated economic development required industrialization and an increased government role in production and investment, many newly independent governments attempted to mobilize revenues for industrial development and an expanded state apparatus by increasing taxes on agricultural output and incomes—especially in the case of export crops whose prices were easily subjected to official control. As the pace of economic activity increased, demand for both final and intermediate goods tended to outstrip domestic supply, and import spending rose faster than foreign exchange earnings. This forced African governments both to accumulate foreign debts and to impose controls on foreign trade and exchange flows. These measures have depressed prices for domestic agricultural goods relative to manufactures and services, discouraged increased agricultural production and reduced farmers' real incomes. Many governments also provided subsidized credit to industrial firms and favored clients and/or protected urban wage rates. Such policies encouraged excessive rural-to-urban migration and overly capital-intensive methods of production and which depressed agricultural output and incomes. Government programs have also typically neglected the rural sector: poor rural infrastructure and badly administered price control and marketing schemes have further disrupted, or depressed, the agricultural sector.

As a result, stagnating agriculture has both failed to generate the foreign exchange, cheap domestic food supplies and increased aggregate savings that are needed to develop other sectors of the economy and contributed little to the growth of the domestic market (Johnston and Mellor 1961). Instead, refugees from rural poverty have flooded the cities and the infant industrial sector, creating urban congestion and un- or underemployment. In the interests of political stability, governments have often employed far more of these people than they could well afford, further straining domestic resources and creating irresistible pressures toward inflationary financial policies.

This diagnosis, which developed from studies of trade policy and industrialization in Asian countries financed by OECD in the late 60's (Little, Scitovksy and Scott 1970), has dominated recent discussion of the African economic situation by the World Bank and other donor agencies (Timmer et al. 1982; World Bank 1981, 1983; USDA 1981). It has also led to a two-pronged debate over possible remedies.

Many economists argue that the first step should be to abandon or reverse the policies which have done so much harm. In their view, African governments should devalue their currencies and dismantle (or reduce) controls on foreign and domestic trade; let commercial banks and/or other private lenders handle credit transactions (with an implied tendency for interest rates to rise, thus limiting access to credit to those who can use it profitably); stop rationing foreign exchange and let the rate fluctuate freely with movements in international market conditions (this will both reduce waste and corruption in the allocation of foreign exchange to domestic buyers and tend to promote "automatic" adjustments in the balance of payments); stop subsidizing urban wages and high-cost domestic producers; reduce agricultural taxation and let agricultural prices rise, and curtail total government expenditure in order to reduce deficit financing and domestic inflation. In short, these economists argue that a significant reduction of state intervention in the domestic economy will create a system of incentives conducive to agricultural expansion and permit the dissemination of improved agricultural technology (Timmer, Falcon and Pearson 1982; Pearson et al. 1981; World Bank 1981). Others, while not disagreeing with these recommendations, make an additional case for selective state intervention in the form of agricultural price supports and increased investment in rural infrastructure and agricultural research (Eicher 1982; USDA 1981; World Bank 1981).

A second approach to the macro-economics of African agriculture accepts much of the first but questions whether governments which have "mismanaged" the economy in the past will be able or willing to reverse their policies or revise them significantly. If we know what the right policies are, some ask, why aren't African governments already moving to adopt them? Is the problem with the governments, the policies or both? (Heyer et al. 1981; Hart 1982). Some who support this line of thinking feel that it is largely a matter of re-educating African policymakers (Morgenthau 1983). Others believe that the behavior of African regimes is governed by systemic forces, that governments are simply not free to rearrange their policies in accordance with the advice of trained professionals and that the food crisis is basically a symptom of an underlying crisis of the state in post-colonial Africa (Boesen, personal communication; de Janvry 1982).

Role of Micro-Studies in Assessing Macro-Policies

This paper will argue that micro-level studies of African farmers, farming systems and rural households can contribute to a critical assessment of the macro-economic arguments outlined above and to the prospects for policy reform. However, not all micro-studies are equally useful for these purposes. Indeed, it may be argued that recent analyses of African agricultural performance and critiques of African governments' policies toward agriculture overemphasize micro-studies of ecological and technical constraints on agricultural production and of African farmers' responses to changes in price. For example, findings that African farmers are producing about as much as they can with locally available inputs or that farmers tend to offer more maize for sale if the price of maize rises are interpreted to mean that policy should concentrate on developing improved technological packages and "getting the prices right" (World Bank 1981; USDA 1981). With appropriate technology and appropriate incentives, it is argued, agricultural output will grow and a secure foundation will be laid for increasing rural welfare, together with diversified, egalitarian development of the national economy.

These conclusions to not necessarily follow. To be useful for macro-analysis, micro-studies must look not only at production methods and price responses but also at the social organization of resource acquisition and resource allocation. Also, if micro-evidence is used to elucidate macro-processes and policy issues, one must do more than average individual farmer's input-output coefficients or add up their partical responses to changes in price. It is clear that we need both farming systems research, as conventionally defined, and studies of intra- (and inter-) household processes. Micro-studies can, in turn, help explain why governments act as they do,[1] as well as the effects of their actions on agricultural performance.

Recent Developments in Micro-Research

Micro-studies of farming systems and household processes have contributed significantly to our understanding of the environmental and technical conditions of agricultural production in Africa. Farming systems research, which is aimed at discovering ways to improve or build on existing farm practices, has aided in the development of appropriate new techniques and has increased agronomists' appreciation of the extent to which indigenous African farming practices constitute viable adaptations to specific ecological and economic constraints. For example, mixed cropping—once denigrated by Western agronomists because yields of individual crops are usually lower in mixed than in sole stands—has been shown to maximize returns to labor, especially in rural economies characterized by sharp seasonal peaks of activity (Norman, 1974); to reduce variations in farm output, thus contributing to farmers' security (Richards 1983; Norman et al. 1979) and, even, in some circumstances to maximize aggregate yields. Similarly, partial clearing, heaping or ridging and mixed cropping all tend to conserve the rather fragile structure of tropical soils, thus helping to maintain productivity over time, in contrast to plowing, which may achieve higher yields in the short run but leaves the soil leached and hardened after a few seasons (Lal and Greenland 1979; Richards 1983).

Farming systems research (FSR) has thus contributed both to documenting actual farming methods in Africa and to demonstrating that they are closely calibrated with local environmental and economic conditions. However, such studies are often narrowly defined. Pressure from funding agencies for quick, programmatic results may lead to an exclusive focus on a single crop or input. For example, the discovery that African practices frequently achieve higher returns to labor than to land has given rise to a single-minded concern with developing "appropriate" labor-saving techniques. Resulting research and policy recommendations range from the suggestion that plant breeders develop long, slender yam tubers (which would be easier to pull than more round varieties) (Terry et al. 1981) to mechanization or the use of herbicides as a substitute for human labor in weeding (Hart 1982). Such suggestions rarely weigh the costs of the required research against alternative uses for the resources involved or consider the implications of recommended labor-saving technical changes for environmental quality, aggregate employment or the balance of payments.

FRS projects seek to identify or develop improvements in farming practices which can be readily undertaken on small, poorly endowed farms. They are accordingly sometimes criticized for pursuing a marginalist approach to rural development which seeks to ameliorate poverty and underdevelopment rather than to eliminate them. However, an incremental strategy of research and technical development can be very effective. In their Chapter (10) on the ILCA project on small ruminants in western Nigeria, Okali and Sumberg show clearly how researchers, working closely with a few farmers over several years, can achieve significant results. The value of farming systems research for the design of rural development strategy is not reduced by its marginalist approach to the development of appropriate technology. However, its value is often limited by its implicit acceptance of the view that individual economic rationality is a sufficient condition for economic development and policy design.

Factors Affecting Responses to Incentives

Most farming systems studies collect detailed data on agricultural inputs and outputs in one or, at most, two cultivation seasons. These are used to show, through analysis of inter-household differences in production coefficients, that farmers' choices of crop mix, input combinations, etc., are consistent with the maximization of expected net returns; they are interpreted to mean that, given appropriate incentives, farmers will alter their production patterns so as to increase production and income. Hence, it is argued, the key to rural development is appropriate technology and appropriate prices.

There are several problems with these arguments:

1. The proposition that farmers act so as to maximize expected net returns has little predictive value unless we can observe expectations independently from behavior—which is impracticable.

2. Cross section analysis is not always a reliable guide to changes over time. For example, the fact that richer households in a given sample

grow more maize for sale than poorer households need not imply that all households would increase maize sales if prices were raised.

3. Both farming systems and supply response studies often focus on a single crop or input, ignoring the extent to which changes in one activity are offset by changes in others. In practice, other things are usually not equal and, the more they change, the less useful is price responsiveness as a general guide to farmers' behavior. The point was made some time ago by Helleiner, who concluded a broad and perceptive critique of the literature on African farmers' supply responses with the statement:

> . . . the *ceteris paribus* assumptions of orthodox micro analysis may . . . not carry one very far. Measuring the response to a change in only *one* of the myriad of influences upon smallholder decisionmaking, even if it is as important a one as output price, is likely to be unrewarding or misleading. . . . The efforts devoted to the establishment of the "price-responsiveness" of smallholders in African agriculture have therefore, despite their relative "youth," probably already reached a point of rapidly diminishing returns (Helleiner 1975, 43–44).

4. Social trends do not equal weighted sums of individual acts— even measurable ones—because of indivisibilities, externalities and market imperfections. Economists recognize this, and most argue that governments must act to promote economic development when markets fail to do so. However, recommended policy interventions are often based on unrealistic assumptions about the ways in which individual actions shape social processes and vice versa. Specifically, it is often assumed that governments can act unilaterally to produce public goods (such as transport networks), which are privately unprofitable but socially necessary, and/or to offset market imperfections which "distort" prices and patterns of resource allocations. But these assumptions are not very realistic. Most markets are "imperfectly" competitive—not because governments do not know when to leave well enough alone but because competition itself gives rise to market controls, as well as to efficient patterns of resource allocation. A competitive environment is a hazardous one: competition not only drives down profits and prices but also impels people to try to protect themselves from its vicissitudes. Hence, people respond to the pressures of competition, in part, by forming alliances or by seeking to exercise authority over the terms on which they buy, sell, work and accumulate. The strategies they use for this purpose often involve political connections or have political repercussions. Thus, price responses have a political dimension, and government officials and

agencies are economic actors—not simply disinterested representatives of the public interest.

Access to Productive Resources

The foregoing considerations suggest that, in order to bring micro-evidence effectively to bear on understanding macro-economic trends and designing rural development policies, we need to incorporate into our thinking about price response evidence on strategies of access to productive resources as well as on patterns of resource allocation. In principle, farming systems researchers could do this. In practice, they usually do not. For example, Norman, Simmons, and Hays (1982) conclude a careful review of the economic and technical advantages of mixed farming—i.e., closer integration of crop and livestock production—in the Nigerian savanna by cautioning that such practices could lead to conflict between farmers and stock owners over competing uses of land or the control of livestock movements (e.g., transhumance vs. kraaling). Clearly, such conflicts could have wide repercussions, not only for the adoption of mixed farming itself but also for the structure of property rights and the distribution of assets among the rural population. However, such issues are considered beyond the scope of farming systems research.

Studies of intra-household processes have often been more directly concerned than farming systems research with documenting and analyzing struggles over access to resources as well as their use, and it may be useful to outline briefly some of the insights to be derived from this literature before turning to their implications for macro-analysis.

In general, people gain access to productive resources by making claims on property and productive services. They do so not only through the market (by means of purchase, leasing, hiring, etc.) but also by drawing on social norms and patterns of authority, obligations and loyalty. Indeed, the effectiveness of the purchasing power derived from income or monetary loans depends on the existence of political institutions, administrative systems and legal and judicial processes which ensure that, once something is purchased, the purchaser may exercise control over its disposition. Thus, access to productive resources depends on the constitution and exercise of rights and responsibilities through a host of social institutions, ranging from the family to the state. As a result, strategies for gaining or defending access to productive resources may encompass efforts to exploit, reinforce or redefine social relationships.

The Role of Social Relationships

If access to land is mediated through kin groups or local polities, opportunities to expand agricultural production may lead to redefinitions not only of the terms on which outsiders (or even different categories of group members) gain access to land but also of the conditions and implications of group membership itself. The spread of tree crop production for export has, for example, often given rise to a separation of rights in land from rights in trees—a process which both facilitates privatization (trees are treated as the property of the individual who planted them and may be mortgaged or sold) and reinforces collective rights in the land itself. Such developments occurred in cocoa and coffee growing areas in West Africa (Berry 1975; Okali 1983; Dupire 1959) and in East Africa (for example, among the Chagga of Northern Tanzania) (Moore 1983). If tree crops remain profitable for some time, leading to increasing demand for permanent cultivation rights on suitable land, the preservation of group rights to land per se tends to reinforce the social salience of landholding groups. Thus, among the Chagga, the growth of demand for good coffee land strengthened the patrilineages who controlled it, enabling them to exercise local political influence throughout the colonial era and afterwards despite TANU's efforts to submerge them in new, centrally defined administrative units (Moore 1983). Similarly, the principle of lineage control over rural land was maintained in the cocoa farming areas of western Nigeria, although the outcome varied from one locality to another. In some places, chiefs were able to manipulate customary principles of adjudication in order to expropriate landholding lineages; in others, heads of certain families rose to political prominence through the adroit accumulation of "lineage land" (Berry 1975).

Access to labor and capital, as well as land, is often mediated through relations of marriage, kinship, seniority, patronage and so forth. Rural emigrants make considerable efforts to establish claims to rural land which they do not wish or cannot afford to farm because such claims serve to validate their membership in the landholding group—and hence their ability to exercise other prerogatives associated with such membership, including claims on the financial assistance, protection, political backing or even labor of other group members (Ross 1982; Spiegel 1980; Berry 1984). Direct access to labor and/or capital may also be obtained through relations of marriage, descent or seniority. Luo or Beti women, who gain access to cultivable land only through their husbands and whose access to agricultural labor is limited to that of their unmarried daughters (Hay 1982; Guyer 1980; Henn 1983), may be extreme examples but the principle that kinship and other relations often define terms of access to productive resources is widespread in rural Africa (Guyer 1981; Berry 1983).

In general, to the extent that access to land, labor and capital depends on social relationships or on established procedures for regulating transactions or solving disputes, we may expect that changing economic incentives will give rise to efforts to reinforce or manipulate those relationships and procedures as well as efforts to re-allocate resources. The fact that the effort is not always successful—the wealth or power of community or descent group may decline; options available to one's wives, sons or other subordinates may expand, etc.—does not obviate the significance of the attempt for the ultimate consequences of changes in economic incentives or technological opportunities.

Effects of Changes in Social Relations

If changes in production incentives lead to reinforcement or alteration of social relationships, changing social relations may also affect the organization of production and/or the allocation of productive resources among alternative uses. Guyer and others have suggested that the rate and pattern of agricultural intensification sometimes depend on the division of labor between men and women (cf., Linares 1981; Henn 1983), and others have shown that changes in the size or structure of farming units may affect cropping patterns or methods of cultivation (Norman et al. 1981; Raynaut 1977). Murray (1981), Beinart (1980), and Peters (1983a) have, for example, documented changes in crop or crop/ livestock combinations which followed the growth of labor migration from rural areas in southern Africa and concomitant rearrangements of relations within and between rural households.

Not only the choice of crops or land/labor combinations but also the intensity of labor effort may be affected by changes in social relations within and among productive units. This is implied by studies which describe various combinations of agricultural technique and domestic organization within a single ecological or economic region (e.g., Linares 1981; Chauveau et al. 1981) and is directly demonstrated by longitudinal studies of rural economic activity. Raynaut (1976), studying a Hausa community in Niger over several years, found that as households' need for cash increased—primarily to pay taxes—household heads began to abdicate their responsibility to meet the financial liabilities of all household members, letting junior men assume responsibility for their own tax payments. Accordingly, junior men began to withdraw their labor from collective household fields in order to seek wage employment off the farm or spend more time cultivating their individual fields. Labor productivity tended to decline on larger fields as well, partly because labor hired to replace that of the junior men was more expensive and partly because of a breakdown in household heads' authority over their dependents.

In sum, the literature on intra-household processes shows that changing economic opportunities often give rise to struggles over the definition and enforcement of property rights or social relations which may be expressed in varied and even contradictory forms and whose outcomes cannot be explained simply in terms of profitability or functional adaptation to economic and social constraints. To cite just one example, Peters' (1983a) study of the long-term consequences of the introduction of boreholes in a dry grazing area of southern Botswana traces the results of increased demand for the use of water points and adjacent grazing lands. Such demand created an impetus for the privatization of rights in water and land as members of borehole-owning syndicates sought to protect their investments (in wells, pumps, and cattle) by restricting non-members' access to wells and adjacent land. However, syndicate members also stood to gain from the principle of open access to grazing areas (especially around natural water sites) and from defending the interests of collectivities through which they derived other advantages (access to labor, influence and status). Accordingly, both their statements and their actions on the question of open or restricted access to land and water have been ambivalent, reflecting the contradictory nature of their own changing interests and economic position (cf., Parkin 1972). This example not only illustrates how changes in economic opportunities and incentives may lead to conflict over access to productive resources but also shows that tensions between alternative principles of access may arise from the contradications of economic expansion itself, as well as from the opposing interests of differently endowed groups of economic actors.

Macro-Uses of Micro-Research

I have suggested above that micro-studies have increased not only our knowledge of the specific social and technical conditions of agricultural production in Africa but also our understanding of the ways in which cultivation practices, social relationships and income-generating strategies interact at the micro-level to shape changing patterns of resource allocation. Such insights can contribute to the discussion of macro-economic processes and policies in several ways.

Getting the Price Responses Right

It is clear from the foregoing discussion that explaining and predicting farmers' responses to changes in relative prices, technical innovations, etc. involve more than measuring costs and returns to alternative productive activities. We also need to understand structures of power and principles of social interaction and how they relate over time to the division and supervision of labor, the definition and management of property rights, and the establishment and enforcement of credit relations, etc. For example, because women play a major role in agricultural production in many African economies, gender relations are centrally important to the organization of agricultural production and patterns of rural resource allocation. Principles and practices surrounding marriage, parentage and the overall definition of men's and women's rights and responsibilities within and beyond the household affect the division of farm and household tasks, the allocation of budgetary responsibilities, the structure of property rights and the terms of access to labor and credit. All these, in turn, shape farmers' responses to policy interventions.

Predicting farmers' responses to policy interventions and tracing their effects on agricultural performance involve more than taking an inventory of those social relations which impose different constraints on different categories of farmer. Policy interventions often touch off struggles over access to resources, or over control of how resources are used, which affect production patterns and/or absorb resources that might otherwise be channelled into raising output and productivity. In Kenya, for example, programs to redistribute European-controlled land to Africans and to increase African farmers' security of title to land in the former African reserves were undertaken, at the time of independence, as part of an effort to encourage increased agricultural production and the adoption of improved farming practices. Often, however, in their rush to take advantage of these new opportunities, Kenyans exhausted their savings by purchasing land, leaving little to invest in improved farming (Heyer 1976). In Nigeria, the Land Use Decree of 1978, which sought to rationalize the land tenure system and promote development by awarding title to disputed land to the claimant who proposed to develop it most effectively, did so by reserving ultimate control over all land to the state. In practice, the measure served to increase the importance of access to the state as a condition for production and investment, thus inducing people to invest in building patronage networks rather than in directly expanding productive activity (Berry 1984; Francis 1981). Similar issues have been raised concerning the long-term effects of the Tribal Grazing Lands Policy in Botswana (Peters 1983a).

Extra-Household Processes

Understanding farmers' responses to policy interventions is not sufficient to explain agricultural performance or the effect of policy changes: we need also to know how farmers and rural households are linked into wider systems of economic and political interaction. Although micro-studies alone may not provide complete information, they raise questions about the adequacy of the conceptual framework underlying current macro-analysis of African agriculture and suggest ways of reformulating it. Those who argue that increased agricultural prices are a necessary (and nearly sufficient) condition for accelerated agricultural growth and equitable development often assume that relations of production can be equated, for purposes of analysis, to a series of market transactions. Just as the "new household economics" seeks to reduce intra-household processes to a series of cost-benefit calculations (Binswanger et al. 1980), so the literature on supply response and appropriate incentives tends to assume that prices, extension services and infrastructure are the only salient variables mediating between household income-generating strategies and aggregate economic policies and performance.

Micro-studies reveal a more complex picture. As we have seen, changes in incentives result in efforts to redefine the rules and relations of access and authority as well as efforts to reallocate resources. It follows that the outcome of many individuals' responses to new incentives does not always correspond to the most profitable individual strategy. Individuals themselves may pursue contradictory strategies, and different individuals (or groups) may respond to the same opportunity in conflicting ways, leading to prolonged and often indecisive struggles over resource allocation rather than to linear, functional adaptations to the new circumstances. Changes in market incentives or technical opportunities may give rise to actual or potential struggles—between cultivators and cattle-owners over land use (Norman et al. 1982), between husbands and wives over allocations of land and labor to cash and staple food crops (Guyer 1980; Haswell 1975) and/or between fathers and sons over the allocation of labor to on- and off-farm employment or the division of authority within the household or descent group (Berry 1984; Raynaut 1976, 1977).

A major theme in the macro-economic literature—namely, the notion that African governments have hindered agricultural development by interfering with competitive market processes—rests on a belief that competition leads to efficient resource allocation, in both the short and the long run.

> . . . the challenge for policy makers in developing and developed countries alike is to break out of the web of restrictive measures that impede agriculture in some countries and overstimulate it in others; to create a trading system in which comparative advantage plays a more important role in production and trade decisions; and to encourage market mechanisms that reduce the risks of participating in the system (World Bank 1982, p. 56).

Yet, as studies of African trading systems and trading enterprises show, some of the most effective marketing systems in Africa have not been unregulated or even particularly competitive. In the past, both local and long-distance indigenous trading systems were often effective because commercial intelligence, brokerage functions and credit were controlled by well-organized kinship or community-based networks (Baier 1980; Lovejoy 1980; Eades 1980; Cohen 1965). These studies are not unknown to economists writing on current macro-economic issues but their significance has not been fully recognized. W. O. Jones (1960, 1977/8, 1980), for example, uses this literature to show that Africans are price responsive, "economic" men (and women) but he largely ignores the evidence it offers on the structure of African marketing systems—i.e., the ways enterprising individuals act, singly or in combination, to establish and exercise control over the conditions of exchange. Indeed, Jones and his colleagues built a whole series of studies of African marketing systems on the assumption that these systems operate under conditions of nearly perfect competition. Harriss (1979) has shown that this assumption led Jones et al., to restrict their evidence to data on prices, quantities and distances between markets. Under conditions of perfect competition, these data would be sufficient to define conditions of market equilibrium but, in actuality, they do not tell the whole story and the results of the Stanford studies are inconclusive. What the studies lack is not only evidence on the organization of markets and marketing systems and on social relations among traders and their "customers" but also any conceptualization of the determinants of differential access to markets (except insofar as this is directly related to distance) or of the management of markets themselves (as distinct from buying and selling units, or enterprises). Macro-economists bemoan the lack of effective management of national economies by African governments; micro-economists recognize that the performance of a farm (or other) enterprise depends on the quality of internal management, as well as the structure of opportunities and constraints external to the farm. But neither has applied the same principle to analyzing those systems of social interaction which link individual enterprise and national economy, of which markets are a prime example.

Just as micro-studies of farming systems and household processes show that social relations impinge on the internal management of farming enterprises, so studies of trading firms and systems can elucidate how markets are organized and how the organization changes with, and influences changes in, legal codes and practices, structures of authority, etc. This is a potential area for application of micro-studies to issues of macro-economic performance which deserves more attention in research on African agriculture—and one which could easily be combined with studies of farming systems and/or household processes since traders often occupy the same villages, compounds and households as farmers, and some traders even farm themselves.

Understanding Agriculture's Role in Economic Development

Johnston and Mellor have argued (1961) that agricultural expansion is a necessary concomitant of economic development because agriculture contributes savings, foreign exchange, wage goods and surplus labor to industrial and/or tertiary sectors of the economy and because rising farm incomes serve to expand the home market for non-agricultural goods. The authors acknowledged the inherent contradiction between raising farmers' incomes to provide a market for industrial goods and extracting surplus from agriculture to finance industrial investment but argued that rapid development of appropriate technology would generate sufficient growth to permit developing economies to have their agrarian cake and eat it too. Experience has shown that this is easier said than done. Struggles to control agricultural surplus have been widespread in post-independence Africa[2] and have given rise to some of the very macro-policies which economists now condemn as undercutting agriculture's contributions to national development.

Micro-level studies suggest some promising ways to think about these questions. As we have seen, policies designed to promote agricultural growth and/or extract agricultural surplus often change incentive structures and thereby affect the conditions of access to productive resources, patterns of resource allocation and division of labor, and the distribution of income and wealth, both within and among households and farms. By tracing these processes into patterns of exchange, conflict, cooperation, etc., between rural households (or communities) and other sectors of the economy, we can move toward an understanding of how intersectoral linkages actually operate, how they affect the level and direction of resource flows and how changes in agriculture actually shape—as well as reflect—developments in regional or national economies.

Investing in Social Relations

As suggested above, productive resources and profitable opportunities in Africa are often mediated through established social relations and regulatory procedures. Colonial regimes frequently introduced new principles and practices to govern the terms on which people gained access to resources and enforced contractual relations. Such colonial interventions did not replace or obviate existing mechanisms of authority and adjudication; rather, they tended to proliferate the political and institutional channels through which people sought access to resources and opportunities. This placed a premium on the question of access. Social rules and relations became objects of investment as people sought access to the means of produciton in order to take advantage of expanding market activities. Both Christine Jones and Pauline Peters, in this volume, cite examples of societies in which cattle are acquired not only for their meat or future sale value but also for their importance to a range of social transactions through which people gain access to credit, labor or leverage over the management of productive activity (Cf., Parkin 1972).

Similarly, in my own research in western Nigeria (Berry 1984),[3] I found evidence of people investing in social relations in order to improve their access to labor, credit and various forms of property. In that study, I found that farmers invested the profits from their cocoa plots in several ways: diversifying their own portfolio of small scale enterprises (usually taking up some trading activity in addition to farming), training their own and their siblings' children for non-agricultural employment or self-employment and contributing to various collective projects (often ceremonial) in their home towns. Such investment patterns not only contributed to the overall expansion of the tertiary sector in Nigeria, since farmers' children usually entered service-type employment, but also reinforced the structure of kinship, community and sectional loyalties and patronage relations through which Nigerians have sought personal advancement since colonial times (or even before). They often served to divert investible resources into patronage relations rather than into the expansion of directly productive activity.

In addition to diverting surplus from directly productive activity, investment in social relations may have long-term effects on output by influencing the organization or management of productive activity (Cf., Peters infra). In both farming and non-agricutural enterprises established by farmers' descendants in western Nigeria, a significant proportion of labor is provided by kin or apprentices who are not paid in cash or commodities, at market determined rates, but who can make future claims for assistance on the proprietor of the enterprise as a reward for their labor—including assistance with establishment of their own economic enterprise (Cf., Okali 1983). Such labor relations are closer in character to clientage than to wage employment and are a crucial means of mobilizing labor in enterprises whose receipts are too low or irregular to permit regular wage payments. But they often place significant constraints on the actual management of labor within the enterprise. One can expect loyalty from clients or children—but not necessarily efficiency.

Together with other studies, my evidence from western Nigeria indicates some of the ways in which investigations of cultivation practices, processes of production, investments and resource acquisition at the household or farm level, when carried out in relation to changing resource flows and shifting economic opportunities and constraints, can sharpen our understanding of the role of agriculture in economic development. These studies suggest that we can move beyond the question of whether, in principle, agriculture can and should provide the incentives and wherewithal for aggregate development to examine how, in practice, patterns of agrarian change affect the uses of agricultural surplus and the process of economic growth and structural change.

Toward Understanding "The Crisis of the State"

Micro-studies can also give insights into the forces that shape the form, as well as the consequences, of resource allocation by the state. Yoruba farmers used their profits primarily to secure, or defend, their access to resources partly because the Nigerian government, in expanding its role in the economy, has politicized the conditions of access to means of production. Dudley Seers pointed out in 1963 that accelerating the pace of economic development in export-oriented, primary producing economies is likely to generate chronic balance of payments deficits and lead to intensification of government efforts to regulate and control transactions. Dunn and Robertson (1973) show that both the colonial and post-colonial regimes in Ghana added new layers of offices or title-holders, with overlapping claims on people or property, to those of pre-colonial Akan society. In Africa, changes in regimes or economic policies have often intensified efforts to mobilize sectional loyalties in pursuit of access to wealth and power. These efforts have perpetuated the proliferation of competing claims on rural land and loyalties and have politicized, rather than rationalized, the processes of resource acquisition and use. To understand why Nigeria's oil wealth has been squandered, we must focus on these processes rather than simply malign the morals of government leaders or bewail their lack of training in economics.

Notes

1. In a recent article in Foreign Affairs, Carl Eicher attributed the African agricultural crisis to "a seamless web of political, technical, and structural constraints which are a product of colonial surplus extraction strategies, misguided development plans and priorities of African states since independence, and faulty advice from many expatriate planning advisors" (Eicher 1982, 157). Like Eicher's metaphor, the argument that the crisis is due to "bad policies" is a description rather than an explanation of the problem, and one which gives us few clues as to how to begin to unravel its causes.

2. The classic case of social and political struggles over disposition of the agrarian surplus—the Russian "debates" of the 1920's—has been wisely discussed, especially in some of Africa's avowedly socialist regimes. The Russian pattern has also been followed, with perhaps inadvertent faithfulness, in countries such as Tanzania and Ethiopia.

3. I began field work in two cocoa farming villages, where most of the farmers were migrants from Yoruba-speaking communities in the savannah. In addition to collecting farmers' life histories of income use, I also mapped out the pattern of economic, social and political linkages between village residents and other socio-economic niches in the regional economy. I then followed up the most important of these, tracing farmers' children into urban and/or non-agricultural occupations, collecting life histories from them, and also following the farmers back to their home towns to trace the role of kinship relations and traditions of origin in the economic activities of this spatially and socially mobile people. A more detailed description of methods and results is given in Berry (1984).

Bibliography

Abbott, Susan. 1976. Full-time Farmers and Weekend Wives. *Journal of Marriage and Family* 38,1:165–173.

Agbonifo, P. O. and R. Cohen. 1976. The Peasant Connection: A Case Study of the Bureaucracy of Agri-Industry. *Human Organization* 35:367–379.

Adam, Michel. 1980. Manioc, Rente Fonciere et situation des femmes dans les environs de Brazzaville (Republique Populaire du Congo). *Cahiers d'Etudes Africaines* 20, 1-2:5–48.

Allen, W. 1965. *The African Husbandman*. Edinburgh: Oliver and Boyd.

Alverson, H. 1982. The Wisdom of Tradition in the Development of Dry-Land Farming in Botswana. Paper presented to the Southern African Research Program Workshop, at Yale University.

———. 1979. Arable Agriculture in Botswana: Some Contributions of the Traditional Social Formation. *Rural Africana* 4-5, Spring.

Ancey, G. 1975. Ni veaux de decision et fonctions objectives en milieu rural africain. *AMIRA* 3. Paris: INSEE.

Arrow, Kenneth. 1951. *Social Choice and Individual Values*. New York: Wiley.

Ay, Peter. 1978. Firewood and Charcoal in the West African Forest: Field Research in Western Nigeria. *Rural Energy Systems in the Humid Tropics: Proceedings of the United Nations University Rural Energy Systems Project, Ife, Nigeria, 10–12 August 1978* (26–38), ed. W. B. Morgan, R. P. Moss, and Gja Ojo. Tokyo: United Nations University Press.

Bader, Zinat. 1975. Women, Private Property and Production in Bukoba District. Master's Thesis, University of Dar es Salaam.

Baier, S. 1980. *An Economic History of Central Niger*. Oxford: Clarendon Press.

Baker, E., E. Modiakgotla, D. Norman, J. Siebert and M. Tjirongo. 1983. Helping the Limited Resource Farmer Through the Farming Systems Approach to Research. *Culture and Agriculture* 19:1–8.

Banaji, Jairus. 1973. Backward Capitalism, Primitive Accumulation and Modes of Production. *Journal of Contemporary Asia* 3,4:393–413.

Bardhan, Pranab K. 1980. Interlocking Factor Markets and Agrarian Development: A Review of the Issues. *Oxford Economic Papers* 32:82–90.

Bardhan, Pranab K. and T. N. Srinivasan. 1971. Cropsharing Tenancy in Agriculture: A Theoretical and Empirical Analysis. *American Economic Review* 51:48–64.

Bartlett, Peggy. 1980. Adaptive Strategies in Peasant Agricultural Production. *Annual Review of Anthropology* 9:545–574.

————. 1980b. *Agricultural Decision Making; Anthropological Contributions to Rural Development.* New York: Academic Press.

Bates, R. 1981. *Markets and States in Tropical Africa.* Berkeley and Los Angeles: University of California Press.

Becker, G. S. 1965. A Theory of the Allocation of Time. *Economic Journal* 75:493–517.

Beeden, P., J. A. Hayward, and D. W. Norman. 1976. A Comparative Evaluation of Ultra Low Volume Insecticide Application of Cotton Farms in the North Central State of Nigeria. *Nigerian Journal of Crop Protection* 2:23–29.

Behnke, R. and C. Kerven. 1983. FSR and the Attempt to Understand the Goals and Motivations of Farmers. *Culture and Agriculture* 19:9–16.

Beinart, W. 1980. Labour Migrancy and Rural Production: Pondonald c. 1900–1950. *Black Villagers in an Industrial Society,* ed. P. Mayer. Cape Town: Oxford University Press.

Bell, Clive. 1977. Alternative Theories of Sharecropping: Some Tests Using Evidence from Northeast India. *The Journal of Development Studies* 13:317–346.

Berry, S. 1984. *Fathers Work for Their Sons: Accumulation, Mobility and Class Formation in an Extended Yoruba Community.* Berkeley and Los Angeles: University of California Press.

————. 1984. The Food Crisis and Agrarian Change in Africa: A Review Essay. *African Studies Review* 27,2:59–112.

————. 1983. Agrarian Crisis in Africa? A Review and an Interpretation. Paper presented for the Joint African Studies Committee of the Social Science Research Council and the American Council of Learned Societies. September. Boston.

————. 1975. *Cocoa, Custom, and Socio-Economic Change in Rural Western Nigeria.* London: Oxford University Press and Oxford: Clarendon Press.

Berg, Elliot J. 1964. The Development of Labor Force in Sub-Saharan Africa. *Economic Development and Cultural Change* 13,3:394–412.

Bienefeld, M. A. 1979. Trade Unions, the Labor Process and the Tanzanian State. *Journal of Modern African Studies* 17,4:553–593.

Bikoi, Achille. 1982. *Notes Provisoires sur l'Impact de SEMRY I (Aspects Agro-Economiques).* Yaounde: Centre de Recherches Economiques et Demographiques.

Binet, Jacques. 1956. *Budgets Familiaux des Planteurs de Cacao au Cameroun.* Paris: ORSTOM.

Binswanger, Hans P. and Mark R. Rosenzweig. 1981. *Contractual Arrangements, Employment and Wages in Rural Labor Markets: A Critical Review.* New York: Agricultural Development Council.

Binswanger, H. P., et al. 1980. *Rural Household Studies in Asia.* Singapore: Singapore University Press.

Bledsoe, Carolyn. 1980. *Women and Marriage in Kpelle Society.* Palo Alto: Stanford University Press.

Boesen, Jannik and A. T. Mohele. 1979. *The "Success Story" of Peasant Tobacco Production in Tanzania.* Uppsala: Scandinavian Institute of African Studies.

Bond, C. A. 1974. *Women's Involvement in Agriculture in Botswana*. Gaborone: Ministry of Agriculture.

Boserup, Esther. 1970. *Woman's Role in Economic Development*. London: George Allen and Unwin and New York: St. Martin's Press.

———. 1965. *The Conditions of Agricultural Growth: The Economics of Agrarian Change under Population Pressure*. London: Allen and Unwin.

Braverman, Avishay and Joseph E. Stiglitz. 1982. Sharecropping and the Interlinking of Agrarian Markets. *The American Economic Review* 72:695–715.

Brown, Barbara. 1983. The Impact of Male Labor Migration on Women in Botswana. *African Affairs* 82:328.

Bruce, K., D. Byerlee, and G. E. Edmeades. 1980. *Maize in the Mampong-Sekudumasi Area of Ghana*. CIMMYT Working Paper, Mexico.

Byerlee, D., L. Harrington, and D. L. Winkelmann. 1982. Farming Systems Research: Issues in Research Strategy and Technology Design. *American Journal of Agricultural Economics* 64, 5:897–904.

Byerlee, D., et al. 1981. On-Farm Research to Develop Technologies Appropriate to Farmers. In *The Rural Challenge*. IAAE Occasional Paper No. 22:170–180. Ed. M. A. Bellamy and B. L. Greenshields. Aldershot: Gower.

Byerlee, D. and M. Collingson. 1980. *Planning Technologies Appropriate to Farmers: Concepts and Procedures*. Londres, Mexico: Centro Internacional de Mejoramiento de Maiz y Trigo.

Byerlee, D., et al. 1979. *On-Farm Research to Develop Technologies Appropriate to Farmers*. CIMMYT.

Byerlee, D. 1974. Rural-Urban Migration in Africa: Theory, Policy and Research Implications. *International Migration Review* 8:543–566.

Caldwell, John C. 1976. Toward a Restatement of Demographic Transition Theory. *Population and Development Review* 2,3.

———. 1969. *African Rural-Urban Migration: The Movement to Ghana's Towns*. New York: Columbia University Press.

Caldwell, J. S. 1983. An Overview of Farming Systems Research and Development: Origins, Applications and Issues. Paper No. 5, *Proceedings of Kansas State University's 1982 Farming Systems Research Symposium, Farming Systems in the Field*, ed. C. B. Flora. Kansas State University, Manhattan, Kansas.

Carl Bro. Int. 1982. *An Evaluation of Livestock Management and Production in Botswana*, with Special Reference to Communal Areas. Gaborone: Ministry of Agriculture.

Casey, Frank and Randolph Barker. 1982. A Course in Farming Systems Research: The Cornell Experience. Review of course, Cornell University, Department of Agricultural Economics.

Chambers, Robert. 1969. *Settlement Schemes in Tropical Africa*. London: Routledge & Kegan Paul.

Chauveau, J. P., et al. 1981. Histoire de riz, histoire d'igname: le cas de moyenne Cote d'Ivoire. *Africa* 51,2:557–595.

Chayanov, A. V. 1966. *On the Theory of Peasant Economy*. Homewood, Illinois: Irwin.

Cheung, S. N-S. 1969. *The Theory of Share Tenancy*. Chicago: University of Chicago Press.

CIMMYT. 1982. Demonstrations of an Interdisciplinary Approach to Planning Adaptive Agricultural Research Programmes. Report No. 5, made November, at Ministry of Agriculture, Zimbabwe, Department of Land Management. University of Zimbabwe/CIMMYT.

CIMMYT Economics Program. 1981. *Planning Technologies Appropriate to Farmers: Concept and Procedures.* CIMMYT. Mexico.

Cleave, John H. 1977. Decision-making on the African Farm. World Bank Reprint Series, No. 32.

————. 1974. *African Farmers: Labor Use in the Development of Small-holder Agriculture.* New York: Praeger.

Cliffe, L. and R. Moorsom. 1979. Rural Class Formation and Ecological Collapse in Botswana. *Review of African Political Economy.* 15–16.

Cliffe, L. 1964. Nationalism and the Reactions to Enforced Agricultural Change in Tanganyika during the Colonial Period. Paper presented to the East African Institute of Social Research Conference, December, at Kampala, Uganda.

Cohen, A. 1965. *Custom and Politics in Urban Africa.* Berkeley and Los Angeles: University of California Press.

Collier, Paul. 1983. Malfunctioning of African Rural Factor Markets: Theory and a Kenyan Example. *Oxford Bulletin of Economics and Statistics* 48:141–172.

Collier, P. and D. Lal. 1980. *Poverty and Growth in Kenya.* Washington, D.C.: World Bank Staff Working Paper No. 389.

Collinson, Michael P. 1982. *Farming Systems Research in Eastern Africa:* The Experience of CIMMYT and Some National Agricultural Research Services, 1976–81. MSU International Development Paper No. 3. Department of Agricultural Economics, Michigan State University.

————. 1981. A Low Cost Approach to Understanding Small Farmers. *Agricultural Administration* 8:433–50.

Comaroff, J. L. 1977. *The Structure of Agricultural Transformation in Barolong.* Gaborone: Botswana Government.

Conti, Anna. 1979. Capitalist Organization of Production through Non-Capitalist Relations: Women's Role in a Pilot Resettlement in Upper Volta. *Review of African Political Economy* 15/16:75–92.

Cooper, D. 1981. A Socio-Economic Geographical Perspective on the Causes of Migration. NMS Conference Paper.

————. 1979. Migration in Botswana Towns: Patterns of Migration of Selebi-Phikwe Mine Workers. NMS Working Paper, No. 3, Gaborone.

Copans, Jane and David Seddon. 1978. Marxism and Anthropology: A Preliminary Survey. In *Relations of Production: Marxist Approaches To Economic Anthropology,* ed. D. Seddon. London: Frank Cass.

Coquery-Vidrovitch, Catherine. 1976. Research on an African Mode of Production. In *The Political Economy of Contemporary Africa* (90–111), eds. Peter Gutkind and Immanuel Wallerstein. Beverly Hills: Sage Publications. (First published in French, in *La Pensee* No. 144:61–78. Subsequently in *Relations of Production; Marxist Approaches to Economic Anthropology* (261–288), ed. D. Seddon (1978). London: Frank Cass.)

Cowen, Michael. 1981. Commodity Production in Kenya's Central Province. In *Rural Development in Tropical Africa*, 121–142, ed. Judith Heyer, Pepe Roberts, and Gavin Williams. London: Macmillan.

Cruise O'Brien, Donal B. 1975. *Saints and Politicians: Essays in the Organization of Senegalese Peasant Society.* Cambridge: Cambridge University Press.

Curtis, D. 1973. The Social Organization of Ploughing. *Botswana Notes and Records* 4:67–80.

Deane, Phyllis. 1949. Problems of Surveying Village Economies. *Rhodes-Livingstone Journal* 8:42–49.

Dey, Jennie. 1981. Gambia Women: Unequal Partners in Rice Development Projects? *Journal of Development Studies* 14:109–122.

Dillon, John, Donald Plucknett, and Guy Vallaeys. 1978. *Farming Systems Research at the International Agricultural Research Centers.* CGIAR.

Dumas, Francoise-Champion. 1983. *Les Masa du Tchad.* Cambridge: Cambridge University Press.

Dunn, J. and A. Robertson. 1973. *Dependence and Opportunity: Political Change in Ahafo (Ghana).* Cambridge: Cambridge University Press.

Dupire, M. 1960. Planteurs autochtones et etrangers en Basse Cote d'Ivoire orientale. *Etudes Eburneennes* 8:7–237.

Dwyer, Daisy H. 1983. *Women and Income in the Third World: Implications for Policy.* New York: The Population Council, The Population Council Working Paper No. 18.

Eades, J. 1980. *The Yoruba Today.* Cambridge: Cambridge University Press.

Economic Commission for Africa. 1983. *ECA and Africa's Development 1983–2008: A Preliminary Perspective Study.* Addis Ababa: Economic Commission for Africa (April).

Eicher, C. 1983. West Africa's Agrarian Crisis. Paper presented for the Fifth Bi-Annual Conference of the West African Association of Agricultural Economists, 7–11 December, at Abidjan, Ivory Coast.

————. 1982. Facing Up to Africa's Food Crisis. *Foreign Affairs* 61:151–174.

Eicher, C. and D. Baker. 1982. *Research on Agricultural Development in Sub-Saharan Africa.* East Lansing: Michigan State University, Department of Agricultural Economics.

Ekeh, Peter. 1975. Colonialism and the Two Publics in Africa: A Theoretical Statement. *Comparative Studies in Society and History* 17,1:91–112.

Eklan, Walter. 1960. *Migrants and Proletarians: Urban Labour in the Economic Development of Uganda.* Oxford: Oxford University Press.

Ernst, K. 1976. *Tradition and Progress in the African Village: The Non-Capitalist Transformation of Rural Communities in Mali.* London: C. Hurst.

Etienne, Mona. 1977. Women and Men, Cloth and Colonization: The Transformation of Production-Distribution Relations Among the Baule (Ivory Coast). *Cahiers d'Etudes Africaines* 65:41–64.

Evenson, R. E., et al. 1980. Nutrition, Work and Demographic Behavior in Rural Philippine Households: a Symposium of Several Laguna Household Studies. In *Rural Household Studies in Asia*, ed. H. P. Binswanger et al. Singapore: Singapore University Press.

Farm Management Surveys. 1978. Reports No. 4 and 5, Monitoring and Evaluation Unit, Rural Development Areas Program. Mbabane, Swaziland. Mimeo.

Feder, Gersho, Richard Just, and David Silberman. 1981. *Adoption of Agricultural Innovations in Developing Countries: A Survey.* IBRD Staff Working Paper No. 4444.

Field, R. F. 1980. *Patterns of Settlement at the Lands: Family Strategy in a Variegated Economy.* Gaborone: Ministry of Agriculture.

Flora, Cornelia Butler. 1982. Women, Agriculture, and Farming Systems in Latin America. Paper presented at Kansas State University's 1982 Farming Systems Research Symposium, at Kansas State University, Manhattan, Kansas.

Fortes, Meyer, R. W. Steel and P. Ady. 1949. The Ashanti Survey 1945–56: An Experiment in Social Research. *The Geographical Journal* 60,4–6:149–179.

Fortmann, L. 1983. Who Plows: The Effect of Economic Status on Women's Participation in Agriculture in Botswana. Mimeo.

———. 1981. *Women's Agriculture in a Cattle Economy.* Gaborone: Ministry of Agriculture.

Foster-Carter, Aidan. 1978. Can we Articulate "Articulation"? *The New Economic Anthropology,* ed. J. Clammer. New York: St. Martin's Press.

Francis, P. 1981. Power and Litigation in a Yoruba Community. Ph.D. diss., University of Liverpool.

Galletti, R., K. D. Baldwin, and I. O. Dina. 1956. *Nigerian Cocoa Farmers.* Oxford: Oxford University Press.

de Garine, Igor. 1964. *Les Massa du Cameroun: Vie Economique et Sociale.* Paris: Presses Universitaires de France.

Gastellu, J. M. 1977. L'absence de differentiation economique en pays Serer. In *Essais sur la Reproduction de Formations Sociales Dominees.* Paris: ORSTOM.

Gilbert, E. H., D. W. Norman, and F. E. Winch. 1980. *Farming Systems Research: A Critical Appraisal.* Rural Development Paper No. 6. Read at East Lansing Department of Agricultural Economics, at Michigan State University.

Goody, Esther. 1970. Kinship Fostering in Gonja: Deprivation or Advantage? In *Socialization: The Approach from Social Anthropology,* ed. Phillip Mayer. New York: Harper and Row.

Goody, Jack. 1983. *The Development of the Family and Marriage in Europe.* Cambridge: Cambridge University Press.

———. 1976. *Production and Reproduction.* Cambridge: Cambridge University Press.

———. 1973. Bridewealth and Dowry in Africa and Eurasia. In *Bridewealth and Dowry* (1–58), ed. J. Goody and S. J. Tambiah. Cambridge: Cambridge University Press.

———. 1971. *Technology, Tradition and the State in Africa.* London: Oxford University Press.

Green, M. M. 1964. *Igbo Village Affairs.* London: Frank Cass.

Gulbrandsen, O. 1980. *Agro-Pastoral Production and Communal Land Use.* University of Bergen, Norway and Rural Sociology Unit. Gaborone: Ministry of Agriculture.

Guyer, Jane I. The Economic Position of Beti Widows. In *Femmes d'Hier et d'Aujourdhui au Cameroon,* ed. J. Barbier and J. Moutome. Forthcoming.

_____. 1984. Naturalism in Models of African Production. *Man* 19,3:371–388.

_____. 1983. Dynamic Approaches to Domestic Budgeting. Cases and Methods from Africa. Ms.

_____. 1981. Household and Community in African Studies. *African Studies Review* 24, 2/3:87–138.

_____. 1980. Female Farming and the Evolution of Food Production Patterns among the Beti of South-Central Cameroon. *Africa* 50:341–356.

_____. 1980. Food, Cocoa, and the Division of Labour by Sex in Two West African Societies. *Comparative Studies in Society and History* 22:355–373.

_____. 1972. The Organizational Plan of Traditional Farming: Idere, Western Nigeria. Ph.D. diss., University of Rochester.

Harrington, L. 1981. *Methodological Issues Facing Social Scientists in On-Farm Farming Systems Research.* Londres, Mexico: Economics Program, CIMMYT.

Harris, John. 1981. A Conceptual Framework for the Study of Migration in Botswana. Boston: *Boston University African Studies Center Working Paper No. 42.*

Harriss, Barbara. 1979. There is Method in My Madness—Or is it Vice Versa? *Stanford University Food Research Institute Studies* 17, 2:197–218.

Hart, Keith. 1982. *The Political Economy of West African Agriculture.* Cambridge: Cambridge University Press.

Haswell, Margaret R. 1975. *The Nature of Poverty.* London: Macmillan Press.

_____. 1973. *Tropical Farming Economics.* London: Longman.

Haugerud, Angelique. The Consequences of Land Tenure Reforms among Small-holders in the Kenya Highlands. In *Rural Africana.* Forthcoming.

Hay, M. 1982. Women as Owners, Occupiers and Managers of Property in Colonial Western Kenya. In *African Women and the Law: Historical Perspectives,* ed. M. Hay and M. Wright. Boston: Boston University African Studies Center.

Hedlund, Hans and Mats Lundahl. 1983. Migration and Change in Rural Zambia. *Research Report No. 70.* Uppsala: Scandinavian Institute of African Studies.

Helleiner, G. 1975. Smallholder Decision Making: Tropical African Evidence. In *Agriculture in Development Theory,* ed. L. Reynolds. New Haven: Yale University Press.

Henn, J. 1983. Feeding the Cities and Feeding the Peasants: What Role for Africa's Women Farmers? *World Development* 11, 12.

Hesselberg, J. 1982. Living at the Lands or the Tap: A Dilemma for the Peasants in Botswana. *Botswana Notes and Records* 14:46–50.

Hesselberg, J. and G. Wikan. 1982. The Impact of Absenteeism on Crop Production and Standard of Living in Two Villages in Botswana. *Botswana Notes and Records* 14:69–73.

Heyer, J., Pepe Roberts and Gavin Williams. 1981. *Rural Development in Tropical Africa.* New York: St. Martin's Press.

Heyer, J., J. K. Maitha and W. M. Senga. 1976. *Agricultural Development in Kenya.* Nairobi: Oxford University Press.

Hildebrand, P. E. 1982. Farming Systems Research: Issues in Research Strategy and Technological Design. *American Journal of Agricultural Economics* 64, 5:905–6.

————. 1981. Combining Disciplines in Rapid Appraisal: The Sondeo. *Agricultural Administration* 8:423–432.

————. 1976. Generating Technology for Traditional Farmers: A Multidisciplinary Methodology. Paper presented at Conference on Developing Economies in Agrarian Regions: A Search for Methodology, 4–6 August, at Rockefeller Foundation Conference Center, Bellagio, Italy.

Hill, Polly. 1978. Food Farming and Migration from Fante Villages. *Africa* 48:220–230.

————. 1975. West African Farming Household. *Changing Social Structure in Ghana: Essays in the Comparative Sociology of a New State and an Old Tradition,* ed. Jack Goody. London: International African Institute.

————. 1972. *Rural Hausa: A Village and a Setting.* London: Cambridge University Press.

————. 1969. Hidden Trade in Hausaland. *Man* 4:392–409.

————. 1963. *The Migrant Cocoa Farmers in Southern Ghana: A Study in Rural Capitalism.* London: Cambridge University Press.

Hindess, Barry and Paul C. Hirst. 1975. *Pre-Capitalist Modes of Production.* London: Routledge and Kegan Paul.

Hodgkin, Thomas. 1956. *Nationalism in Colonial Africa.* London: Frederick Muller.

Holdcroft, L. E. 1981. The Role of External Aid. *Africa Report* 26:15–18.

Horton, Douglas E. 1983. *Social Scientists as Agricultural Researchers.* International Potato Center. Lima, Peru.

Hyden, Goran. 1983. Approaches to Cooperative Development: Blueprint Vs Greenhouse. Paper presented to the Symposium on Cooperative and Rural Development at the 11th International Congress in Anthropological and Ethnological Sciences, August, in Quebec.

————. 1984. The Political Economy of Small-Holder Agriculture in Africa. Conference Paper.

————. 1980. *Beyond Ujamaa in Tanzania. Underdevelopment and an Uncaptured Peasantry.* Berkeley and Los Angeles: University of California Press and London: Heinemann Educational Books.

Iliffe, John. 1979. *A Modern History of Tanganyika.* Cambridge: Cambridge University Press.

ILO. 1972. *Employment, Incomes and Equality: A Strategy for Increasing Productive Employment in Kenya.* Geneva: ILO.

IRRI. 1982. The Role of Anthropologists and Other Social Scientists in Interdisciplinary Teams Developing Improved Food Production Technology. Workshop at Los Banos.

ISRA. 1977. *Recherche et Development Agricole: Les Unites Experimentales du Senegal.* Bambey, Senegal: Institute Senegalis de Recherches Agricole.

Izzard, W. 1979. Rural-Urban Migration of Women in Botswana. NMS Final Fieldwork Project.

Jaeger, W. J. 1983. Animal Traction and Resource Productivity: Evidence from Upper Volta. Paper presented at Farming Systems Research Symposium, Kansas State University. Mimeo.

Jahnke, H. E. 1982. *Livestock Production Systems and Livestock Development in Tropical Africa.* Kiel: Kieler Wissenschaftsverlag Vauk.

de Janvry, A. 1982. *The Agrarian Question: Reformism in Latin America.* Baltimore: Johns Hopkins University Press.

Janzen, John M. 1969. The Cooperation in Lower Congo Economic Development. In *The Anthropology of Development in Sub-Saharan Africa,* ed. David Brokensha and Marion Persall. Lexington: Society for Applied Anthropology.

Jeffries, R. 1982. Rawlings and the Political Economy of Underdevelopment in Ghana. *African Affairs* 81, 324.

Johnston, Bruce and Peter Kilby. 1975. *Agriculture and Structural Transformation: Economic Strategies in Late-Developing Countries.* New York: Oxford University Press.

Johnston, B. and J. Mellor. 1961. The Role of Agriculture in Economic Development. *American Economic Review* 51:566–593.

Johnston, B. F. 1958. *The Staple Food Economies of Western Tropical Africa.* Palo Alto: Stanford University Press.

Johnson, G. L. 1982. Small Farmers in a Changing World. In *Small Farmers in a Changing World: Prospects in the Eighties* (7–28), ed. W. Sheppard. Manhattan: Kansas State University.

Jones, C. 1983. Mobilization of Women's Labor for Cash Crop Production: A Game Theoretic Approach. Ph.D. diss., Harvard University.

Jones, W. O. 1980. Agricultural Trade Within Tropical Africa: Historical Background. In *Agricultural Development in Africa,* ed. R. Bates and M. Lofchie. New York: Praeger.

————. 1977/78. Turnips, The Seventh Day Adventist Principle, and Management Bias. *Stanford University Food Research Institute Studies* 16:142–157.

————. 1960. Economic Man in Africa. *Stanford University Food Research Institute Studies* 1,2:107–134.

Kafando, T. W. 1972. *Les Perspectives du Development Rural de l'Est Volta.* Paris: IEDES.

Kang, B. T., G. F. Wilson, and L. Sipkens. 1981. Alley Cropping Maize (*Zea mays* L.) and Leucaena (*Leucaena leucocephala* Lam.) in Southern Nigeria. *Plant and Soil* 63:165–179.

Karanja, W. W. 1983. Conjugal Decision Making: Some Data from Lagos. In *Female and Male in West Africa,* 236–241, ed. C. Oppong. London: Allen and Unwin.

Kerven, C. 1979. Urban and Rural Female-Headed Households' Dependence on Agriculture. Gaborone: Central Statistics Unit and Rural Sociology Unit.

King, Kenneth. 1977. *The African Artisan: Education and the Informal Sector in Kenya.* London: Heinemann Educational Books.

Kleene, F. 1976. Notion d'Exploitation Agricole et Modernisation en Milieu Wolof Saloum. *Agronomie Tropicale* 31:63–82.

Knight, J. and G. Lenta. 1980. Has Capitalism Underdeveloped the Labour Reserves of South Africa? *Oxford Bulletin of Economics and Statistics* 42, 3.

Korten, David C. 1980. Community Organization and Rural Development: A Learning Process Approach. *Public Administration Review* 40,5.

Kossoudhi, Beth and E. Mueller. 1981. The Economic and Demographic Status of Female-Headed Households in Rural Botswana. Research Report 81-10. Population Studies Center. University of Michigan.

Lagermann, Johnannes. 1977. *Traditional Farming Systems in Eastern Nigeria: An Analysis of Reaction at Increasing Population Pressure.* Munich: Weltforum Verlag.

Lal, R. and D. Greenland, eds. 1979. *Soil Physical Properties and Crop Production in the Tropics.* Chichester: Wiley.

Lancaster, K. 1966. Change and Innovation in the Technology of Consumption. *American Economics Review/Supplement* May: 14–23.

Law, Robin. 1977. *The Oyo Empire c. 1500 – c. 1936: A West African Imperialism in the Era of the Atlantic Slave Trade.* Oxford: Clarendon Press.

Lele, Uma and W. Candler. 1981. Food Security: Some East African Considerations, In *Food Security for Developing Countries,* ed. A. Valdes. Boulder: Westview Press.

Le Plaideur, A. 1977. *Structures et premiers elements des systemes de production des exploitations agricoles du Centre-Sud.* Yaounde: SODECAO.

Leys, Colin. 1975. *Underdevelopment in Kenya.* London: Heinemann Educational Books.

Lightfoot, C. 1982. Agricultural Research for Development of Small Farmers: A Closer Look at Traditional Technology. *Botswana Notes and Records* 14.

Linares, O. 1981. From Tidal Swamp to Inland Delta: On the Social Organization of Wet Rice Cultivation among the Diola of Senegal. *Africa* 51,2:557–595.

Litschauer, J. G. and W. F. Kelly. 1981. *The Structure of Traditional Agriculture in Botswana.* Gaborone: Ministry of Agriculture.

Little, I., T. Schitovsky, and M. Scott. 1970. *Industry and Trade in Some Developing Countries: A Comparative Study.* London: OECD.

Little, Kenneth. 1973. *African Women in Towns: An Aspect of Africa's Social Revolution.* London: Routledge & Kegan Paul.

Lonsdale, John. 1981. States and Social Processes in Africa: A Historiographical Survey. *African Studies Review* 24, 2/3.

Lovejoy, P. 1980. *Caravans of Kola.* Zaria: Oxford University Press.

Low, Allan. 1984. Household Economics in Southern Africa. Mbabane, Swaziland. Typescript.

Low, A.R.C. 1982a. A Comparative Advantage Theory of the Subsistence Farm-Household: Applications to Swazi Farming. *The South African Journal of Economics* 50:136–157.

———. 1982b. Farm-Household Theory and Rural Development in Swaziland. Development Study No. 23, Department of Agricultural Economics and Management, University of Reading.

———. 1982c. Agricultural Development in Southern Africa: A Household Economics Perspective. Ph.D. diss., Department of Agricultural Economics and Management, University of Reading.

McLoughlin, Peter. 1970. *African Food Production Systems: Cases and Theory.* Baltimore: Johns Hopkins University Press.

Mahoney, N. 1977. Contract and Neighbourly Exchange among the Birwa of Botswana. *J. African Law* 21, 1.

Mamdani, Mahmood. 1976. *Politics and Class Formation in Uganda.* New York: Monthly Review Press.

Marris, Peter and Anthony Somerset. 1972. *The African Entrepreneur: A Study of Entrepreneurship and Development in Kenya.* New York: Africana Publishing Corporation.

Marshall, G. 1964. Women, Trade and the Yoruba Family. Ph.D. diss., Columbia University.

Mascarenhas, Ophelia and Marjorie Mbilinyi. 1983. *Women in Tanzania: An Analytical Bibliography.* Uppsala: Scandinavian Institute of African Studies.

Matlon, P. J. 1977. The Size, Distribution, Structure and Determinants of Personal Income Among Farmers in the North of Nigeria. Ph.D. diss., Cornell University.

Matthewman, R. W. 1980. Small Ruminant Production in the Humid Tropical Zone of Southern Nigeria. *Trop. Anim. Hlth. Prod.* 12:234–242.

Maymard, J. 1974. Structures Africaines de Production et Concept d'Exploitation Agfricole Premier Partie. Un Example de Terroir Africain: Les Confins Diolamanding aux Board du Sonngrongron. *Cahiers ORSTOM (Serie Biologie)* 24:27–64.

Meillassoux, Claude. 1981. *Maidens, Meals, and Money.* Cambridge: Cambridge University Press.

———. 1964. *Anthropologie economique des Gouro de Cote d'Ivoire.* Paris: Mouton.

Miracle, Marvin. 1966. *Maize in Tropical Africa.* Madison: University of Wisconsin Press.

Mitchell, John C., ed. 1969. *Social Networks in Urban Situations.* Manchester: Manchester University Press.

Moock, Joyce. 1978. The Content and Maintenance of Social Ties Between Urban Migrants and their Home-Based Support Groups: The Maragoli Case. *African Urban Notes* 3 (Winter).

Moore, S. 1983. Lecture given at the Harvard Institute for International Development, At Harvard University.

Moreno, R. I. and J. J. Saunders. 1978. *A Farming Systems Research Approach for Small Farms of Central America.* Turrialba, Costa Rica: CATIE.

Morgenthau, R. 1983. Food Policy in Africa. Paper presented at the Harvard Center for International Affairs, at Harvard University.

Moris, J. 1983. Lecture given at a workshop on Research Priorities for Rural Development, AID, at Washington, D.C.

Moris, Jon R. 1981. *Managing Induced Rural Development.* Bloomington: International Development Institute.

———. 1976. The Transferability of the Western Management Tradition to the Non-Western Public Service Sectors. *Philippine Journal of Public Administration* 20,4.

Muntemba, Shimwaayi. 1982. Women as Food Producers and Suppliers in the Twentieth Century: The Case of Zambia. *Development Dialogue* 1,2.

Murray, Colin. 1981. *Families Divided: The Impact of Migrant Labour in Lesotho.* Johannesburg: Ravan Press and Cambridge: Cambridge University Press.

Muth, R. F. 1966. Household Production and Consumer Demand Functions. *Econometrica* 34:699–708.

Mutsaers, H.J.W., P. Mbouemboue, and Mouzong Boyomo. 1978. Shifting Cultivation in Transition. Food crop growing in the Yaounde area. Communication No. 6, University of Yaounde, ENSA, Department of Agriculture.

Nash, June. 1983. Implications of Technological Change for Household Level Rural Development. Working Paper No. 37, read in October, at Michigan State University, East Lansing.

Nicholas, G. 1960. Un Village Haosa de la Republique du Niger: Tussao Haossa. *Cahiers d'Outre-Mer* 13:421–450.

Norcliffe, Glen. 1983. Operating Characteristics of Rural Non-Farm Enterprises in Central Province, Kenya. *World Development* 2, 11.

Norman, D. W. 1983. Helping Resource Poor Farmers: the agricultural technology improvement project, Botswana. Department of Agricultural Research, Sebele. Mimeo.

————. 1983. Institutionalizing the Farming Systems Approach to Research. IITA Conference. Mimeo.

————, Emmy B. Simmons, and Henry M. Hays. 1982. *Farming Systems in the Nigerian Savanna. Research and Strategies for Development.* Boulder: Westview Press.

————. 1982b. The Farming Systems Approach to Research. *Farming Systems Research Paper Series, No. 3, Kansas State University.* Mimeo.

————, Mark Newman, and Ismael Quedraogo. 1981. Farm and Village Production Systems in the Semi-Arid Tropics of West Africa: An Interpretive Review of Research. *Research Bulletin No. 4, Vol. 1.* October. Patancheru, Andhra Pradesh, India: International Crops Research Institute for the Semi-Arid Tropics.

————, Mark Newman, and Ismael Quedraogo. 1981. *Farm and Village Production Systems in the Semi-Arid Tropics of West Africa.* 2 vols. Hyderabad: ICRISAT.

————, David H. Pryor, and Christopher J.N. Gibbs. 1979. *Technical Change and the Small Farmer in Hausaland, Northern Nigeria.* East Lansing: Michigan State University, Department of Agricultural Economics.

————. 1974. Rationalizing Mixed Cropping Under Indigenous Conditions: The Example of Northern Nigeria. *Journal of Development Studies* 11,1.

————, Mark Newman, and I. Ouedraogo. 1971. *Farm and Village Production Systems in the Semi-Arid Tropics of West Africa.* Research Bulletin 4, 1. Hyderabad, India: ICRISAT.

Obbo, Christine. 1980. *African Women: Their Struggle for Economic Independence.* London: Zed Press.

Ogionwo, William. 1978. *Innovative Behavior and Personal Attitudes: A Case Study of Social Change in Nigeria.* Boston: G. K. Hall & Company.

Okali, C. 1983. *Cocoa and Kinship in Ghana: The Matrilineal Akan of Ghana.* London: Kegan Paul for the International African Institute.

Oppong, C., C. Okali, and B. Houghton. 1975. Woman Power: Retrograde Steps in Ghana. *African Studies Review* 18,3:71–84.

Oram, P. A. 1983. Workshop of Financing the Recurrent Costs of Agricultural Services. 20 May, at the Hague ISNAR.

Ottenberg, P. V. 1959. The Changing Economic Position of Women Among the Afikpo Ibo. *Continuity and Change in African Cultures,* ed. W. R. Bascom and M. J. Herskouits. Chicago: University of Chicago Press.

Pala Okeyo, Achola. 1979. Women in the Household Economy: Managing Multiple Roles. *Studies in Family Planning,* special issue entitled "Learning about Rural Women." New York: The Population Council 10,11/12:337–343.

Palmer-Jones, R. 1981. How Not to Learn from Pilot Irrigation Projects. *Water Supply and Management* 5, 1.

Parkin, D. 1972. *Palms, Wine and Witnesses.* San Francisco: Chandler.

Parson, J. 1980. The "Labor Reserve" in Historical Perspective: A Political Economy of the Bechuanaland Protectorate. Paper presented at ASA Meeting, 15–18 October, at Philadelphia.

Pearson, S., et al. 1981. *Rice in West Africa.* Stanford: Stanford University Press.

Peters, P. E. 1983a. Cattlemen, Borehole Syndicates and Privatization in the Kgatleng District of Botswana: An Anthropological History of the Transformation of a Commons. Ph.D. diss., Boston University.

———. 1983b. Gender, Developmental Cycles and Historical Process: A Critique of Recent Research on Women in Botswana. *Journal of Southern African Studies* 10,1, October.

———. 1983c. Promoting Research Contributions to Knowledge about Households and Women. In *Knowledge-Building for Rural Development: Social Science and the Cooperative Agreements,* ed. J. M. Cohen et al. HIID/AID.

———. 1984. Household Management in Botswana: Cattle, Crops and Wage Labor. Conference Paper. Bellagio, Lake Como, Italy.

Radcliffe-Brown, A. R. and D. Forde, eds. 1950. *African Systems of Kinship and Marriage.* London: International African Institute, Oxford University Press.

Ralston, Lenore, James Anderson, and Elizabeth Colson. 1983. *Voluntary Efforts in Decentralized Management: Opportunities and Constraints In Rural Development.* Berkeley: University of California, Institute of International Studies.

Ramond, D., M. Fall, and T. M. Diop. 1976. *Programme Moven Terme Sahel Main-d'Oeuvre et Movens de Production en Terre, Materiel et Cheptel de Traction des Terroirs de Got-Ndiamsil Sessene-Lahaye (Enquete 1975).* Bambey, Senegal: CNRA.

Ranger, Terence. 1967. *Revolt in Southern Rhodesia 1896–97.* London: Heinemann Educational Books.

Raynaut, Claude. 1977. Aspects socio-economiques de la preparation et de la circulation de la nourriture dans un village hausa (Niger). *Cahiers d'Etudes Africaines* 17,4:569–598.

———. 1976. Transformation du system de production et inegalite economique: le cas d'un village haoussa (Niger). *Canadian Journal of African Studies* 10,2.

Reining, Priscilla, et al. 1977. *Village Women: Their Changing Lives and Fertility: Studies in Kenya, Mexico and the Philippines.* Washington, D.C.: American Association for the Advancement of Science.

Remy, G. 1977. *Enquete sur les Mouvements de Population du Pays Mossi. Rapport de Synthese, Fascicules I et II.* Ouagadougo, Burkina Faso [formerly Upper Volta]: ORSTOM.

Rhoades, Robert E. 1983. Breaking New Ground: Anthropology in Agricultural Research. History and Overview, International Potato Center.

Richards, Paul. 1983. Ecological Change and the Politics of African Land Use. *African Studies Review* 26, 2:1–72.

———. 1983. Farming Systems and Agrarian Change in West Africa. *Progress in Human Geography* 7,1.

Roberts, Richard. 1980. Long-Distance Trade and Production: Sinsani in the Nineteenth Century. *Journal of African History* 21,2:169–188.

Robertson, A. F. and C. A. Hughes. 1978. The Family Farm in Uganda. *Development and Change* 9:415–438.

Robinson, Ronald. 1977. European Imperialism and Indigenous Reactions in British Africa, 1880–1914. *Expansion and Reaction: Essays on European Expansion and Reactions in Asia and Africa,* 141–163, ed. H. L. Wesseling. Leiden: Leiden University Press.

Roe, E. and L. Fortmann. 1982. Season and Strategy: The Changing Organization of the Rural Water Sector in Botswana. Ithaca: Cornell University, Rural Development Committee.

Ross, P. 1982. Land as a Right to Membership: Land Tenure Dynamics in a Peripheral Area of the Kano Close-Settled Zone. Paper presented at a Social Science Research Council Conference on State and Agriculture in Nigeria, at Berkeley, California.

R.U.C. (United Republic of Cameroon). 1978. National Nutrition Survey. Final Report.

Rugumisa, S. M. 1973. Mutual Aid Groups and Their Potential For Agricultural Development in Bukoba District with Special Reference to Bukabuye Village. Paper presented to the Ninth Social Science Conference of the East African Universities, December, at Dar es Salaam.

Ruttan, Vernon. 1982. Agricultural Research Policy. St. Paul: University of Minnesota.

Rweyemamu, Justinian. 1973. *Underdevelopment and Industrialization in Tanzania.* Nairobi: Oxford University Press.

Sahlins, M. 1972. *Stone Age Economics.* London: Tavistock.

Saint, W. S. and E. W. Coward. 1977. Agriculture and Behavioral Science. Emerging Orientations. *Science* 197:733–737.

Sandbrook, Richard. 1982. *The Politics of Basic Needs: Urban Aspects of Assaulting Poverty in Africa.* London: Heinemann Educational Books.

Sanjek, Roger. 1982. The Organization of Households in Adabraka: Towards a Wider Comparative Perspective. *Comparative Studies in Society and History* 24, 1:57–103.

Schultz, Theodore W. 1974. Fertility and Economic Values. *Economics of the Family: Marriage, Children and Human Capital,* ed. Theodore W. Schultz. Chicago: The University of Chicago Press for the National Bureau of Economic Research.

———. 1964. *Transforming Traditional Agriculture.* New Haven: Yale University Press.

Scott, James C. 1976. *The Moral Economy of the Peasant: Rebellion and Subsistence in Southeast Asia.* London and New Haven: Yale University Press.

Shaner, W. W., P. F. Philipp, and W. R. Schmehl. 1982. *Farming Systems Research and Development. Guidelines for Developing Countries.* Boulder: Westview Press.

Shepherd, A. 1981. Agrarian Change in Northern Ghana: Public Investment, Capitalist Farming and Famine. *Rural Development in Tropical Africa*, ed. J. Heyer, et al. New York: St. Martin's Press.

Shumba, E. 1983. The Crop-Livestock Interrelationship in Farmer Adaptation to Problems of Reduced Cattle Numbers and Lack of Dry Season Feed in Communal Areas of Zimbabwe. CIMMYT Technical Networkship, October, at Ezualwini, Swaziland.

Sisson, Andrew B. and Theodore H. Ahlers. 1981. *The Socio-Economic Impact of SEMRY I: Economic Aspects*. Yaounde: Centre de Recherches Economiques et Demographiques Research Report No. 1, June.

Skinner, Elliott P. 1974. Voluntary Associations in Ouagadougou: A Re-Appraisal of the Function of Voluntary Associations in African Urban Centers. *African Urban Notes*, Series B, No. 1 (Winter).

Solway, J. S. 1979. Socio-Economic Effects of Labor Migration in Western Kweneng. NMS Workshop Papers.

Spiegel, A. 1980. Rural Differentiation and the Diffusion of Migrant Labour Remittances in Lesotho. In *Black Villagers in an Industrial Society*, ed. P. Mayer. New York and Cape Town: Oxford University Press.

Sumberg, J. E. 1983. Leuca-Fence: Living Fence for Sheep Using *Leucaena leucocephala*. *World Animal Review* 47:49.

Technical Advisory Committee. 1978. *Farming Systems Research at the International Agricultural Research Centers*. Washington, D.C.: Technical Advisory Committee, Consultative Group on International Agricultural Research.

Terry, E., et al. 1981. *Tropical Root Crops: Research Strategies for the 1980s*. Ottawa: IDRC.

Tessema, S. 1983. Animal Feeding in Small Farm Systems. CIMMYT Technical Networkship, October, at Ezulwini, Swaziland.

Timmer, P., et al. 1982. *Food Policy Analysis*. Baltimore: Johns Hopkins University Press.

Tripp, Robert. 1983. Anthropology and On-Farm Research. CIMMYT. Mexico.

Upton, M. 1984. Models of Improved Production Systems for Small Ruminants. Paper presented at the Workshop on Small Ruminant Production Systems in the Humid Zone of West Africa, January, at Ibadan, Nigeria.

USDA. 1981. *Food Problems and Prospects in Sub-Saharan Africa*. Washington, D.C.: United States Department of Agriculture.

USDA/AID. 1980. *Food Problems and Prospects in Sub-Saharan Africa: The Decade of the 1980s*. Washington, D.C.: USAID/AID.

Van der Wees, C. 1982. Rural Labour Withdrawal: A Study on Migration and Arable Agricuture. *Botswana Notes and Records* 14.

Verdon, Michel. 1980. Descent: An Operational View. *Man* (N.S.) 15:129–150.

Vincent, V. and R. G. Thomas. 1960. The Agro-Ecological Survey in the Federation of Rhodesia and Nyasaland. Harare, Zimbabwe [formerly Salisbury, Rhodesia].

de Vletter, F. 1981. Report of a Sample Survey. USAID, Mbabane, Swaziland.

Wallace, T. 1981. The Challenge of Food: Nigeria's Approach to Agriculture, 1975–1980. *Canadian Journal of African Studies* 15,2:239–258.

Watson, V. 1983. Farming Systems on Swazi Nation Land: Results of Extension Field Officer Survey September–November. Cropping Systems Research and Extension Training Project, at Malkerns, Swaziland. Mimeo.

Weisner, Thomas. 1976. The Structure of Sociability: Urban Migration and Urban Ties in Kenya. *Urban Anthropology* 5,2:199–223.

Whitehead, Ann. 1981. I'm Hungry, Mum: The Politics of Domestic Budgeting. *Of Marriage and the Market: Women's Subordination in International Perspective*, ed. Kate Young, Carol Wolkowitz, and Roslyn McCullagh. London: CSE Books.

Winkelmann, D. and E. Moscardi. 1979. Aiming Agricultural Research at the Needs of Farmers. Paper presented at the Seminar on Socio-Economic Aspects of Agricultural Research in Developing Countries, 7–11 May, at Santiago, Chile.

Winter, G. 1970. *Methodologie des Enquetes "Niveau de Vie" en Milieu Rural Africain.* Bilan des 3 enquetes efectuees de 1961 a 1965 au Cameroun. Paris: Orstom.

Wolf, Eric R. 1981. The Mills of Inequality: A Marxian Approach. *Social Inequality: Comparative and Development Approaches,* ed. G. Berreman. New York: Academic Press.

Wolpe, H. 1972. Capitalism and Cheap Labour Power in South Africa: From Segregation to Apartheid. *Economy and Society* 1.

World Bank. 1983. *World Development Report 1983.* Washington, D.C.: World Bank.

––––––. 1983. *World Development Report 1982.* Washington, D.C.: World Bank.

––––––. 1981. *Accelerated Development in Sub-Saharan Africa.* Washington, D.C.: World Bank.

Wrigley, Chris. 1978. Sketch Maps of African Economic History. Paper presented at History Department Seminar, 14 December, University of Nairobi.

Zandstra, H. G. 1978. Cropping Systems Research for the Asian Rice Farmer. *Agricultural Systems* 4:135–153.

––––––, et al. 1981. *A Methodology for On-Farm Cropping Systems Research.* Los Banos, Philippines: International Rice Research Institute.

Znaniecki, Florian. 1967. *The Social Role of the Man of Knowledge.* New York: Octagon Books.

About the Contributors

D. C. Baker, assistant professor of economics at Kansas State University, is a farming systems economist for the Agricultural Technology Improvement Project in the Department of Agricultural Research, Government of Botswana.

Sara Berry is associate professor of history and economics at Boston University.

John D. Gerhart is deputy vice president of the Ford Foundation and was formerly its representative for the Middle East and North Africa.

Jane I. Guyer is associate professor of anthropology at Harvard University.

Goran Hyden is a staff member of the Ford Foundation and formerly its representative for Eastern and Southern Africa.

Christine W. Jones, an economist, is an associate at the Harvard Institute for International Development.

Allan Low is a regional economist with CIMMYT's Eastern and Southern Africa Economics Program.

Katharine McKee is a program officer with the Ford Foundation.

Joyce Lewinger Moock is associate director of agricultural sciences at the Rockefeller Foundation.

D. W. Norman, professor of economics at Kansas State University, is team leader of the Agricultural Technology Improvement Project in the Department of Agricultural Research, Government of Botswana.

C. Okali, formerly socio-economist and team leader at the ILCA Humid Zone Program in Ibadan, Nigeria, is a visiting scholar at the African Studies Center, Boston University.

Pauline E. Peters holds a joint appointment as assistant professor of anthropology at Harvard University and associate at the Harvard Institute for International Development.

Mandivamba Rukuni is deputy dean of agriculture in the Department of Land Management at the University of Zimbabwe.

Marie Angélique Savané, a Senegalese sociologist, is the president of the Association of African Women for Research and Development.

J. E. Sumberg is an agronomist with the ILCA program in Nigeria.

Helga Vierich is principal social anthropologist of the ICRISAT program in Ouagadougou, Burkina Faso.